Mies van der Rohe

CRITICAL ESSAYS

Mies van der Rohe

CRITICAL ESSAYS

Edited by Franz Schulze

Contributions by

Franz Schulze
Wolf Tegethoff
Richard Pommer
Fritz Neumeyer
James Ingo Freed

The Museum of Modern Art, New York

Distributed by The MIT Press, Cambridge, Massachusetts

The publication of this book has been made possible
in part by a generous grant from the
National Endowment for the Humanities,
Washington, D.C., a Federal agency.

Library of Congress Catalogue Card Number: 89-061122
ISBN 0-87070-569-5
The MIT Press ISBN 0-262-19287-X (trade edition)

Edited by Harriet Schoenholz Bee
Designed by Steven Schoenfelder
Production by Susan Schoenfeld
Type set by Graphic Composition, Inc., Athens, Georgia
Printed and bound by The Murray Printing Company, Westford, Massachusetts
Jacket printed by Eastern Press, Inc., New Haven, Connecticut

The Museum of Modern Art
11 West 53 Street
New York, New York 10019
Printed in the United States of America

Contents

Dedicated to Arthur Drexler

Foreword

In the centennial year of Ludwig Mies van der Rohe's birth, The Museum of Modern Art presented the most comprehensive exhibition ever devoted to this architect, one of the great pioneers of modern architecture. Initially, two publications were planned in conjunction with the exhibition: an illustrated catalogue of the exhibition and a book of essays examining various aspects of the architect's work, including its philosophical and political significance.

Arthur Drexler, the late Director of the Museum's Department of Architecture and Design and the director of the 1986 *Mies van der Rohe Centennial Exhibition*, was to have written the first of these volumes and edited and contributed an essay to the second. Sadly, he was unable to complete either task because of illness, and before his untimely death in 1987, he asked Franz Schulze, author of a highly respected biography of Mies van der Rohe, to assume the editorship of the book of new writings on the architect.

The dedication of this volume to Arthur Drexler recognizes his primary role in its conception and plan. However, we owe deep gratitude to Franz Schulze for his expert stewardship of the project. He brought to it his thorough knowledge of Mies and his work, and he also contributed the illuminating introductory essay. He deserves our admiration as well as our warm thanks.

Finally, we are also most grateful to the National Endowment for the Humanities. Without its generous assistance and patience this publication would not have been possible.

Richard E. Oldenburg
Director
The Museum of Modern Art

Acknowledgments

One of the principal events marking the 1986 centennial of Ludwig Mies van der Rohe was the retrospective exhibition held at The Museum of Modern Art between February 10 and April 15, 1986. Organized by Arthur Drexler, the late Director of the Museum's Department of Architecture and Design, the exhibition was the largest ever devoted to Mies's work. It not only reenforced his position as one of the most illustrious architects of modern times, but aroused renewed interest in his career among observers both in Europe and the United States.

This reception suggested to Drexler that the best of the new scholarship on Mies be documented. The present volume is the result of his vision. He had begun work on it as early as 1986 but his serious illness intervened, and shortly before his death in 1987 he invited me to assume the editorship of the project.

Primary credit for the book must therefore go to the man who inspired it, Arthur Drexler. Appropriately, it is dedicated to him. The authors of the four contributions that comprise it join me in acknowledgment of his deep admiration of Mies and his unsurpassed knowledge of Mies's singular creative accomplishments. The authors have also earned my personal gratitude as well as my abiding respect: Professor Wolf Tegethoff of the Zentralinstitut für Kunstgeschichte in Munich, Professor Richard Pommer of the Institute of Fine Arts of New York University, Professor Fritz Neumeyer of the Technical University of Dortmund, and James Ingo Freed, a partner in the architectural firm of I. M. Pei & Partners in New York.

Thanks are no less due members of the staff of The Museum of Modern Art: to Harriet Schoenholz Bee for her informed and insightful reading and scrupulous editing of the manuscripts; to Steven Schoenfelder for his sensitive design of the book; to Susan Schoenfeld for painstaking care in its production; to Stuart Wrede, the present Director of the Department of Architecture and Design, for having sustained the Museum's formal commitment to the project; and to Lacy Doyle and Penny Perkins of the Department of Development, who provided invaluable help in maintaining the liaison between the Museum and the National Endowment for the Humanities, whose generous grant assistance made publication of the book possible.

I would like to express appreciation as well to the staff of the Mies van der Rohe Archive of the Department of Architecture and Design, who have been consistently available for information and advice: Robert Coates, Steven Bluttal, Pierre Adler, and Eric Mendlow. Their colleagues in the department have likewise offered their time and wisdom: Marie-Anne Evans, Cara McCarty, and Matilda McQuaid. Additionally, I am indebted to other Museum staff members: Nancy Kranz, Kristin Teegarden, Dylan Neubauer, Amy Ellis, and Daniel Starr; and to Brunhilde Mayor for her guidance in translations from the German.

To Dirk Lohan, Mies's grandson and a leading architect in Chicago, a special note of gratitude is due for the photographs of Mies's provocative drawings for his 1934 project for the Brussels Pavilion, published in this book for the first time.

Franz Schulze

FRANZ SCHULZE

Introduction

It can hardly be said that we failed to seize the opportunity to question Ludwig Mies van der Rohe while he was alive, or that he neglected to respond to our attentions. He was famous and we were in awe of him. He had, moreover, a substantially more seigneurial image of himself than his shyness and taciturnity would have seemed to suggest (Fig. 1). Hence the procession of interviewers to Berlin and Chicago, the pilgrimages of students, the courtesies of colleagues, the venerations of critics and scholars. Hence too, however, the irony that we find ourselves—just a generation after Mies died—with so many questions that we might have asked but never did because the certainties we thought we had accumulated tended to foreclose doubt.

To a degree such a condition is to be expected, since reassessment, especially of figures as dominant in their times as Mies was in his, is a tropism of survivors. With Mies, however, the issues prove to be more open-ended and the judgments more debatable than they might be with many other artists of comparable importance.

He was, at last and despite all the traffic to his door, the most reticent and least forthcoming of the great modern architectural masters, expressing him-

1. *Ludwig Mies van der Rohe, 1947*

self with Delphic compactness in words and actions alike and even persuading us as he went along that self-expression was an inappropriate characterization of what he did. Such an insistence on impersonality kept us from realizing until much later that his way was just that: a style, a manner, a personal procedure rather than a rationally incontrovertible method. It is enough to recall his 1953–54 project for a Convention Hall (Fig. 2), a monumental exercise in structural virtuosity and one of his most impressive works. Had it been built, it would likely have been functionally perverse, a vast unitary space breathtaking to behold but ill-suited to the variety of events it was presumably meant to accommodate. The Convention Hall was a stupendous display of rationality in constructive means so magnified in scale yet so reductively simplified in form as to create an irrationality of effect.

It is Mies's art, then, and not his fabled logic, that has proven his most enduring merit. After he emigrated to the United States and became renowned as an educator, his architecture was widely promoted as the most teachable of all modern types. In fact, it may have been maximally difficult to pass on to

2. *Convention Hall, Chicago. Project, 1953–54. Detail of model*

others, since he composed it of so few elements that anything less than a sensibility to materials and proportions equal to his own was liable to result in the look of formula, sterility, or outright cheapness. Thirty years ago we did not see it this way. Reductivism was an accepted affirmative at that time, an expressive end associated with the noblest strivings of modern art and widely believed to be endowed with the aesthetic equivalent of a moral imperative. It is little wonder that Mies, like the de Stijl group, the Constructivists, or any number of other truth-seekers in art before him—even the Surrealists—upheld the inevitability, not just the preferability, of his position.

Clearly an opposite attitude prevails today, although it is probably no less a reflection of prejudice. The late twentieth century has witnessed, at times in dismay, at others with satisfaction, the dissolution of imperatives in art. St. Augustine's phrase, "Beauty is the splendor of truth," which Mies quoted often and with conviction, is seldom remembered today, still less frequently invoked. The priority of the avant-garde has given way to the unavoidability of pluralism, the latter an unheroic condition less driven by self-righteousness than the former, but easier, freer, and more disabused, at its best capable of producing an architecture of exuberance, at its worst one of licentiousness. And just as any building that resembled the Miesian archetype had an a priori aesthetic advantage in the 1950s, even some of Mies's own most celebrated works are frequently met with a chilly reception now.

Either way, whether one continues to admire him for reasons dear to the 1950s or resists him in keeping with the disposition of the 1980s, the very nature of Mies's art calls forth a widely differing variety of assessments and readings. For any expression that is made up of few formal components and little apparent associative content—any art, that is to say, which conceals art— is likely to induce a perceptual horror vacui in the interpreter, tempting him to fill in the space that the art has emptied out, as it were, and thus to account for the emptying.

This is less the case with Frank Lloyd Wright than with Mies, since Wright's art is one of an overt and plenteous sort, copious in its ideas and in the ever-changing proliferation of forms those ideas took on. Since there appears to be more on the face of it, the critic finds it safe to take it more nearly at face value. In this respect Le Corbusier stands between Wright and Mies, but was himself, especially in his later works, a sufficiently additive artist that, like Wright, he appeals more to the additive predilections of today than Mies does. Mies, laboring to make his architecture as formally spare as possible and thus to gain impact proportionate to the subtlety, elegance, and determination with which he cut away any excess from it, leaves us conjecturing more actively than we would about Wright and Le Corbusier as to the ultimate meaning and deeper intent of his work. It has been customary to affirm that he sought to dematerialize architecture, a paradoxical objective that prompts explanations extending from architecture into philosophy. Mies himself summoned up the spirits of philosophers in his own verbal statements more than the other major architects of his time did. He regarded his works as objectifications of philosophical concepts, not just as buildings that functioned at the practical or aesthetic level.

In the 1950s his admirers were less taken with his ruminations about philosophy than with the aspects of his work that spoke to their condition.

Convinced of the worthiness of reductivism, and therewith of the primacy of abstraction, critics and architects of the 1950s concentrated attention on Mies as a maker of structure, the property of building that he so artistically distilled to a formal essence. Through structure he rationalized the abstraction of architecture. Yet, as we have lately begun to raise questions about the character and effect of Mies's rationality, we are similarly uneasy with many of the old generalizations about his commitment to structure. It turns out that much of his European production, about which we knew less in the 1950s than we know now, reflected no more a devotion to structure than a preoccupation with the plan, or with massing, or with untectonic qualities like monumentality. The Brick Country House project, the Barcelona Pavilion, and the Reichsbank project provide evidence of that, as the essays in this book confirm. Even the curtain wall of his American highrise buildings is less an expression of structure than a functional device that facilitates heating and air-conditioning. If the cage of the 860–880 Lake Shore Drive Apartments in Chicago is a formal abstraction of architecture, the curtain wall that replaced it in the late 1950s and in the 1960s masks the cage and is notable for its symbolic effect rather than for its structural candor. Much the same can be said of the famous corner detail in the Alumni Memorial Hall at Illinois Institute of Technology (Fig. 3). It is hardly surprising, then, with the tastes of the 1980s running less to formal abstraction than to symbolic and associative meaning in art, that the philosophical implications of Mies's work attract us more than they ever did.

Attention has been drawn lately as well to other subjects that would have been passed over thirty years ago or not discussed at all, either in deference to the Mies myth or in ignorance of the facts, or both. The 1986 Mies van der Rohe centenary turned out to be more than an occasion for dusting off ancient catechisms about the master (Fig. 4). Rather, it prompted a renewal of scholarly and critical investigations, with results that ranged from praise to censure, the best of them drawn from data or representative of viewpoints that were unavailable to us when The Museum of Modern Art held the first retrospective exhibition of Mies's work in 1947–48 (Fig. 5).

This book contains four of the most provocative and informative of these recent commentaries on Mies. On balance, their judgment of him is affirmative; each of the contributors proceeds from the assumption that Mies was a figure of vital and lasting consequence to the history of architecture. But admiration is sometimes qualified or even overshadowed by disappointment, or is marginal if not irrelevant to the main issue. Disagreement among the writers can be inferred at times, especially in their more speculative judgments. In seeking to determine in Mies a deeper meaning, which we have called uncommonly fugitive because what shows on the surface of his work is so minimal and so secretive, several of the essays take strikingly long leaps of interpretation, no less thoughtful or instructive for all of that. Others meanwhile offer an abundance of straight information that until now has been simply inaccessible, neglected, oversimplified, or covered up.

The opening piece by Wolf Tegethoff, which deals chiefly with Mies in the 1920s, is the longest of the four and appropriately so on several counts. For one thing, Mies gained international prominence during that decade, and an account of his ascendancy based on the most informed scholarship is fitting both

3. *Alumni Memorial Hall, Illinois Institute of Technology, Chicago. 1945. Corner detail*

4. *Installation view of* Mies van der Rohe Centennial Exhibition, *The Museum of Modern Art, New York, 1986*

for its own sake and as a keynote to the contributions that follow. For another, the very fame that has accrued to him in consequence of that period of his life is the source of much of the mythologizing about him. The renown attached to the five great projects of the early 1920s—the Friedrichstrasse Office Building, the Glass Skyscraper, the Concrete Office Building, the Concrete Country House, and the Brick Country House—has only facilitated the transformation,

5. *Installation view of* Mies van der Rohe, *The Museum of Modern Art, New York, 1947–48*

not to say hardening, of observation into conventional wisdom, thence into dogma. A similar process can be discerned with respect to his built work of the second half of the 1920s, culminating in the one work widely regarded as his masterpiece, the German Pavilion erected for the Barcelona International Exposition of 1929.

Tegethoff accepts that much of the image: the Barcelona Pavilion does emerge in his essay as the crowning achievement of Mies's European career. Yet the route Tegethoff pursues to that end covers ground that previous writers have been too often content to presume was well trod already. Not so, and here again is a paradox: because we have thought we knew so much about the 1920s we knew too little. And this ignorance applies not only to Mies but to the modern movement itself, indeed to the whole architectural landscape of the Weimar years. Tegethoff thus subjects not only Mies but the *Neue Bauen* (new architecture) to a probing re-examination in the course of which both become more complex phenomena rather than less.

We had reason to anticipate such a study from Tegethoff, recalling his 1981 book *Die Villen und Landhausprojekte von Mies van der Rohe* (*Mies van der Rohe: The Villas and Country Houses,* 1985) in which he scrutinized the master's residential designs more thoroughly than anyone had before. His purpose here is to trace the maturation of Mies's thought during his most fruitful and important European period and to seek evidence of that process chiefly in Mies's architecture. Thus, he dwells on commercial buildings as well as on houses, omitting material already offered up in his book as well as any reference to efforts, like the Monument to the November Revolution (the Karl Liebknecht–Rosa Luxemburg Monument), that are not, strictly speaking, architecture.

Most of Tegethoff's essay consists of arguments based on formal and functional analysis. He suggests, for example, that plan rather than structure seems to have inspired Mies in his design of both the Friedrichstrasse Office Building and the Glass Skyscraper, thus that the architect's own claim to the structural concept as the "essential function" of his design in both cases is open to serious question. On the other hand, he gives Mies more credit than one normally hears for adjusting the Glass Skyscraper to the neighborhood context in which it would most likely have found itself.

He disputes other standard notions as well, not least the influence Wright may or may not have exerted on the Brick Country House. "Any discernible similarities . . . are outweighed by demonstrable differences," Tegethoff writes, contrasting the respective concepts of space of Wright and Mies, with interior space for the former shown to be more fixed and protected, for the latter, more fluid and extroverted. Yet the very fluidity of space in the Mies villa enables the dweller to establish himself more freely in the center of the dwelling— although in a position more "open and adaptable to change"—than would be possible in one of Wright's Prairie Houses.

Tegethoff also answers a question that is seldom raised in discussions of the 1920s: when Mies finally was able to build in the modern manner, not simply to conjure projects as he had in his unfettered if isolated way during the first half of the decade, what gaps separated his drawing-board dreaming from the technology available to him, and how well did he bridge them? With difficulty, concludes Tegethoff, and he suggests a creative crisis hinted at by Mies himself when he referred to 1926, the year construction began on his first

6. *Wolf House, Guben, Germany (destroyed). 1925–27. Terrace*

completed modern commission, the Wolf House (Fig. 6), as "the most significant" of his Weimar career, one "of great realization and awareness."

Mies began to pass the crisis in his next important assignment, the organization and supervision of the Weissenhof settlement (*Weissenhofsiedlung*) in Stuttgart, which opened to the public in 1927. The most obvious effect of that event was its spectacular success in validating the internationalization of the modern style in architecture. If this much is textbook knowledge, Tegethoff adds to it consideration of a general question, the extent to which Mies consciously sought to produce the consolidation of modernism at Stuttgart; and a specific one, the ultimate effect on his own architecture of the skeletal frame that supported the apartment block he designed as his personal contribution to the colony (Fig. 7).

7. *Apartment Building, Weissenhofsiedlung, Stuttgart. 1925–27. Garden facade*

The lessons Mies learned from that apartment building were manifest in the Barcelona Pavilion, to which the final section of Tegethoff's essay is devoted. It begins with another challenging contrast, between Mies and Le Corbusier (Fig. 8), and ends on a note that transcends the otherwise coolly analytic temper of his essay. Acknowledging "a certain mystic and ethereal quality" in the Barcelona Pavilion (Fig. 9) and mindful as any writer on Mies must be that the master equated the materiality of architecture with the immateriality of philosophy—even as he endeavored to avoid all overt simulacra of meaning in design—Tegethoff ponders the iconographical implications of the work. He finally shies away from any interpretation more specific than Mies's recognized pursuit of the *geistig* (spiritual), while leaving no doubt that a spiritual dimension is essential to any measurement of the famous structure that was rebuilt in 1986 in Montjuich Park in Barcelona.

In the second essay, Richard Pommer likewise takes up the issue of spirit in Mies's work of the Weimar years, but he examines it in an ideological rather than philosophical context. Of all the questions pertinent to Mies's career, none has been more inaccurately recorded, vaguely accounted for, sidestepped, or ignored outright, than the evidence of his personal political sympathies. Pommer is also critical of our previous understanding of the politics of several other major architects in Weimar Germany and, by extension, of the modern movement itself. The faulty reporting can be blamed partly on the prejudices and preconceptions of earlier observers, although as Pommer points out, even more confusion has resulted from careless weighing of the variables in the case, these being more numerous than we have taken the trouble to recognize. Political views of the period, while distinguishable from aesthetic and philosophical doctrines, sometimes overlapped both and varied, moreover, from individual to individual and group to group, not to mention from phase to phase in the lives of both individuals and groups.

Thus cautioned, Pommer begins his study by rejecting as simplistic the widespread notion that the modern movement grew collectively from socialist roots and kindred left-wing associations. He moves quickly to Mies, whose ideology proves to be identifiable enough, although more convoluted and delicately shaded than one might presume from all that has been written about it. Nor was that ideology subject to any less change than the architecture Mies created to embody it. Pommer takes Mies's career back to the years prior to the First World War, at which point he finds that Mies was not part of the debates that stirred the councils of the Deutsche Werkbund following its founding in 1907, but felt their backwash as an assistant in the office of Peter Behrens, one of the Werkbund's leading figures. Although affected by the neoclassical tastes of Behrens as well as by the aesthetics of the doctrine of cultural reform that circulated in prewar Germany, Mies steered clear of any socially oriented movements, remaining indifferent to them as well as to radical modernist style until several years after the war ended. When he finally embraced modernism in the early 1920s, the argument he presented for it reflected the mood of the *Neue Sachlichkeit* (new objectivity) in all that movement's antiromantic, nonexpressionist aspects. He saw building as a self-referential activity connected to society only by its inescapable dependence on modern technology. Nonetheless, his own claim to *Sachlichkeit* was qualified, if not undercut, by his will to exalt the building process, to lift it to an idealized level.

8. *Le Corbusier and Mies van der Rohe, Stuttgart. 1927*

9. German Pavilion, International Exposition, Barcelona. 1929. View toward enclosed pool

His objective, in any case, was a depoliticized architecture, although even that generalization does not take into account a shift in his thinking during the mid-1920s when he exhibited a brief but demonstrable interest in social housing and a perceptible loyalty to the programs of the German Democratic Party, a centrist group with a laissez-faire right wing that appealed to him probably because it favored cultural over social reform. The intricate relationships of ideologies—both political and cultural—in Germany during the 1920s are reviewed at length by Pommer, who shows in what respects and at what times Mies was close to some of his colleagues and distant from others, and how he began in 1927 to stake out a more distinctly personal position.

Once again the factor of the spiritual was central to his new stance, although the key terms he employed in defining it were freedom and order. The formative elements of this "explicit credo," as Pommer calls it, were various and complex, chief among them Mies's disillusionment with several causes he himself had earlier championed. By 1928–29 he had become persuaded that modern society was threatened, on the one hand, by mechanization, which he saw as an ill-disciplined child of the Industrial Revolution—that is, as technology unbridled—and, on the other, by a gulf between "hyper-individualism" and the mass culture—a condition he traced to the Renaissance. The chaos of modern architecture could be overcome, he believed, only by the preservation of a coherent set of values that would at the same time ensure man the liberty of his own movement and encourage his sovereign interaction with nature. Pommer sees this Miesian view "with its potential signification of freedom and order and of tradition and modernity" made manifest in the classicist style and the steel-and-glass technique of the Barcelona Pavilion and the Tugendhat House. In both works man was meant to engage nature even as he controlled it.

If patently idealistic, Mies's position was also politically middle-of-the-road, as we would now call it, although Pommer likens it to the propensity of many Weimar liberals at the end of the 1920s to "withdraw into [a] cultural neutralism," thus protecting themselves from attacks from either the political left or the right. The attacks were mounted, however, increasing as the Depression worsened, so that a split in the modernist ranks, between architects of a socially-minded, materialist point of view and those like Mies who leaned more toward formalism or idealism, paralleled the crisis that deepened within the national economy.

The argument itself was not so much resolved as beaten into irrelevance, with the accession in 1933 of Hitler and the rigidification a year or two later of the Nazi attitude toward the arts. Pommer conducts a painstaking examination of a subject sufficiently incendiary to have produced far more heat than light in the past: Mies's efforts to endure and even to continue a professional life in the midst of a society that grew steadily more repressive. The narrative is too complicated to be submitted here to the simplifications that have been the very cause of its inaccurate accounting in the past. It is certain at least that this chapter of Mies's ideological adventures ended unhappily, like most stories in which German modernist culture either attempted to oppose Nazi doctrine or sought accommodation with it. Suffice it to add that Pommer's exhaustive account should put in the shade the numerous ill-considered attempts to picture Mies either as a liberal proponent of artistic freedom, as a mere opportunist, or as a Nazi sympathizer.

The attentive reader will note a number of ironic likenesses and divergences, several of them sobering if not surprising, that emerge in the course of Pommer's essay. The Nazis, it develops, shared with Mies a measure of faith in the modernist style, adopting the manner for certain buildings they associated with the new technology. For again like Mies, they upheld as a cultural ideal the blending of tradition (neoclassical style) and modernity (steel-and-glass technique). Furthermore, they believed that one of the hallmarks of modern society was its impersonal and collective character. And so did Mies. But so did the Marxists. And so did other major modernist architects in Germany.

Yet as soon as these similarities are admitted, far deeper clefts swallow them up. The doctrinal differences between Nazism and communism and between Nazism and modernism as a whole, or communism and modernism, were irreconcilable, and Pommer leaves no doubt of it. Mies, moreover, in the course of the 1920s, shifted the subject of his attentions from the impersonal collective to human freedom, the latter, however, of a private and metaphorical sort that had nothing to do with the cause of political and social justice as espoused by Walter Gropius, Bruno Taut, and Ernst May. It is in these terms that we understand the bitterness that persisted between Gropius and Mies, even as both endeavored to rationalize remaining in Nazi Germany, and even as both finally emigrated to America.

In fact, the cultural ideal of tradition united with modernity was enunciated earlier than the 1920s and 1930s and in yet another context, as Fritz Neumeyer affirms in the third essay. On the surface Neumeyer's piece confines itself to several of Mies's earliest buildings but at its heart addresses the master's lifework. If Pommer's method is analytic, Neumeyer's is synthetic.

Until now only a handful of writers have taken Mies's first residential design, the Riehl House in Potsdam, of 1907, seriously enough to praise it, and even so have regarded it as little more than the work of a gifted apprentice. Neumeyer is vastly more impressed. While his principal objective, like that of Tegethoff and Pommer before him, is to show that the house was philosophy concretized, he goes further than they, interpreting it not just as an object reflective of a point of view but as an expression in its entirety and its smallest details of a complex architectural typology, the material counterpart of a specific and finely constructed *Weltanschauung.*

The origin of Mies's thought, according to Neumeyer, lies in the relationship he struck up with his client, Alois Riehl, a professor of philosophy in Berlin and one of the leading Nietzsche scholars of his day. Mies had developed a taste for philosophy on his own when he was still a teenager, and he had read Riehl's writings before the two men ever knew each other. Their meeting was an accident of fate, but the commission that followed appears to have been affected to a degree by Riehl's realization that the young designer he had hired was not only deeply interested in the professor's lifework but by inclination sympathetic to Riehl's personal understanding of it. Thus Riehl made a spiritual protégé of the man who was his architectural provider.

The Riehlian world view addressed the tensions that had troubled the modern Western spirit ever since ancient values—the a priori order—collided with the "insistence of the modern self on making its own laws." Nietzsche, Neumeyer recalls, had responded radically to this conflict, calling for a full-scale revolution of world values. Riehl, on the other hand, a more moderate thinker, proposed an ethic that allowed for new values only as they evolved from old ones: "The ancient Good—hold fast to it! The new Good is but a transformation of the old."

Neumeyer sees Mies's youthful preference for neoclassicism—the manner in which the Riehl House is built—as aesthetic evidence of his shared respect for what Riehl called "the ancient good." But the element of transformation is no less discernible in the design of the house. Following a careful examination of the two façades of the building, its longer, closed front and shorter, open side, Neumeyer concludes that the former is meant to convey the impression of a traditional block, the latter the covert configuration of a more nearly modern, skeletally framed pavilion. Two spirits thus coexist, although the more original of them—metaphorically, the new good shaped by the transformation of the old—is that of the pavilion, a form that became a central instrument of Mies's mature architecture, apparent as late as his last major work, the New National Gallery in Berlin (Fig. 10). The search for a union of tradition and modernity, which Pommer associated with Mies in the late 1920s, is seen by Neumeyer as adumbrated in Mies's earliest built efforts, and is traceable to Riehl's philosophy.

But Neumeyer finds several other influences, chiefly architects, acting upon Mies in the Riehl design. The first of these was Peter Behrens, whose Crematorium in Hagen gained widespread recognition in the profession following its completion in 1906–7. Although Mies was not yet in Behrens's employ, he must have known this work well enough to bow to it in the Riehl House, albeit with enough independence of intent to suggest that he was as free of Behrens's rationale as he was mindful of the form Behrens gave it. The second influence is Karl Friedrich Schinkel, dead for more than a half-century when

10. New National Gallery, Berlin. 1962–68

Mies was laboring for Riehl but a figure of immense consequence to German architecture, not only of the nineteenth century but of the early years of the twentieth. In the decade prior to the First World War Schinkel's neoclassicism inspired a generation of German architects in their efforts to liberate themselves from the burdensome historicism of the late 1800s and the still later stylistic excesses of the Jugendstil.

Mies found more in Schinkel than neoclassicism, and it took the form of another duality. For neoclassicism was but one element in Schinkel's larger Romantic vision, itself a reflection of German Idealist philosophy of about 1800. Neumeyer detects a Romantic sensibility in Schinkel's inclination to regard architecture as a mediating force that both expresses and facilitates the mutuality of man and nature, the complementarity, that is, of the autonomous, conscious, reasoning self and its surrounding world—man's "other." The block, as it addresses its setting, is understood to stand for the self in reciprocal relation with nature. Schinkel's Charlottenhof Palace in Potsdam serves as an example. There the manor house takes the form of a block that is connected to its environment by a three-sided portico, similar in effect to a pavilion, and an asymmetrically attached pillared pergola. Neumeyer takes note of the block/

pavilion analogy in the Riehl House, adding that Schinkel achieved a similar end in an urban situation with his Altes Museum in Berlin, in which the cubic mass of the building communicates with the plaza space before it through the intermediary device of a powerful frontal colonnade. Thus Schinkel sought not only to translate his understanding of the reflexive-self/nature relationship into architectural form, but to ensure the duality that was a necessary expressive aspect of that relationship. By inference, then, Mies saw in the Riehl House the possibility of effecting yet another unification, between the philosophies of the two men he admired, Riehl and Schinkel.

Still, the autonomous pavilion freed of its connection with the block was the end product of the process initiated in the Riehl House. It was followed in Mies's next residential design, the Perls House of 1910–11, and carried forward in the skeletal buildings of the 1920s and later. Neumeyer argues the seminal importance of the pavilion form to the history of modern architecture, maintaining that "the urge to pierce the block" was part of the effort to effect a closer union of building and landscape. He further notes that the pavilion in its stripped post-and-lintel configuration amounts to a "distillate of architecture." Thus the recognition of its place in the unfolding of abstract art in general and in Mies's own contribution to that development is crucial to the understanding of Mies's goals. Neumeyer contends that those objectives were attained when modern materials and modern construction made possible such works as the Barcelona Pavilion, the Tugendhat House, S. R. Crown Hall, and the New National Gallery. There, he concludes, Mies sought a "higher unity" of man, building, and nature, a quest traceable to his lifelong devotion to the spirit of German Idealism.

Neumeyer's definition of this search is expressed in more consistently sanguine terms than those employed by James Ingo Freed in his comments on its outcome. To be sure, Freed is largely occupied with two subjects—Mies the educator and Mies the architect in America—with which Neumeyer is only marginally concerned. The two men locate their respective problems for the most part in different places, and their interpretations can be compared only at occasional crossing points. Still, Mies spent fully thirty years of his professional career, indeed the mature half of it, in the United States, where he apparently had freedom and authority enough to pursue his creative and intellectual goals as both architect and teacher. How well he performed in both roles is a question reasonably asked in the light of all that Neumeyer and Freed, as well as Tegethoff and Pommer, have to tell us.

At the outset of his interview, Freed takes care to emphasize distinctions rather than unities. He begins with the need to differentiate among Mies's roles as educator, builder, and artist. After speculating that Mies would have shaped a different architecture school at Harvard University than at Armour Institute of Technology (later Illinois Institute of Technology)—chiefly because of dissimilar student constituencies in the two institutions—he asserts his belief that Mies's outlook and work would have been the same regardless of where he settled.

Freed's highest tribute to Mies is his argument that his work was based on principle, a term which he defines only at length in the course of his remarks, but which he treats in terms more of building than of ideology. Nevertheless, he acknowledges that Mies's principle, insofar as it was "a moral way of behaving when you build," did have a philosophical base in the conviction that architecture is the most significant visual record of the spirit of a civilization: the *Zeitgeist*. Reflecting on the modern *Zeitgeist*, Mies reasoned that technology is an elemental and inescapable fact of modernity; we are therefore obliged to derive our process of building from it. If we refine the process, we make poetry out of technique. The poetry and the technique, together comprising architecture, reflect, objectify, and make manifest the *Zeitgeist*.

We are here reminded of the aforementioned view of Mies that was common to the 1950s. Freed, however, considering his former teacher from the standpoint of the 1980s, has his doubts about Mies's view of the *Zeitgeist*. He calls it "frozen and fixed," and adds that we are today not so certain of facts, still less sure of their universal meaning and application; rather, we are compelled, in the spirit of pluralism, to acknowledge a global variety of opinions, often equal in urgency and persuasiveness if not in credibility. "Mies was an absolutist," declares Freed in a judgment that can be taken as differing from Neumeyer's interpretation of the dualities and complementaries that Mies based on the examples of Riehl and Schinkel.

But at this juncture Freed is perhaps not so distant from Neumeyer after all. Instead of concluding that Mies's absolutism marks his American work as frozen and fixed, as many recent critics might maintain, he makes a detailed case for Mies's own personal freedom from rigidity and inflexibility in his best American buildings. Freed regards the Seagram Building as a masterpiece of contextuality, the very factor that Mies is so often accused of having ignored (Fig. 11). Similar compliments are paid the 860–880 Lake Shore Drive Apartments in Chicago. They are not only admirably responsive to their immediate urban environment, Freed submits, but as a pair of buildings—one building, as he puts it—they are exceptional in the "lambent" spatial relationship they create: "not so much a building *in* space as a building that *makes* space."

Reflecting on his experience as Mies's student at IIT, Freed goes on to recall that Mies could be as undogmatic in his teaching as in his designing, since he tended in the atelier to instruct more by example than by theory. Yet before ever coming to IIT he had put together a meticulously constructed program that seemed to him so clear and consistent, so airtight, that he believed his colleagues and assistants could rely on it in their own educational assignments and thus teach it as well as he.

And therein lurked a fatal flaw. The program was indeed clear and consistent. Mies saw to it that it was less experimental even than the classic Bauhaus curriculum, reasoning that subjective elements might weaken the structure of presumably immutable fact upon which his understanding of the *Zeitgeist* rested. In order to arrive at an optimally trustworthy system of architectural education, he sought to reduce the components of the craft to primary forms. In the mind of a master, such a grammar could be manipulated with admirable effectiveness. His students, however, and his fellow teachers, proved to be more constrained by the intransigence of the program than illuminated by its clarity and precision. In practice, the Miesian discipline shrank their options rather than sharpened their visions, with the lamentably ironic result that Mies's efforts to create an educational order with overtones of a brotherhood of builders in the service of the *Zeitgeist* had the effect only of widening the gap between the master's art and that of his apprentices.

11. Seagram Building, New York. 1954–58

It is understandable that the experiences of the 1930s would have shaken any artist who watched the momentum of modernism as a whole decreased if not arrested outright by the forces of Depression and dictatorship. One can hardly wonder, then, remembering Pommer's observation that order replaced freedom at the head of Mies's architectural priorities when he came to the United States in 1938, that his subsequent work would tend toward closed, compact, symmetrical volumes—primary forms, Freed has called them—and that his educational methods would exhibit a kindred tendency toward fixity.

But Freed notices signs of this inclination in Mies even before the end of the 1920s. He speculates that the search for an absolute system began when Mies recognized the contrary implications of an open-endedness readable in the plan of the Brick Country House of 1924, and pulled back from them. Other motives seem to have prompted him in his 1928 project for the Remodeling of Alexanderplatz in Berlin. There, a group of slablike highrise buildings arranged "independent of the old street system" prefigured a post–Second World War development in America to which Mies himself contributed and which had the effect of shredding the urban fabric. The deference Mies showed the environment of the Seagram Building seems quite missing in the Alexanderplatz plan, and Freed suggests that Mies in conceiving it may have felt the influence from one, maybe two, phenomena of the Weimar years. On the one hand, his interest in the freestanding building as expressed in the Alexanderplatz group may have been a reflection of the revolutionary intentions of the *Neue Sachlichkeit* as Freed sees them, which stood for a rejection of the old city pattern and the introduction of "a new kind of space to live in." On the other hand, the Alexanderplatz project in its grim monumentality could just as easily have stood for the "bureaucratization of society," a process Mies may have sensed even before the worldwide totalitarianism of the 1930s set in. In any case, Freed assigns Mies a substantial measure of responsibility for the Americanization of the freestanding slab during the post–Second World War years, and its unhappy, antiurbanistic consequences. Once again, speaking from the viewpoint of the 1980s, he takes note of the failure of modernist planning to make a liveable urban environment, and concludes that the contemporary city with its relatively free-wheeling diversity is a better place than the windy stretches of urban renewal plans that grew all too often a generation ago from the modernist tower-in-the-park concept.

Yet Freed insists that modernism, despite its follies and broken hopes, is not bankrupt. It still has much to teach us, and nothing more important than the lesson Mies provided in his work and in his devotion to his work. "What he stood for," says Freed, "was the principled, ethical worker—architect, designer, or craftsman—who possesses the will to build to last." The permanence of form Mies sought and the poetry of form he evoked, together with a matchless sense of space: these are the richest elements of a legacy traceable to a principled approach to architecture, which is instructive independent of the Miesian "style" or any other.

Clearly Freed ends his statement on an affirmative note. Nevertheless, in sum, he is more critical of Mies than are the other contributors to this volume, especially Tegethoff and Neumeyer. Pommer, for that matter, reproaches Mies chiefly for his politics, not his art. Freed has little to say about freedom as a guiding principle in Mies's career—Tegethoff, Pommer, and Neumeyer are transfixed by it—and far more about the search for an absolute architectural system. Pommer comes nearer Freed's position in arguing that Mies put order ahead of freedom after 1938, while Neumeyer makes no such distinction. He believes that Mies respected the context of his buildings more consistently than Freed is willing to acknowledge, and he adds emphatically that, "Reciprocal perfectability and autonomy combined with responsibility toward the whole" were "principles Mies honored most in his philosophy of serving in freedom." Meanwhile Pommer has his own interpretation of Mies's concept of freedom, which he defines as private, metaphorical, and little related to serving, although Pommer and Neumeyer agree on Mies's desire, especially at the turn of the 1930s, to create an architecture conducive to man's interaction with nature. A major consonance occurs between Neumeyer and Freed on the issue of responsibility, which Freed grants Mies at least in his attitude toward building in the abstract. While Pommer and Freed appear in similar accord about Mies's idealizing tendencies, the former emphasizes Mies's "depoliticized" architecture and the latter sees evidence in the Alexanderplatz project of a sympathy with revolutionary—presumably political—inclinations in the *Neue Sachlichkeit* to remake the pattern of city space.

Even in minor points disagreements crop up here and there. For example, Tegethoff regards the colors used in the interior of the Barcelona Pavilion— black carpet, red drapery, gold onyx wall—as symbolic of Weimar Germany's national flag, while Pommer doubts the scheme had any iconographical significance at all. What shall we make of these diverging arguments? It seems to me that the sober reader would be more suspicious of the four authors if they were in total unison rather than occasional discord. Paradoxically in fact, their differences are evidence of a major recent consensus: that Mies van der Rohe was an artist not only of surpassing subtlety but of immense, at times even confounding, complexity, one to be neither examined in haste nor explained in simplified terms. Aside from the intrinsic value of the four statements, which help to fill in the portrait of Mies with more detail and discriminating tonality than we have enjoyed in the past, they remind us that their subject is rich enough to require and reward continued study by future generations of scholars and architects.

WOLF TEGETHOFF

From Obscurity to Maturity: Mies van der Rohe's Breakthrough to Modernism

With his first independent work, the Riehl House of 1907, published in two respectable periodicals, Ludwig Mies (later, Mies van der Rohe) made an imposing architectural debut. For a talented 21-year-old who had just left provincial Aachen for the bustling German capital this early recognition must have engendered considerable self-confidence. Conditions could hardly have been better for the start of a promising career: Berlin was in the midst of a building boom, and commissions were plentiful and easy to obtain. Nevertheless, Mies felt reluctant to try his hand at independent practice, and after a brief period on his own he sought employment with Peter Behrens.

Perhaps he recognized the distance that still lay between him and social status in the authoritarian, static society of Berlin. As the son of a stonemason, he lacked the classical education commonly expected of professionals in upper-class German intellectual circles. Clients as open-minded and venturesome as the philosopher Alois Riehl were the exception to the rule.

But Mies learned conventional proprieties quickly, absorbing more from Behrens than he would later admit. Yet with his urbane upper-class colleague Walter Gropius also in Behrens's office, he must have felt somewhat the underdog. Reared in a typical petit-bourgeois, Rhenish Catholic environment imbued with traditional values, including that of aspiration to social advancement, Mies was disinclined to take a radical stance or to associate himself with the advocates of the underprivileged. If history regards him as a progressive architect, he might better be characterized as a liberal with conservative leanings.

His path to maturity was hardly as straight as Mies in his later years wanted the public to believe. The Perls House of 1910–11 as well as his competition entry for the Bismarck Monument of 1910–11, and his Kröller-Müller House project of 1912 all attest to extraordinary qualifications. Yet they do not compare in audacity with the revolutionary design of Gropius's 1911 Fagus Factory, built about the same time. As late as 1920 Mies was still a rather insignificant Berlin architect who, after what had been a promising start, seemed somehow to have failed to catch up with the more adventurous spirits in his field. Before 1925 he had built a number of houses equal to the highest craftsmanly standards of the day, but they were stylistically conservative: the Riehl, Werner, Urbig, Kempner, Feldmann, Eichstaedt, and Mosler houses.

While attempting a reconstruction of Mies's career from obscure local professional to a leading figure of modern architecture—as well as an examination of the driving forces and circumstances that guided him—I will focus on those designs that mark the crucial stages of his ascendancy. Following the discussion of Mies's famous five early projects, which contained the nucleus of his radical architectural intentions (even though they were conceived in rapid succession during the period of the conventional Kempner and Mosler houses), the question of how successfully these visionary concepts translated into practice will be explored, beginning with the Wolf House in Guben. Conceived in late 1925, and thus just prior to Mies's "most significant year . . . of great realization and awareness,"[1] the Wolf House was, in fact, his first executed building to which the stylistic term *modern* may truly apply.

Mies's master plan and supervision of the Deutsche Werkbund's Weissenhof exhibition of 1927, which brought him international recognition, was a clear artistic breakthrough for himself and for modern architecture in general. It was at Weissenhof that the various groupings of the European avant-garde finally converged. Thus I will direct attention to a close-up view of the actions and aims of Mies and the people involved with him in that ground-breaking endeavor.

The Barcelona Pavilion of 1929, which concludes the essay, has been accepted almost unanimously as Mies's masterpiece. On the strength of its architectural detailing, constructive principle, and spatial layout it constituted the prototype for all his residential projects of the 1930s (including the Tugendhat House) and many structures of his later years in America. At the same time, however, the Pavilion embodied some irritating, if not irrational, features, never to occur again in Mies's oeuvre, which might be attributable to the spiritual atmosphere of his formative years. In more than one respect, then, 1929 serves as an appropriate point at which to conclude this essay.

Many projects of the decade under study could only be touched upon in a cursory way, and some—like Mies's unexecuted designs for office buildings and department stores of the second half of the 1920s—have not been dealt with at all. Nevertheless, I think that the areas of focus I have chosen reflect Mies's own preoccupations in that decade. As to the 1930s, intensive research is still to be done.

Prelude to an Architect's Career

The collapse of imperial Germany in November 1918 released the creative vigor of a generation of architects whose ambitions had suffered a four-year suspension during the war that effectively marked the end of nineteenth-century Europe. Initially, those who had shaped the previous epoch were paralyzed by the sudden vacuum created by the disappearance of protégés and opponents alike. Hans Poelzig for a short time seemed to be the father figure of the Expressionist movement, and Peter Behrens, in his administration building for I. G. Farben in Frankfurt-Hoechst, begun in 1920, showed great flexibility in adjusting his formal conceptions to the new spirit of postwar Germany. But it fell to Walter Gropius and Bruno Taut, the angry young men of the Deutsche Werkbund conference of 1914, to assume the leading role within the architectural avant-garde—the former through his position as head of the newly created Bauhaus in Weimar, the latter as founder of the *Gläserne Kette* (Glass, or Crystal, Chain), which for a brief period was one of the major movements dedicated to social reform through the arts.

Both Gropius and Taut believed architecture should provide an environment in which a modern society could flourish. However, Taut and his circle allowed themselves to be carried away by utopian fantasies which soon proved inadequate to the practical needs of the day, whereas the Bauhaus curriculum established by Gropius at least kept a back door open to a rational approach.

Nevertheless, disastrous inflation, which reached its peak in Germany in

1923, marked a turning point in their fortunes. Although war and revolution had deeply shaken the political convictions of the German bourgeoisie, the nation's social structures had remained more or less intact. Now, with their economic base undermined by inflation, the middle class no longer felt inclined to tolerate, let alone follow, the radicals' path toward an architecture idealistically expressive of modern society. Architects like Gropius and Taut, therefore, had to rely on public, as opposed to private, commissions, which left little room for utopian extravagance. The resultant brief alliance of progressive politicians and socially-minded architects helped to shape the architectural-cultural image of the Weimar Republic, which was no more reflective of most contemporaneous private buildings than it was of the Expressionist experiments that dominated the early postwar years.

Looking back on one of the most theoretically active although practically unproductive periods in German architecture (1919 to 1922), one may be surprised that Mies van der Rohe had virtually no part in it. The shortlived Work Council for Art (*Arbeitsrat für Kunst*) of 1918–22, an association of progressive Berlin artists, patrons, and architects led successively by Taut, Gropius, and the critic Adolf Behne, which tried to establish a union of all the arts under the aegis of architecture, never listed him among its members. Neither did he hasten to associate himself with the less politically inclined Novembergruppe, which he joined only in 1922 by which time it had turned into a mere lobby for promoting the Berlin representatives of the modern movement.[2] For a while he played an active role in the Brandenburg section of the *Bund Deutscher Architekten* (BDA), the traditional association of German architects, and a moderate if not conservative society at that. On August 13, 1923, he accepted election to the regional board of the BDA but resigned early in 1926 following extended quarrels with the leadership over the organization's future policy.[3] Thus it was left to the Werkbund to provide the platform for Mies's rise within the field of modern architecture.

Mies was formally invited to join the Werkbund on March 22, 1923.[4] In contrast, Gropius and Taut had already held important positions in the group before the outbreak of the First World War, and both were present at the Werkbund's conference in Cologne in 1914 when Henry van de Velde launched his famous attack on Hermann Muthesius.[5] There is strong evidence that Gropius, backed by the Hagen banker and patron of the arts Karl Ernst Osthaus, engineered this open controversy between Muthesius, the advocate of industrial standards, and van de Velde, who defended the artist's right to individuality. Judging from the correspondence in the Karl-Ernst-Osthaus-Museum, van de Velde served mainly as a figurehead for the revolt by a younger generation of architects against a complacent Werkbund establishment represented by Muthesius, its eloquent if doctrinaire partisan.[6] The young Gropius was ready for a break, but van de Velde and Osthaus accepted a compromise before the whole affair was finally cut short by the war. After 1918 Gropius repeatedly complained about the Werkbund's weak policies, and practically withdrew from its activities; by 1923 the organization seemed almost paralyzed.[7] The *Arbeitsrat* and the Novembergruppe filled the gap, although both lacked the potential political power of the Werkbund with its unique interaction among artists, industrialists, and public representatives. In 1923 what the Werkbund most needed was leadership.

In March 1924, exactly one year after Mies had joined the Werkbund, the latest palace revolution took place, and he was in the middle of it. On March 22 he wrote to Friedrich Kiesler in Vienna: "Here in Berlin, a group of young artists is about to attempt a regeneration of the Deutsche Werkbund, i.e., these younger forces want to decide what is to be done. The Werkbund has promised to support these efforts, and to back events of all kinds. I, too, was contacted and asked to participate. I think that this may turn out to be a useful means for realizing the concept of elementary design [*elementare Gestaltung*]."[8]

The initiative behind this thrust had been taken by the politically radical Berlin sculptor Paul Henning.[9] In contrast to the events of 1914, there seems to have been no serious opposition from the leading members of the Werkbund, who must have felt a rejuvenation was inevitable if the organization was going to survive. Even more revealing in the letter to Kiesler is Mies's overwhelming concern with an architectural ideal as distinct from the realization of personal ambition—with an opportunity, that is, which participation in the Werkbund administration promised to offer. And he got his chance: once a member of the executive board, he was, on June 26, 1925, elected artistic supervisor for the Werkbund exhibition in Stuttgart, at that time planned for 1926. Later in the year, on October 26, Gustav Stotz, the association's regional representative in Stuttgart, wrote to Mies that the executive secretary of the Werkbund, Otto Baur, wanted him (Stotz) to come to Hannover, "so that, before the meeting, a small circle could talk about how to get the organization of the Berlin exhibition into the hands of the young generation. It is my impression that he, too, realizes the critical situation of the Werkbund, and that he himself is anxious to convert the Werkbund into a vigorous and up-to-date movement. He places all his hopes in you and [Hugo] Häring. I told him that his plans absolutely conform with ours and that in any case [Peter] Bruckmann will be on our side. While still forced to work with the old group today, Baur himself can, of course, not enter into negotiations with you on his own initiative. But this is not even necessary, since the affair should start from here. Just take care that [Richard] Lisker and Miss [Lilly] Reich are present at the meeting. If you know somebody else on the executive board who is on our side, make him come."[10]

The following year, on June 23–27, 1926, Mies was elected first vice president of the Werkbund, a position he retained until 1932.[11] At his insistence the presidency reverted to Peter Bruckmann, a southern German manufacturer of silverware and a founding member of the Werkbund who had held the chair almost continuously since 1909.[12] The decision was wisely made. Bruckmann's reputation and conciliatory personality helped to placate the established members who had grown increasingly conservative over the years. Moreover, there was hardly any risk he would interfere with the architectural intentions of Mies van der Rohe. Stotz's letter leaves no doubt that Bruckmann was on Mies's side from the beginning. Besides, as an industrialist, he was scarcely familiar with questions of artistic choice. Mies, in turn, from his own point of view, may have welcomed a certain counterweight to keep the radicals from his heels.

By the time Mies, as the spokesman of the young generation, finally occupied a leading position in one of the foremost cultural organizations of Weimar Germany, he was already forty years old. Compared to Gropius and Taut, who were more or less the same age, he was a latecomer, a characterization applicable to his architectural career as well. It is nonetheless remarkable how swiftly he rose to power once he decided to enter the field.

Mies in the 1920s must have been a different personality from the taciturn grand old man of modern architecture feeding his audience cryptic bits of architectural philosophy. Or was it just his unwillingness to get entangled in the thicket of daily politics that made him acceptable to both factions of the Werkbund? He may have been a charismatic figure whose aura derived from his very composure in the midst of frantic activity. Above all, he was an architect, a creative spirit who offered to replace the falseness and pretension of modern society with a rare and compelling honesty. Next to so many who constantly talked about art and society, Mies was one of the few who preferred to act. For him action meant building.

At some point in late 1925 or early 1926, Mies directed his assistant Sergius Ruegenberg to climb to the attic of his studio at Am Karlsbad 24 and destroy all the old plans and drawings that had been stored there.[13] In an architect's career such a gesture must be taken as a sign of a profound change in outlook. The volume of paper could not have been that great, judging from the limited number of commissions Mies had worked on, but the story recalls others in which artists have thus demonstrated a radical break with their past.

Surely Mies had done nothing during the three years immediately following the end of the First World War that pointed to a reorientation of his artistic convictions. The single possible exception is the published version of a drawing for the unexecuted Petermann House, which Paul Westheim (writing in 1927) dated to 1921.[14] The Kempner Villa in Berlin-Charlottenburg, Mies's first major postwar commission, was finished in 1922. Badly damaged during the war, this building did not survive. A preliminary version, done in 1919, and also illustrated by Westheim,[15] shows a flat-topped brick design of one and a half stories in a modified neoclassical style. The design is not without interest, yet its tall rectangular windows and arcaded loggia have little in common with the basic principles of a later modern architecture. The final working drawings for the Kempner Villa have only recently been discovered, and they suggest that the executed building was even less stylistically advanced.[16] Thus, there must have been good reason for Mies to keep silent about this project in his later years. The same is true for the Eichstaedt House of 1922, a modest stucco building still standing on Dreilindenstrasse in Berlin-Wannsee, and not much more than a variation of the Perls House of more than a decade earlier.[17]

The first truly modern project by Mies that has come down to us with a reliable date is thus his entry in the competition for the Friedrichstrasse Office Building of December 1921. The slightly Expressionist aspect of its jagged plan and skyline notwithstanding, it remains without precedent both in contemporaneous German architecture and in the oeuvre of Mies van der Rohe himself. Conceived when he was thirty-five, it was the initial project of five that laid the foundations of his rise from anonymity to the leading ranks of the European avant-garde. Only once before, in 1912, had Mies been on the verge of an artistic breakthrough: when Mrs. Helene Kröller-Müller decided to entrust him with a proposal for her estate at Wassenaar, near The Hague. At the time Mies was project architect for Peter Behrens, whose own design had already failed to satisfy the patron. In accepting her offer, Mies broke with Behrens and went on to produce one of the outstanding examples of German neoclassical architecture of the period. Although it was largely a revised version of the Behrens scheme, Mies's project surpassed his master's in the serene austerity of its massing (Fig. 1). Conceived for a setting in the dune country of the Dutch coast, it evokes the image of the ideal antique country house transferred to a distant northern shore.

Neoclassicism had inspired a still earlier project, a competition entry of 1910–11 for the design of the Bismarck Monument on the cliffs of the Rhine River, opposite Bingen (Fig. 2). The balanced grouping of exedra, pylons, and pillars set on an enormous substructure and enclosing an inner Court of Honor, did not lack monumentality, yet it was free of the patriotic pathos to which the majority of his more than three hundred competitors took recourse.[18] While his entry passed a preliminary review by the jury, it was later rejected on grounds of "obviously excessive building costs."[19]

However, Mies sustained a serious blow to his self-confidence not over the latter rejection but when Mrs. Kröller-Müller's advisor Hendrik Peter Bremmer rejected his design for Wassenaar in favor of a proposal by Dutch architect Hendrik Berlage. Ironically, Mies had always held Berlage in the highest esteem, but Bremmer's withering comment, "This is art [pointing to Berlage's model], and [turning to Mies's] this is not" (as reported by Salomon van Deventer),[20] was most likely too much to bear for a young man who had come so

1. Kröller-Müller House, Wassenaar, The Netherlands. Project, 1912. Original photograph of full-scale wood and canvas model. The Museum of Modern Art, New York, Mies van der Rohe Archive. Gift of the architect

2. Bismarck Monument, Bingen-am-Rhein, Germany. Competition project, 1910–11.
Court of Honor. Drawing. Whereabouts unknown

close to realizing his first major creative effort in architecture. The fact that Mies later asked the famed art critic Julius Meier-Graefe in Paris for an independent opinion on his plans betrays how deeply he must have been hurt.[21]

We cannot know exactly what inspired the massive shift in Mies's thinking that is evident in his revolutionary design for the Friedrichstrasse Office Building, but we may at least speculate. In February 1919 Mies responded to a letter from Gropius, who was soliciting material for the *Exhibition of Unknown Architects* (*Ausstellung für unbekannte Architekten*), organized by the *Arbeitsrat:* "I gladly comply with your kind request and send some photos of the Kröller-Müller House in The Hague. The project was, admittedly, conceived some seven years ago, and I wonder if it qualifies for your purposes. Other projects, especially those that serve the collaboration of all the arts, I do not have at hand right now. At a later date I could offer you some other projects."[22]

According to Sandra Honey, Mies's offer to exhibit the Kröller-Müller drawings was flatly rejected.[23] A project for a bourgeois country house probably seemed out of place in the midst of the numerous utopian daydreams that were more in accord with the exalted revolutionary spirit of the day.

What happened over the next year and a half is unknown, since almost all documentary evidence has been destroyed. But in December 1921 (at the latest by January 1922, the closing date of the competition) Mies came up with his proposal for the Friedrichstrasse skyscraper. As he himself recalled in the 1960s, his project was no more cordially received by the jury than his earlier designs had been, but at least it got a friendly mention in an article by Max Berg,[24] the architect of the famous Breslau Centennial Hall of 1912–13. This time, however, Mies was not perceptibly disturbed by the rejection. The next months found him working on a revised version of the design that took the form of a curvilinear structure later known as the Glass Skyscraper. The proposal for a Concrete Office Building was soon to follow. Two country house projects, of 1923 and 1924, marked the point of departure to his greatest achievements in the second half of the decade, confined mostly to the residential field. Within this sequence of works that have come to be known as the five early projects, the Brick Country House of 1924 was surely the last. Thus it coincided with,

3. *Mosler House, Potsdam-Neubabelsberg. 1924–26*

or even preceded, the Mosler House in Potsdam-Neubabelsberg, which, in spite of its fine proportions and generous size, turned out to be a rather conventional building with a hipped roof, symmetrical layout, and altogether traditional detailing (Fig. 3).[25]

Thus Gropius's rejection of the Kröller-Müller project in 1919 and the destructive campaign in the attic of 1925–26 may be regarded as the dates bracketing an evolutionary process that fulfilled, albeit in fits and starts, the architectural prospects opened up by the Friedrichstrasse Office Building.

The Five Projects

Between 1920 and 1922 the argument was advanced that building regulations should be eased, in a limited number of cases, to allow skyscrapers, or *Turmhäuser* (tower buildings), to be erected in major German cities.[26] The concentration of business and administration within a few multistory buildings seemed to promise an improvement in the tight housing situation.[27] The expectation was that former residential areas now occupied by commerce and industry could be regained for the housing market by providing a sufficient amount of new and attractive office space elsewhere, presumably in tall buildings. Other perceived advantages of skyscrapers were more visionary. For many Germans the outcome of the war had proved the clear superiority of the American economy, whose tangible image took the form of the highrise buildings that rose so dramatically in downtown Manhattan. The skyscraper represented economic efficiency, not to mention national self-assurance, and it appeared to be the ideal model for a modern democratic Germany. As a symbol for economic progress it promised to compensate for the traumatic experience of losing the war.

Nevertheless, the American prototype was not accepted without reservation. Its German advocates objected to its stylistic eclecticism,[28] and they criticized the inadequate building regulations (although the New York zoning law of 1916 was welcomed as a first step in the right direction). To avoid the unhealthy light and air conditions that plagued Manhattan's financial district, architects and critics generally agreed that the erection of skyscrapers in Germany should be limited to carefully selected sites within the centers of major cities. As modern landmarks they would counteract the monotony of the nineteenth-century urban environment, while interfering as little as possible with the neighborhood they were meant to dominate. Thus, three different but interconnected objectives animated the skyscraper discussions of the early 1920s: the furthering of private enterprise as the source of common welfare, the concept of the latter controlling the former, and the advocacy of planning as the integrating factor of both, thus guaranteeing a systematic and orderly development of the city. Mies's two skyscraper projects, extreme examples among countless proposals for German skyscrapers of the time, must be seen in light of these issues.

As early as 1914 Bruno Möhring had presented a proposal for a highrise building to be erected on a vacant lot opposite the Friedrichstrasse Station in Berlin. Alternative projects were soon to follow, since the idea was sustained throughout the war.[29] In 1920 Möhring was asked to analyze the situation, and the speech he delivered to the Prussian Academy of Civil Engineering (*Preussische Akademie des Bauwesens*) on December 12 prompted an immediate reaction by the prevailing political institutions.[30] A decree issued by the Prussian Minister of Public Welfare (*Preussischer Minister für Volkswohlfahrt*) on January 3, 1921, allowed for the erection of multistory buildings exceeding Berlin's official height limit of 72 feet (22 meters), provided such a variance were granted by the minister himself.[31]

With so many practical advantages, the Friedrichstrasse site seemed likely to acquire the first skyscraper in Germany. Bordered on the south by the central metropolitan railroad station, on the north by the Weidendamm Bridge across the Spree River, and on the east by Friedrichstrasse itself, the triangular area was central to one of Berlin's most heavily trafficked neighborhoods (Fig. 4). Yet it lacked an important architectural accent, which was exactly what the projected skyscraper could offer. The closest buildings included the station—a simple utilitarian structure of limited architectural value—and those buildings on the opposite side of Friedrichstrasse that would presumably have suffered only slightly from a change in contextual scale. However, the principal vistas were to be enjoyed from the north and west where there was sufficient space (rather than from the adjacent street itself): from the other end of the Weidendamm Bridge and from a point west of the elevated tracks that crossed Friedrichstrasse before entering the station (Fig. 5).[32]

After preliminary studies pointed to a profitable amortization rate for highrise buildings as well as a lively demand in the local business world, the Tower Corporation (*Turmhaus Aktien-Gesellschaft*) was established, which went on to acquire the property from the city. The company's decision to hold a competition, open to all members of the BDA, was officially announced on November 1, 1921. The conditions included a number of requirements that may help to explain some of the features of Mies van der Rohe's first skyscraper project.[33]

In spite of its emphasis on a simple and unambiguous solution for the basic plan, the program provided only a generalized definition of what the building was to be used for. While the ground floor was intended exclusively for stores,

4. *Aerial view of Friedrichstrasse competition site, Berlin, c. 1921*

5. *Friedrichstrasse Office Building, Berlin.
Competition project, 1921. Photomontage.
Whereabouts unknown*

the upper levels were to accommodate offices as well as exhibition spaces or showrooms. A number of optional facilities like restaurants, cinemas, storage spaces, garages, and studios were also mentioned. The layout was to allow for maximum flexibility, and architects were asked to present alternative solutions for the various floors. The maximum requisite height of 262 feet (80 meters) was imposed on the building because of the geological instability of the area, which is notorious for its sandy soil interspersed with cavities and layers of putrescent mud from ancient river beds. The importance of the town-planning aspects of the program may be inferred from the stipulation that the new building harmonize with its surroundings. In order to attract sufficient customers for the stores and to assure easy access to the station from the Weidendamm Bridge, a passage at street level was suggested. Elevators would provide access to a proposed subway station below.

The following drawings were required: a site plan, floor plans, sections, two elevations, and two perspective views at 6 feet (2 meters) above ground from fixed points nearby. All were to be executed in simple freehand drawings accompanied by a brief commentary and specifications.

The deadline for submission was January 2, 1922. Entries were exhibited for review by the public at the old Berlin City Hall.[34] For purposes of identification, Mies's project bore the name *Wabe* (honeycomb). The surviving documents include no section, and only one set of identical and rather schematic floor plans, which in all likelihood were drawn for publication after the competition (Fig. 6).[35] Of the two large perspective renderings in charcoal one is certainly a presentation drawing. It probably constituted the principal element of the entry (Fig. 7). The other is more sketchy in character and may have been rejected by Mies in favor of the first. The single surviving side elevation is scaled to 1:200 as required by the jury, whereas the photomontages (*see* Fig. 5) show the actual siting.

Although the key position of the Friedrichstrasse Office Building within the early history of modern architecture has never been seriously challenged, critical opinion on it has always been divided. Ever since the publication of Philip Johnson's monograph on Mies in 1947, the curtain wall as a transparent skin sheathing the skeleton structure has frequently been hailed as a pioneering breakthrough. Other views of the building, stressing its supposedly Expressionist plan, have seen it as a somewhat less adventurous effort. In fact, the project has never been regarded in a broad context. Thus measured, Mies's proposal for Friedrichstrasse is radically modern in more than the one respect emphasized by Johnson.

Contrary to almost all of his competitors (Fig. 8), Mies decided against a stepped-back elevation, which would have been more in scale with the neighboring structures. Instead, he designed an all-glass curtain wall that rises continuously to a full height of twenty stories, "as though cut by shears."[36] While Louis Sullivan, in proposing a definition for the skyscraper, had modeled its elevation after the tripartition of the classical column, Mies chose a homogeneous and almost unarticulated skin that neutralized the soaring effect of the tower. Sullivan typically used a two-story base and a heavy cornice of at least another story to balance the vertical shaft of the skyscraper in between. Mies worked the other way around, so to speak, breaking up the facades into vertical

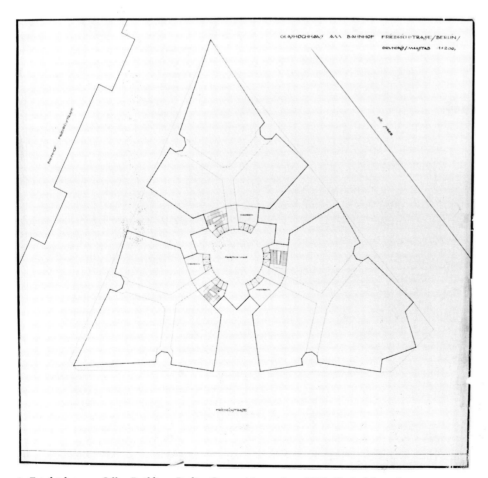

6. *Friedrichstrasse Office Building, Berlin. Competition project, 1921. Typical floor plan.*
Ink on tracing paper. The Museum of Modern Art, New York, Mies van der Rohe Archive.
Gift of the architect

7. *Friedrichstrasse Office Building, Berlin. Competition project, 1921. Perspective, north and east sides. Charcoal and pencil on brown paper. The Museum of Modern Art, New York, Mies van der Rohe Archive. Gift of the architect*

planes in order to produce a dynamic effect. Sullivan, in his design for the Wainwright Building of 1890–91 (Fig. 9), has given an identical articulation to structural piers and non-bearing "mullions," thus contradicting his own principle of "form follows function." From the strictly functionalist point of view, Mies also would have left himself open to criticism for not differentiating floors with clearly dissimilar functions. The ground floor, intended as a shopping arcade, looks the same as the others, even in height. It is not known where he would have accommodated the cinemas and other facilities cited in the program. Instead of a complex solution responding to the various spaces inside, Mies, like Sullivan before him, favored the uniform shape of the compact tower, which in its monotonous sequence of identical stories presents itself foremost as an office building.

8. Hans Scharoun: Friedrichstrasse Office Building, Berlin. Competition project, 1921. Drawing. Akademie der Künste, West Berlin

Unlike Sullivan, however, he disapproved of the use of traditional surface patterns and insisted that the form evolve totally from the nature of the new building type itself.[37] According to Mies, it was not the functional requirements but the steel skeleton that constituted the essential precondition for the skyscraper: "The new structural principle of those buildings comes to the fore only when glass is used for the nonsupporting outer walls of today."[38]

In spite of this straightforward constructivist confession, Mies seemed well aware of the formal consequences imposed by the all-glass curtain wall, as his further remarks on the Friedrichstrasse project reveal. Because of the triangular site, he wrote in 1922, "a prismatic form adjusted to the shape of the triangle appeared the right answer to me. To avoid the dull and lifeless effect that often results from glass being applied to large surfaces, I set the individual planes of the facade at a slight angle. While experimenting with a glass model, I soon came to realize that it is not the effect of light and shadow but an abundant ripple of reflections that matters with the material."[39]

Revealing as it is, Mies's first article, from which the above quotations are taken, gives a somewhat one-sided account of the factors that motivated his design. In fact, the faceted contour of the skyscraper was determined largely by the interior development of the building. The only author to have commented incisively on the importance of the plan has been Arthur Drexler,[40] who noted that the Friedrichstrasse skyscraper actually consists of three independent towers grouped around a cylindrical core, which serves as a communication area for each individual level. Vertical access to the different floors is established by means of smaller connecting parts containing staircases and elevator shafts. All elevators open toward the circular lobbies on each floor, from which **Y**-shaped corridors branch off in three directions to end at the polygonal recesses that subdivide the facade. Since the corridors at street level were probably meant to issue from secondary entrances, visitors could gain access to the building from virtually every possible point.

9. Louis Sullivan and Dankmar Adler: Wainwright Building, St. Louis. 1890–91

The radial system of passageways superimposes a linear plexus upon the triangular shape of the skyscraper (see Fig. 6). Reaching out in one direction like the roots of a gigantic tree, the corridors converge in another at the trunk of the vertical core, then branch out again on the different floor levels, allowing for convenient access and circulation throughout the building. Indeed, the peculiar plan of the three towers closely resembles the configuration of ivy leaves, whose veins would be equivalent to the forked corridors that connect them to the stem. Although this conception is unique in Mies's oeuvre, the biomorphic

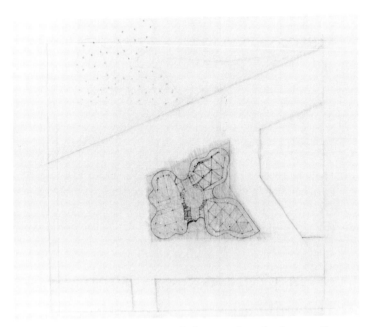

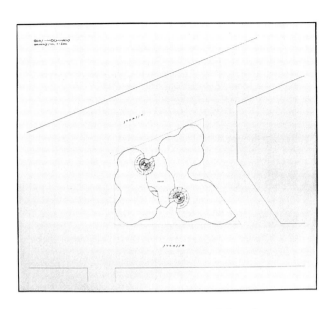

10. *Glass Skyscraper. Project, 1922. Preliminary floor plan (structural).*
Pencil on tracing paper. The Museum of Modern Art, New York, Mies van der
Rohe Archive. Gift of the architect

11. *Glass Skyscraper. Project, 1922. Typical floor plan.*
Ink on tracing paper. The Museum of Modern Art, New York,
Mies van der Rohe Archive. Gift of the architect

image works out too well to be discarded as a possible source. In any case, it appears no less convincing than the perhaps unconscious influence of Jean (Hans) Arp's biomorphic reliefs on the plan of the curvilinear Glass Skyscraper of 1922, a connection initially suggested by Johnson and repeated later by others.[41]

According to Mies, his second skyscraper project was an immediate consequence of his continued experiments with the all-glass curtain wall. The preliminary plan (Fig. 10) shows a layout similar to that of the first project, with a circular hall that was only later replaced at its core by the bipolar arrangement of two cylindrical shafts (Fig. 11). These shafts contain elevators and ample spiral staircases at their centers. An irregularly shaped lobby runs between them. Each of the cylindrical elements serves half of the tower and is situated next to an indentation in the facade, providing an entry on each side of the building; this makes it possible to enter the staircases directly from the outside. Horizontal circulation is provided on each floor by a spacious lobby, whose shape looks somewhat arbitrary, especially where the partition walls meet the elevators. The undulating contour of the curtain wall produces a more economical interior layout than that of the Friedrichstrasse skyscraper because it avoids both the awkward, sharp-angled corner spaces and the uneven lighting conditions of the latter project.

Werner Graeff, who in 1923–24 was one of the editors of the Constructivist journal *G*, recorded what Mies had told him about the genesis of both projects: "When working on a model, he came to realize that at this particular site, and with the sun at a certain position, a huge, plane surface of glass would blind pedestrians and carriage horses all along Friedrichstrasse. He therefore tried to break up the surfaces into angular planes and, in his second skyscraper project, to further divide them into even smaller strips, from which that undulating plan was derived."[42]

The story sounds too simple: why use an all-glass curtain wall to reveal a structure that nobody would see because of the strong reflections peculiar to the material, and why then go to great lengths to keep the glistening effect at a tolerable level, yet still not achieving the transparency necessary to meet the Constructivist point of departure? In fact, the curtain wall does not reveal, but only implies, the steel skeleton behind it; and it is not the transparency but, rather, the fragile, untectonic nature of the glass that demonstrates its non-bearing character. Furthermore, neither the Friedrichstrasse plan nor the published version of the curvilinear plan gives any indication whatever of the structural system. Mies's clumsy attempts in the preliminary plan betray the fact that "the structural concept as the essential foundation of the artist's design"[43] has not been seriously tackled at all, let alone solved. On the other hand, much care was devoted to the functional layout, with priority given to accessibility and lighting. One wonders if it was not the advantage of the continuous floor plan that initially suggested the curtain wall to Mies. Site and orientation also must have played a part in the conception of the skyscraper. In a contemporary article—the first written about Mies—Carl Gotfrid arrived at a similar conclusion, supposedly drawing on information gained directly from the architect: "The shape of the building emerged from the conditions of a given site. It was [further] determined by the lighting of the interior, as well as by the effect of glass and by the grouping of masses in relation to the urban situation."[44] The final design thus clearly represented a synthesis of many previous decisions, among which the formal problem of how to handle a continuous glass surface should be regarded as just one aspect.

Drawings and a model of the Glass Skyscraper were first shown at the annual *Berlin Art Exhibition* (*Grosse Berliner Kunstausstellung*) in 1922.[45] Since this exhibition opened on May 20, the project must have been designed in the early months of that year. Few photographs of the original model survive, while the model now owned by the Bauhaus-Archiv, Berlin, is a more recent reproduction. Much attention has been drawn to the striking contrast between the pure, technical form of the tower on the one hand, and on the other the crude plaster models of typical turn-of-the-century townhouses that crouch around its base, and the huge trees, totally out of scale, which stand in the background. Some critics, believing the disproportion to be intentional, have concluded that Mies meant the photographs as a polemic attack on the traditional urban environment. In one of the photographs the tip of a cupola rising behind the trees can be identified as the top of the so-called Marine-Panorama (Fig. 12).[46] This circular building, now destroyed, was once situated in the vicinity of the exhibition hall at Lehrter Bahnhof, where Mies's model was on display in the summer of 1922. The model must have been moved into the park by the photographer, who simply wanted to take advantage of the better lighting conditions outside. Although Mies may have consciously invited the contrast with the older buildings, there is insufficient reason to ascribe a polemical intention to it. For a while, he even favored a retouched print in which the background trees had been blocked out.[47]

Unlike Le Corbusier, Mies never liked grand schemes conceived in their entirety on the drafting board. He always concentrated on the specific site addressed by his design, as we have inferred from Gotfrid's comments about the curvilinear skyscraper project. The irregular street configuration seen in the

12. Glass Skyscraper. Project, 1922. Photograph of original model

preliminary plan points to an authentic site, possibly in Berlin, even though attempts to locate the site on a 1920s map of the city have so far proved fruitless. Be this as it may, there can be no doubt that Mies intended his skyscrapers to be seen as integral parts of an existing urban environment. Werner Graeff reports that "Mies made a point of having the adjacent structures . . . scaled down to the model and placed next to it for investigation and for shooting pictures. At that time, he had them molded by a sculptor from contemporary Berlin streets. His comment was as follows: 'I want to know what my buildings really look like on the vacant lot in question, however hideous their vicinity may be. Others usually indicate the surroundings in heavily adjusted shapes.' This is also the reason why Mies preferred to have photos made that showed the anticipated site from various positions, and why he ordered huge enlargements of them, of which those parts had to be left blank which he intended to draw by using the same perspective. Even in photographs, many of his early projects were thus exactly placed in their proper neighborhood."[48]

The carefully balanced perspectives of the montages as well as the large charcoal drawing of the first of the two projects are based on photographs taken from opposite positions on Friedrichstrasse. The distant and slightly diagonal views were apparently deliberately chosen in order to compensate, by means of foreshortening, for the soaring effect of the skyscraper. In spite of the continuous height of twenty stories, its skyline seems to drop below the eaves of the much lower buildings in the foreground. The actual distance of the tower from the flanking masonry structures is hard to judge, so that there is no direct clue as to its real scale. Besides, in the presentation drawing the surroundings appear in dark silhouette only where they form a striking contrast to the delicate shading of the crystalline skyscraper. The tower's mass, occupying a whole block, is barely apparent, since its airy appearance is counterbalanced by the stout, down-to-earth architecture of the adjacent buildings. There is no question that the impression would have been quite different in reality, especially if one approached along the street. But while from afar the individual towers of the skyscraper shrink to a uniform prism, they separate again at closer view so as to establish a rhythmic sequence of slender shafts which progressively join in different configurations.

The curvilinear skyscraper project was, likewise, conceived as a volumetric body that would reveal its true form only when one moved around the building. Although the photograph of the original model could depict only a limited number of views, the photographs showing different arrangements of the plaster models from different angles do convey a notion of the ever-changing combinations perceivable in an actual urban environment. It is this multifaceted, changing aspect, responding to the fluctuating life of the modern city, that distinguishes Mies van der Rohe's skyscraper designs from those of other architects of the early 1920s.

Conceived between December 1921 and early May 1922, the two glass skyscraper projects had no architectural precursors, nor did they exert an immediate impact on the functional building mode that began to emerge the following year in Germany. Provided that its dating to about 1919 is correct, an early watercolor by Hans Scharoun showing glistening prismatic shapes may have served as a possible source of inspiration.[49] However, aside from formal analogies, the comparison will do little to explain the specifically architectural qualities of Mies van der Rohe's design. Actual examples of Expressionist glass architecture were extremely rare and usually alluded to the translucent, rather than to the transparent and reflective, nature of the material. This is also true of numerous other projects and architectural fantasies of the period. It is, therefore, to a different kind of architecture that one must turn to trace the genesis of Mies's idea.

One of the most radical examples of an early all-glass curtain wall could be found within walking distance of the Friedrichstrasse site. Bernhard Sehring's facade of the Tietz Department Store on Leipzigerstrasse, erected in 1899–1900, had two continuous, nonbearing glass walls four stories in height, each measuring about 59 by 84 feet (17.5 by 26 meters) (Fig. 13). Sehring's glass wall, however, was only an oversized window, as one can see by its architectural encasement. The curtain wall flanked by slender neo-Baroque limestone bays is framed by a heavy cornice, which corresponds neither with the conventional visual norms nor with the new structural system employed.[50] The first truly plastic curtain wall made its appearance in the unsupported corner bays of Gropius's Fagus Factory of 1911. But as the office block of his model factory at the Cologne Werkbund exhibition of 1914 shows even more conspicuously, the influence of neoclassicism on Gropius's prewar career was too strong for him to have fully grasped the architectural potential of the curtain wall. In both instances, the suspended glass walls were attached to what still appears to be a traditional post-and-lintel structure.[51] The excellence of the Fagus Factory notwithstanding, the inherent conflict between curtain wall and post-and-lintel structure became only too clear with the Cologne office block, which failed to match the formal consistency of the earlier work except in the superb glass-enclosed staircases at its corners.

13. Bernhard Sehring: Tietz Department Store, Leipzigerstrasse, Berlin. 1899–1900

Mies must have eagerly followed the career of his former colleague in the Behrens office, ready to pounce on every shortcoming that might be deemed a lapse into formalism, a deviation, that is, from the path toward a truly modern architecture. The struggle against eclecticism and the pastiche—major issues of the formative years of the Werkbund—had by 1920 been undertaken even by the more conservative architects. All direct borrowing from traditional stylistic patterns was commonly considered anachronistic, and there was an unspoken agreement among German architects that building meant more than decorating facades at random. In contrast to the slightly later Chicago Tribune Tower competition, virtually none of the (published) entries for the Friedrichstrasse skyscraper had direct recourse to historical prototypes.

The deteriorated state of affairs in the design profession at the turn of the century, of which the proliferation of mass-produced period styles was symptomatic, thus constituted only one aspect of the situation against which the early projects of Mies van der Rohe have to be measured. Much of their impetus was, by contrast, derived from a constant grappling with the most advanced solutions of his own day. Mies's worry about a new kind of formalism lurking behind the professed functionalism of many of his fellow combatants was openly expressed in a letter to Werner Jakstein of November 1923: "To some extent, Gropius with his austere shapes is still as formal as is Häring with his curves; with neither of them does the form evolve as the final consequence. Gropius claims to work constructively, and Häring thinks himself an organic architect, but in my opinion both are still formalists to a large degree. I do not see the difference between an agitated and an austere form. In relation to Gropius, Häring is a Baroque character, while Gropius in relation to Häring is a classicist."[52]

Mies's judgment of Gropius was based on his impression of the *International Architecture Exhibition (Internationale Architekturausstellung)* held in Weimar between August 15 and September 30, 1923, as part of the famous Bauhaus exhibition.[53] As the following quotation demonstrates, this first comprehensive survey of the modern movement, organized by Gropius, confirmed Mies's disillusionment with what so far had been offered to open up new paths for twentieth-century architecture. It seems to have been this disappointment, rather than the constructivist leaning often associated with his articles in *G*, that caused the radical intonation of Mies's early statements:

"Of all things, it was the chaotic constructivist formalism which I saw in Weimar, and the nebulous artistic indistinctness dominating that place that prompted me to once again explain my point of view in *G*—especially since, by mistake, part of what I had written was not published in the first issue. In the forthcoming number of *G* there will be stated:

"Form is not what we are aiming at, it is merely the outcome of our work.

"There is no form by itself; form as an end in itself means formalism, and that we reject.

"Really perfect form is always conditioned, is deeply rooted in the task; in fact, it is its most elementary expression."[54]

Unfortunately, the last part of this statement was omitted in the translation of the *G* article that Johnson made for his monograph on Mies. Consequently, the negative aspects of form appeared accentuated. But Mies, in fact, acknowledged the inherent aesthetic quality of architectural design.[55] And for him the formal component was not to be treated in isolation or, even worse, to be understood as a mask that could be applied to a structure at random. Form would evolve automatically if all functional, structural, and technical problems were tackled and solved in the most comprehensive way, and ultimately it would express the very nature and relationship of these conditioning factors.

Strictly speaking, this is almost a paraphrase of the statement Otto Wagner made several decades earlier. According to Wagner, the architect must subscribe to a number of rules, without which he will never achieve a work of art that vitally corresponds in style to the "art of our time." In particular he demanded: "1) careful understanding and perfect fulfillment of the purpose—down to the smallest detail; 2) happy selection of materials, which must be easy to obtain and process, durable, and economical; 3) straightforward and economical construction, and, only after these three principal points have been considered; 4) the form derived from the above preconditions. It will flow from the pen by itself, and it will always be easily intelligible."[56]

Wagner's conviction was certainly known in prewar Werkbund circles,[57] if not in most of the avant-garde movements of the day. Yet the effect of Mies's strikingly parallel view is noteworthy. For one thing, his timing was well chosen: the cold conciseness of his words may have appealed to a public increasingly tired of Expressionist ravings. More than that, however, his written statements in combination with his architectural conceptions helped to clarify his larger intentions. Thus, in the first *G* article referred to in his letter above, the argument shifted from dogmatic assertions to a detailed description of the project illustrated (the Concrete Office Building), and it is hard to say whether text or project was meant to be the manifesto (Fig. 14).

In any case, who among Mies's contemporaries reading the following lines

Jede ästhetische Spekulation,
jede Doktrin,   lehnen wir ab.
und jeden Formalismus

Baukunst ist raumgefaßter Zeitwille.
Lebendig.   Wechselnd.   Neu.

Nicht das Gestern, nicht das Morgen, nur das Heute ist formbar.
Nur dieses Bauen gestaltet.

Gestaltet die Form aus dem Wesen der Aufgabe mit den
   Mitteln unserer Zeit.

              Das ist unsere Arbeit.

B Ü R O H A U S

      Das Bürohaus ist ein Haus   der Arbeit   der Organisation   der Klarheit   der Ökonomie.
Helle weite Arbeitsräume, übersichtlich, ungeteilt, nur gegliedert wie der Organismus des Betriebes. Größter Effekt mit geringstem Aufwand an Mitteln.
      Die Materialien sind   Beton   Eisen   Glas.
      Eisenbetonbauten sind ihrem Wesen nach Skelettbauten. Keine Teigwaren   noch Panzertürme. Bei tragender Binderkonstruktion eine nichttragende Wand. Also Haut- und Knochenbauten.
      Die zweckmäßigste Einteilung der Arbeitsplätze war für die Raumtiefe maßgebend; diese beträgt 16 m. Ein zweistieliger Rahmen von 8 m Spannweite mit beiderseitiger Konsolauskragung von 4 m Länge wurde als das ökonomischste Konstruktionsprinzip ermittelt. Die Binderentfernung beträgt 5 m. Dieses Bindersystem trägt die Deckenplatte, die am 'Ende der Kragarme senkrecht hochgewinkelt Außenhaut wird und als Rückwand der Regale dient, die aus dem Rauminnern der Übersichtlichkeit wegen in die Außenwände verlegt wurden. Über den 2 m hohen Regalen liegt ein bis zur Decke reichendes durchlaufendes Fensterband.
      Berlin, Mai 1923   Mies v. d. Rohe

14. Concrete Office Building. Project, 1922–23. Publication in the first issue of G, *July 1923*

would have seriously questioned the statement that the building's appearance was determined by anything but strictly functional and structural reasoning?

"We flatly reject all aesthetic speculation, all doctrine, and any kind of formalism.

"Architecture is the will of the time in its spatial manifestation—animated, changing, new.

"Not the past nor the future, only the present can be shaped. Only if this has been accepted, will there be creative building.

"Create the form out of the nature of the problem, with the means of our time: This is our task.

"The office building is a house of work, of organization, of transparency, of economy; light and ample spaces to work in, easy to take in at a glance, undivided, arranged according to the organization of the company. Maximum effect with minimal possible means.

"The materials are concrete, steel, glass.

"Buildings of reinforced concrete are by their very nature skeletal structures; to be treated neither as 'gingerbread' nor as armored turrets; load-bearing girder construction allows nonsupporting walls; skin and bone construction is the consequence.

"The most efficient layout of the working area determined the depth of the space, which measures 16 meters [52 feet, 6 inches]. A double-supported frame spanning 8 meters [26 feet, 3 inches], with a cantilever of 4 meters [13 feet, 2 inches] on each end, was calculated to be the most economical constructive device. The girders, 5 meters [16 feet, 5 inches] apart, carry the floor slabs, which also form the outer skin by turning upward at the edge of the cantilevered beam. Thus they encase the filing cabinets that have been transferred from the inside of the space to the outer walls, so as to retain the transparency of the interior. Above the shelves, two meters high, there runs a continuous band of windows, which reaches right up to the ceiling."[58]

15. *Concrete Office Building. Project, 1922–23. Perspective. Charcoal and crayon on tan paper. The Museum of Modern Art, New York, Mies van der Rohe Archive. Gift of the architect*

The article, dated May 1923, coincided with the first public appearance of the project in the annual *Berlin Art Exhibition*. Thus it seems unlikely that the conception extended far back into 1922. A wood model also existed,[59] as did the large charcoal perspective usually illustrated (Fig. 15). As Werner Graeff recalled, the model was painted gray with stripes of Venetian red, a scheme which may have been intended to separate visually the nonbearing "skin" of the parapet walls from the "bones" of the structural frame.[60]

Subsequent to the Berlin exhibition, the project was shown at the Bauhaus in Weimar (Fig. 16). It was scheduled to be seen in the fall of the same year, 1923, at Léonce Rosenberg's gallery L'Effort Moderne in Paris, where Theo van Doesburg had organized a comprehensive presentation of de Stijl architec-

16. *Installation view of* International Architecture Exhibition (Internationale Architekturausstellung), *Bauhaus, Weimar, 1923. Models of Mies's Concrete Office Building and Glass Skyscraper can be seen at the left*

ture.[61] However, because of the tense political situation following the French occupation of the Ruhr, all materials had to be shipped to Paris via The Hague. Mies therefore refrained from mailing the model, but sent two additional drawings instead (including a section), of which no trace has survived.[62] One has thus to rely on Mies's own description in G to get a notion of the building's actual layout. Ludwig Glaeser's reconstruction of the plan, which presumes four sections around a central court, seems reasonable although suppositional, since the perspective drawing provides no direct evidence of an inner court. According to this reconstruction, the building would have enclosed a rectangular court about three bays (roughly 49 feet, 2 inches [15 meters]) wide, but, like the entrance facade, which is partly hidden from view, of an undetermined length.[63] According to Graeff, the main entrance was placed off center in the model, in response to the square that the drawing depicts in front of the site.[64]

First seen, the outer shape of the building seems to bear out Mies's programmatic declaration, that is, it represents a perfectly rational constructivist design. The strict separation of bearing and nonbearing members not only stands for structural honesty and probably more efficient building methods, but also allows for optimal flexibility in the interior layout. The undefined purpose of the Concrete Office Building would be consonant with an open plan, free of the usual segregation created by supporting walls. Thanks to the skeleton system, Mies was able to achieve an even distribution of well-lit spaces which could be subdivided and rearranged at will. Most features of markedly formal impact, such as the deep recess of the ribbon windows, can also be ascribed to practical considerations: the projecting slab of the ceiling functions as a *brise-soleil* against direct sunlight. The end bays were given a much larger interval and, with their pillars strengthened by additional corbels to support the cross girders, firmly terminate the regular rhythm of the facade. Although highly "reminiscent of classical solutions" (Glaeser), this simply reflects the perpendicular interpenetration of two contiguous sections as demanded by the structural system. Furthermore, in repeating the 26-foot, 3-inch (8-meter) span of the main girder in its end bays, each facade reveals its section in elevation and so provides a perfect demonstration of the skeleton structure.

Yet there remain a number of features that cannot be explained except on aesthetic grounds, as the following will bear out. To begin with, the building is deprived in the drawing of a solid visual foundation, a condition even more striking than in the case of the earlier skyscraper designs. On the ground floor only the continuous window strip rises above street level, visually isolating the upper stories from the ground.[65] This seems to be the only level in the building from which the occupants might glimpse more than clouds and sky, since the parapets were said to be 6 feet, 7 inches (2 meters) high. Similarly, the top floor has been considerably reduced in height, leaving only a narrow slit of window between parapet and ceiling. Consequently, the top-floor interior would have been quite dark and not a little conducive to claustrophobia.

Furthermore, one would have entered the building at the first-floor level by passing through a kind of inverted portico that cuts back deeply into the structure. A flight of stairs emphasized by freestanding pillars and spanning almost five bays gently ascends to a landing that stretches between additional rows of pillars, where a transparent wall of glass separates the entry from the interior. This treatment is anything but purely and simply functional. Rather, its effect and most likely its motive appear to be architectural monumentality.[66]

The floating character of the Concrete Office Building has been remarked upon by contemporary critics.[67] As Mies would have claimed, this was but a logical consequence of the cantilevered skeleton frame relieving the walls of their load-bearing function.

Why, then, did he give so much physical prominence to the walls, while almost hiding the structural system inside? In fact, everything else has been done to enhance the floating effect. The sunken ground floor and the deep recess of the entry leave a void where one would normally expect a solid foundation. The massive parapets of the floors, which project increasingly as they rise, hover above fragile strips of glass, so as to emphasize the weightlessness of what seems otherwise a heavy element. Moreover, what reason did Mies have for the considerable reduction of the top-floor height, unless he wanted to achieve a cornicelike effect by linking the roof slab visually to the parapet below? In strong contrast to the building's "open base," this deliberate allusion to a rather conventional motif essentially serves to counterbalance the structure's floating character, and thus constitutes a firm termination (*see* Glaeser) to its rising sequence of stories.

How far Mies intended the airy appearance of the structure to compensate for its enormous mass, which neglects the scale of the neighboring buildings, remains open to speculation. In any case, his apodictic statements need to be modified. Architectural conceptions simply do not work without a certain degree of aesthetic intuition. Some formal features will always creep in that cannot be deduced completely from (but that may fully harmonize with) the functional or structural predeterminants of a building.

By early 1923, when Mies was occupied with his fourth pioneering project (Fig. 17), the country house as a genre was in little demand. While a number of private houses were built in and around Berlin after the First World War, public interest tended to be focused on other building tasks. It would not have been surprising if Mies, having produced several designs for office buildings, had continued with another sequence of urban concepts, like apartment houses or projects for low-income housing, which were social necessities of the first order. But this was not the case. In the same *Berlin Art Exhibition* where he

17. Concrete Country House. Project, 1923. Perspective, garden side. Charcoal and pencil on cream colored paper. The Museum of Modern Art, New York, Mies van der Rohe Archive. Gift of the architect

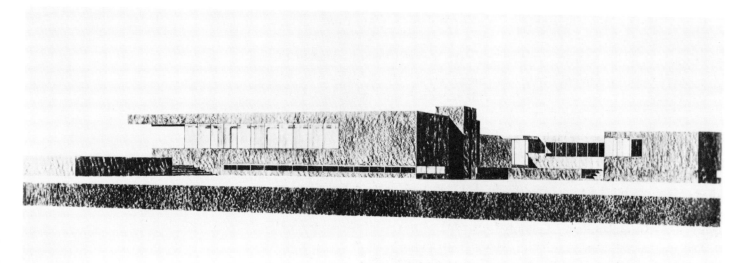

exhibited the Concrete Office Building in May 1923, he also contributed a design for the Concrete Country House. A second example, in brick, followed the next year. These two works initiated a series of residential projects, only a few of them actually executed, which culminated in his American commissions, the Resor and Farnsworth houses of the late 1930s and 1940s.

The origins of the two country house projects have been dealt with in a different context to which one may refer for a more detailed discussion.[68] There is strong evidence that both were initially intended as preliminary designs for the architect's own residence. As early as 1914, Mies had toyed with the idea of building a house for himself. The site was to be at Werder, a small island town in the middle of the Havel lakes, a few miles west of Potsdam. Of the two sketches that have come down in reproductions,[69] one depicts a flat-roofed, one-story building of symmetrical layout with two projecting wings opening toward a terraced garden area (Fig. 18). The central section of the Concrete Country House (without the open entrance hall and the living-room wing, which form clearly separate units) shows a similar U-shaped arrangement, except that the tall French windows have been replaced by larger, sharply cut openings of horizontal extension (Fig. 19).

Since only the entrance area and the living room annex possess technically advanced cantilever construction on freestanding pillars (Fig. 20), one may assume that Mies indeed had initially returned to the Werder project as a source of inspiration. Written evidence is extremely scarce for the period in question, but a small number of letters survive which may be connected to the two residential projects under discussion.

On February 14, 1923, Mies offered his services to a Mr. Albrecht, a factory owner from Thuringia, who had just acquired a piece of real estate on the banks of Lake Jungfern in Potsdam. Mies remarked that in the summer of 1922 he had entered into negotiations (ultimately fruitless) with the owner to purchase the same land for his own purposes, and that he was thoroughly familiar with the positive and negative aspects of the site.[70] In March 1923, Mies addressed the municipal authorities of Potsdam with an inquiry about another site, on Höhenstrasse, also overlooking Lake Jungfern (Fig. 21), and not too far from the first property. The response he received was encouraging,[71] but he must have decided against the purchase, for by the end of April he wrote to Albrecht again, after the industrialist's plans had come to naught: "In case you intend to sell the plot, I would very much appreciate it if you would let me know the details."[72]

Mies's continual efforts to acquire a piece of land in one of the most attractive areas on the outskirts of Berlin casts the Concrete Country House in a new light. As the only unidentified project dating from the same period as the above correspondence, it may originally have been related to one of the sites mentioned there.

It is not certain that Mies had enough money to build his own house, nor is it clear how he might have gotten it. He had a few lucrative commissions during the inflationary period and he did bill his clients in goldmarks, but was this enough to enable him to finance a building the size of the Concrete Country House? In mid-July, Mies ordered his bank to buy a block of stocks and bonds, but since the amount indicated was the nominal value and not the market price, his actual expense is impossible to determine.[73] On the other hand,

18. House for the Architect, Berlin-Werder. Project, 1914. Perspective drawing. Whereabouts unknown

53

19. *Concrete Country House. Project, 1923. Model viewed from the rear. Whereabouts unknown*

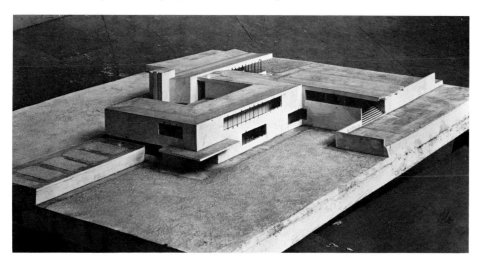

20. *Concrete Country House. Project, 1923. Model viewed from the front. Whereabouts unknown*

Hans Richter, the Dada artist and co-editor of G,[74] once related that he had visited Mies at his office on Am Karlsbad hoping to secure financial support for an upcoming issue of the journal. He was led to a huge drafting board on trestles, on which Mies kept his library. Several piles of books were removed before Mies lifted the board, and to Richter's great surprise, "between library-shelf and trestles, Mies kept a supply of dollar bills that without difficulty would have enabled him to buy up the whole fashionable street of Am Karlsbad."[75] Richter may have exaggerated; it did not take much to impress a poor artist and publisher in 1923. But the suspicion remains that Mies was probably rather well off by the standards of the day. Given the fragmentary nature of the sources quoted here, it must be left to the reader to follow the author's conviction that there existed some kind of connection between them and the Concrete Country House.

With the Brick Country House of 1924 the situation is different. In an early photograph of the plan and perspective (Fig. 22) the former bears an original inscription in the upper left-hand corner, identifying it as a drawing for a house in Neubabelsberg[76]—a residential district near Potsdam, where Mies had already built a number of houses for Berliners.[77]

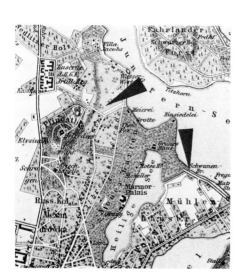

21. *Detail from a map of Potsdam, c. 1910. Triangles indicate possible locations for Mies's Concrete and Brick Country houses.*

No definite site is known for the Brick Country House, but according to one reliable source, the prospective client was none other than Mies himself. When in early 1925 Paul Westheim's *Das Kunstblatt* published the drawings, the project was referred to as a house for the architect.[78] Westheim has provided valuable information on Mies's early work,[79] which suggests that he got his data directly from the architect. Thus, the notion that the Brick Country House and probably the Concrete Country House as well were purely theoretical must be discarded—at least as far as Mies's motivations are concerned.

The two projects vary considerably in structure and character. The earlier has a homogeneous concrete shell, with walls perforated by large but conventional windows. The second design consists of solid masonry walls that carry a flat roof, while the glazed floor-to-ceiling openings have neither sills nor lintels and thus are not properly "windows." In layout, too, there are remarkable differences. Common to both, as well as to modern architecture in general, is the free plan with asymmetrical but carefully balanced massing. Furthermore, each plan has been keyed to a pivotal center of gravity, replacing the usual system of axes that traditionally determines a building's layout. The wings of

22. *Brick Country House. Project, 1924. Elevation and plan. Installation view of* New Types of Architecture (Typen neuer Baukunst), *Mannheim Municipal Art Gallery, Mannheim, Germany. 1925*

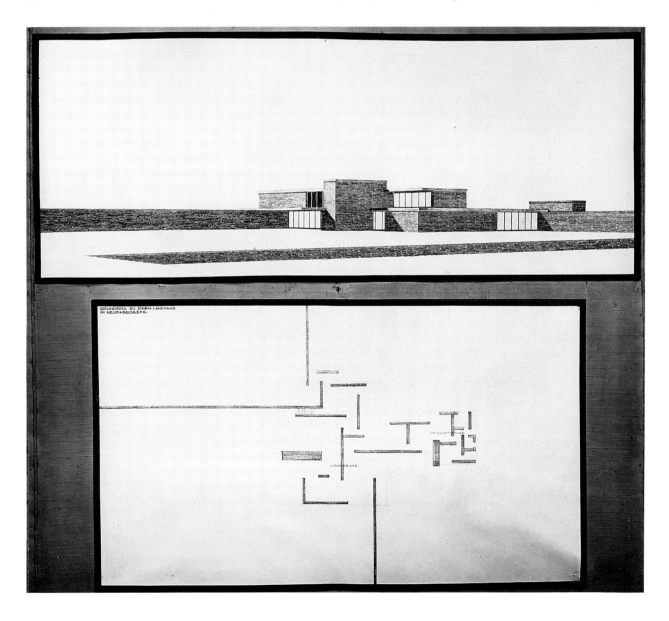

the Concrete Country House branch out in opposite directions, but their dynamic thrust is curbed by the right-angled turns of their end sections. By contrast, the Brick Country House forms a dense two-story agglomeration around two eccentrically placed chimney blocks. Linear wall elements project outward from it, continuing apparently to infinity. The surroundings appear tied to the structural core, which, due to large sections of transparent wall and an ingeniously devised system of transitional zones, pushes outward, extending the interior spaces into the garden area.

One is inclined to detect here the influence of Frank Lloyd Wright, whose early work Mies knew from the Wasmuth portfolio of 1910 and the monograph published the next year.[80] But efforts to pinpoint the exact nature of the influence have yielded little. While the built-in filing cabinets in the Concrete Office Building obviously derive from Wright's Larkin Building,[81] the Concrete Country House bears no close or clear resemblance to any of Wright's designs. Mies did not develop the open plan until 1924, and there is no evidence that it grew out of a debt to Wright's Prairie Houses. In fact, in the Brick Country House, any discernible similarities with Wright's work are outweighed by demonstrable differences. For example, the chimney block: for Wright the fireplace symbolized home ("It comforted me to see the fire burning deep in the solid masonry of the house itself"),[82] and like the primitive hearth, it usually occupied the very center of the house (Fig. 23). Apart from this symbolic significance, for Wright the chimney "provides a solid core of masonry to anchor the building to the ground and also the pivot of the whole composition at the crossing of the axes. It is the point of absolute mass about which are organized all the varieties of more or less open interior and exterior space."[83]

In the Brick Country House the oversized chimney blocks are focal points of mass, but they have been deliberately placed off center, compressing the house between them, so as to lend structural stability to the fluid and dynamic spatial configuration of the interior.[84] Sculptural solids that they are, they contribute an element of repose that serves to counterbalance the horizontal spread of the extending walls.

To Wright space meant first of all a universal dimension of primarily horizontal extension. Thus architectural space was the void between solids that in some way or other had to be enclosed and shielded against the outside—hence Wright's preference for leaded glass to screen off the openings. As Mies saw it, space was something very different from that, a positive and expansive quantity which the architect could channel and bind, but never isolate from the outside world. The difference is essentially one of orientation. Wright's Prairie Houses pay tribute to their natural setting, and they do so handsomely; their interiors, however, are always protective and introverted, fixed on the fireplace.

Mies's spaces, by contrast, are extroverted, clearly oriented toward a garden or, wherever feasible, to the open landscape beyond, seeking to catch as much of a view as possible. Even when he did use a chimney, seating was always arranged parallel to the fireplace to face one of the larger openings to its side (Fig. 24). One casual remark of his, reported by Ruegenberg, "I need to have a wall at my back," is symptomatic of this inclination.[85]

Vincent Scully has remarked that in Wright's architecture the massive solid of the chimney has replaced the Palladian cylindrical void and thus pro-

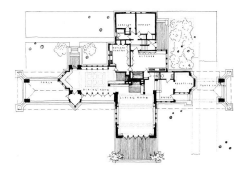

23. *Frank Lloyd Wright: Willits House, Highland Park, Illinois. 1902. Plan*

01

24. *Gericke House, Berlin-Wannsee. Project, 1932. Interior perspective of dining area and living room as seen from court. Pencil on illustration board. The Museum of Modern Art, New York, Mies van der Rohe Archive. Gift of the architect*

hibited the human being from firmly establishing himself in the center.[86] This applies to the axial relationships as well. In his residential buildings, Wright never allowed a single axis to dominate, so that one feels constantly urged to readjust one's position. There, finally, lies another characteristic trait that distinguishes the Brick Country House from Wright's earlier conceptions. Its outward-extending walls, lacking a common point of origin, do recall the shifted layers of cross axes of the Prairie Houses, but here it is no longer the walls but the space between them that counts. Because of the project's asymmetrical composition—the strictly rectangular arrangement of its individual elements notwithstanding—axial relationships have been deliberately avoided throughout. Consequently, it is on spatial and not on abstract linear terms that communication is established with the surrounding space outside; and it is from the inside that space gradually develops and expands. The interior has thus become the nucleus of a force field which, by means of brick walls reaching out in all directions, fixes the coordinates of the environment and defines it with exclusive reference to the viewer inside.[87]

In the Brick Country House, man is again allowed to inhabit a central position, albeit a position no longer fixed by geometry and enclosed, as in a Palladian villa, but open and adaptable to change. Free of the imposing hierarchical order of an axial layout the occupant may choose his position at will, in the expectation that the architectural setting will readjust and respond accordingly, each time offering a new spatial sensation.

It has been observed that Mies's private commissions and projects were conceived essentially for occupancy by a single client.[88] Wherever a couple or even parents with children had to be provided for, the prerogatives of family life did not affect the principal portion of Mies's house designs but were relegated instead to separate quarters. With an extensive roof terrace serving as a playground (as, for example, in the Tugendhat and Gericke houses) children were obviously expected to keep to themselves and, under the care of a nurse, to stay away from the major living area and possibly the more intimate parts of the garden, too (Fig. 25). Children and adults thereby remain within their own spheres of life. With little concern for the habits and ideals of the average client, Mies must have envisioned a rather different type of man for his buildings; and the clue to that notion is likely to be found in his own personality.

Significantly, the conception of the two early country houses coincided with his decision to leave his family for good and to live by himself for the remainder of his life.[89] Nonetheless, although single by disposition, he was hardly inclined to lead a hermit's existence. Thus, when planning a house for himself he conceived it neither as a retreat nor as a family home, but rather as an architectural demonstration of the very freedom and independence which he thought he had gained. In their openness and control of exterior space, the two projects reflect the self-confidence of an architect aspiring to nothing less than a reinterpretation of social behavior and of man's basic attitude toward nature in general.

25. *Tugendhat House, Brno, Czechoslovakia. 1928–30. Children at play on the roof terrace*

Projects and Buildings, circa 1925

By the mid-1920s Mies had secured a strong position within Germany's leading artists' and architects' associations: the Werkbund, the Novembergruppe, and the BDA. His early projects, frequently shown at exhibitions at home and abroad,[90] had already gained wide recognition and, re-enforced by his own published statements, contributed to his reputation as a leading figure of the modern movement. Yet his achievements were confined to paper work. The Mosler House, nearing completion by 1925,[91] bears witness to the conservative taste of its client (*see* Fig. 3). Mies's first chance to put his pioneering concepts into practice was still to come—and he spoiled it thoroughly.

Unlike the banker Georg Mosler, the art historian and Constructivist artist Walter Dexel was sympathetic to the principles of modern architecture. As head of the Jena *Kunstverein* he had organized an exhibition of German avant-garde architects in November 1924 at which Mies was invited to give the opening lecture. On the pretext of illness Mies, who never enjoyed speaking in public, declined on short notice, and Gropius's associate Adolf Meyer stood in for him.[92] This minor episode presaged the more serious trouble the Dexels were to face when, in January 1925, they commissioned Mies to design a house for them.[93] The reservations expressed by the critic Adolf Behne, whom Dexel had consulted, soon proved to be justified: "I would probably choose Mies— but Gropius is closer, Berlin a long way away."[94] Time was running short, since tax requirements dictated the completion of the building by the fall at the latest. Mies had promised to present some general proposals in January, but they were not forthcoming. Upon repeated inquiry from the clients, he declared categorically: "The project must be worth something or I won't allow it to leave the studio."[95] Although the deadline was repeatedly postponed, he failed to come up with anything but a couple of small preliminary sketches. Dexel finally wearied of urging him and passed the commission on to Adolf Meyer, whose plans were submitted to the Jena building authorities in May 1925. As matters developed, Meyer's project was denied a building permit, and the whole affair came to naught.[96]

Whether it was for similar reasons that the Eliat House project was also turned down remains a matter of speculation. The crucial documents are missing, and even Mrs. Eliat, the client's wife, did not remember what finally caused its failure.[97] As in the case of the Dexel project, contact was established in January 1925. Eliat had already hired another architect, but Mies succeeded in securing the job. This time, at least, he was able to present a developed concept, although he may not have started working on it before the spring (Fig. 26).[98] Plans dated June 17 were obviously intended for submission to the local authorities for approval. The flat-roofed house shown in the drawings consists of a complex configuration of wings set around an approximately square central communication and service area which is clearly designated in the elevation by its slightly sunken roof line. Each wing was assigned a different function so as to separate the various spheres of daily life. On the other hand, ample connection between the spaces, provided wherever necessary, suggested an efficient organization of the household.

Situated in the bank of Lake Fahrland near Nedlitz in the Potsdam region, the site may have resembled those already mentioned in connection with Mies's country house projects of 1923 and 1924. Indeed the general layout of the plan (Fig. 27) reminds one of the Concrete Country House, from which the arrangement of the Eliat entry hall and dining room, including their deeply projecting roof slabs, have obviously been derived. Even the lower floor, where the kitchen and servants' and guest rooms face the lower terrain in the rear of the living room area, has been adopted from the earlier project. For all of that, however, the plan lacks the ease of its predecessor. In contrast to the Concrete Country House's generous disposition of separate wings, which seem to freely possess the surrounding space, the densely interlinking parts of the Eliat House, with their abruptly changing orientation, appear a bit forced. So do the harsh juxtapositions of diverse elements, for example: the projecting bay of the pantry opposite the balcony of the dressing room, the entryway cramped between abutting spaces, and the outside chimney piece curiously intersecting the cantilevered roof slab of the garden terrace.

Mies's apparent difficulty in matching the standard of his own pioneering projects may have been that here, at the advanced stage of the planning process of the Eliat House, all aspects of a "modern" building had to be given meticulous treatment down to the last detail. A plan of the Concrete Country House has not survived (and, with the possible exception of working drawings for office use only, in all likelihood never existed); and although the photographs of the model allow a reasonable reconstruction of the building's interior layout,[99] one is obliged to suspect that the extensive use of separate wings would have reduced the convenience of daily living while increasing the technical problems that a homogeneous concrete shell entailed. In the case of the floor plan of the Brick Country House, with its rather cursory designation of the living and service areas, any attempt to relate it exactly to the corresponding perspective (see Fig. 22) is futile.[100] If one presumes that the plan belongs to a different stage of development, a second story necessary to accommodate the bedrooms would in any case have caused serious structural problems. In other

26. *Eliat House, Nedlitz (near Potsdam). Project, 1925. Perspective. Whereabouts unknown*

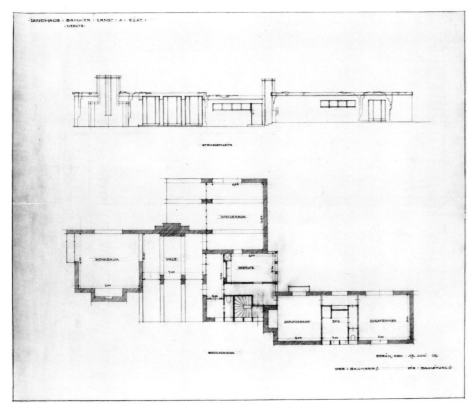

27. *Eliat House, Nedlitz (near Potsdam). Project, 1925. Plan and elevation (street side).*
Pencil on tracing paper. The Museum of Modern Art, New York, Mies van der Rohe Archive.
Gift of the architect

words, Mies's original conception would hardly have survived the subsequent stages without major alteration. Thus, aside from the poorly documented Lessing House project of 1923,[101] the Eliat House was the first commission in which Mies was compelled to submit his unconventional ideas to a critical test. Moreover, while in this instance he was once again denied tangible proof of his capacities as a modern architect, the next, more promising project was already underway.

29. *Wolf House, Guben, Germany (destroyed).*
1925–27. View from the north

28. *Wolf House, Guben, Germany (destroyed). 1925–27. View from the south*

Erich Wolf's attention had been drawn to Mies early in 1925 by the warm recommendation of a former client, Mrs. Maximilian Kempner. Contact with the architect was established on January 26, very shortly, that is, before Mies was in touch with Eliat, and while he was already involved in the Dexel affair.[102] However, definite steps appear not to have been taken before late summer: a first set of drawings signed by Wolf, Mies, and Hermann John-Hagemann, Mies's assistant and his local supervisor in Guben, was dated October 1925. These drawings underwent minor changes in the following months. Construction must have started sometime in the spring of 1926, and lasted almost another year before the building was finally ready for occupancy.

The city of Guben—an hour's drive southeast of Berlin—occupies the west bank of the Neisse River, which now marks the border between East Germany and Poland. The house, located on Teichbornstrasse on a narrow but exceptionally long strip of land, was reportedly destroyed at the end of the Second World War.[103] A number of drawings and blueprints and a handful of photographs are all that remain of Mies's first building in a clearly modern style.

Situated some distance off the street and taking up the whole width of the plot, the Wolf House was erected on the crest of a terraced slope that descends steeply toward the south (Fig. 28). The first impression gained from the photographs is that of a confusing agglomeration of interlinking cubes, which on closer inspection seem to pile up to a blocklike three-story core abutting the vacant property to the west. Remarkably, it is only from a rather inconspicuous point in front of the kitchen court that the actual height of the building can be seen fully (Fig. 29); elsewhere perspective overlaps, irregular window formats, and large sections of blank wall leave one uncertain about the sequence of stories as well as their relationship to different parts of the building. (It takes some time to realize that the house, indeed, has a uniform floor level throughout.)

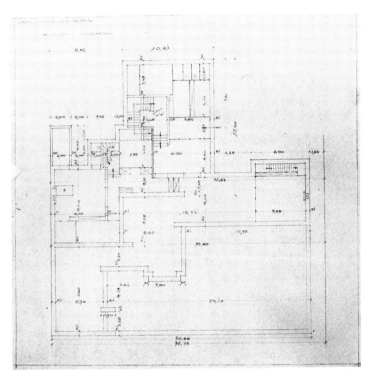

30. *Wolf House, Guben, Germany (destroyed). 1925–27. Ground-floor plan. Print. The Museum of Modern Art, New York, Mies van der Rohe Archive. Gift of the architect*

In its highly irregular composition, the plan (Fig. 30) bears a faint resemblance to that of the Eliat House project. Certain features of the latter, adopted with only minor changes, include the positioning of the dining room with its cantilevered roof slab, and the stepped, projecting chimney blocks. However, the original restrained detailing underwent further purification during the various planning stages. The only elements to remain the same in the Wolf House were the notched corners of the chimneys. Even the cornicelike tops of the walls were replaced by a simple vertical layer of brick to retain the smoothness and homogeneity of the enclosing skin. Like the Eliat project, the Wolf House was conceived mainly from within, with utmost care devoted to the organization of its functional program—sometimes, one feels tempted to say, to the disadvantage of the overall composition. The Teichbornstrasse facade (actually regarded as the rear of the building) turned out surprisingly well. Similarly successful was the limited view of the house as seen from the main terrace (Fig. 31). It was probably from the lower edge of the property, that is, from the south, that Mies intended his building to provide the most dramatic effect. The horizontal layers of setback stories, with secondary vertical accents established by the chimney blocks, terminated in the lower retaining walls, thus producing a cascading sequence of garden terraces. Viewed from below, on the other hand, almost all of the lower partitions disappear behind the parapet of the main terrace. Thus the design is flawed by a somewhat one-sided orientation, and its masses, now concentrated in the western half, appear slightly out of balance. That Mies seems to have had difficulty in conceiving a building from below is also evident in his design for the Tugendhat House of some years later (Fig. 32).

Some further shortcomings of the Wolf House should be noted. Negligible as they may seem relative to the overall quality of the design, they reveal the

31. *Wolf House, Guben, Germany (destroyed). 1925–27. Terrace*

problems of an architectural conception that was, in fact, several steps ahead of the technical methods of its time. For one thing, the cantilevered beam on the veranda is much too sturdy for the lightweight slab it is called upon to carry. Mies probably wanted to be sure the roof would hold up, although it is possible that the building authorities insisted he reinforce the girder.[104] Furthermore, heavy wood casements used for the larger openings form a peculiar contrast to the smooth, skinlike brick facing of the structure. Resembling ordinary windows punched through walls, they interrupt the continuity of the surface so that one almost misses some kind of architectural framing to reestablish the tectonic character of the wall. Metal casements, which Mies later used in the

32. *Tugendhat House, Brno, Czechoslovakia. 1928–30. View from the garden*

Lange and Esters houses, would have solved the problem, but they were available only for industrial application at that time.

Supposedly small problems like these have often been overlooked in previous discussions of Mies's architectural achievement. For the sake of argument, it may be worth imagining the replacement of the slender girders and window sashes as well as the fine profiles of the projecting roof slabs that characterize the early country house projects with the comparatively clumsy features of the Wolf House: the difference could hardly be more striking. "Form follows function," or, as Mies, following Gottfried Semper, might have put it, form is the mere effect of function, material properties, and the available structural or technical devices duly considered and correctly employed. There are still some myths to be surrendered or at least radically modified, when considering the history of the modern movement: the technical possibilities, no doubt, were there, but it required great effort on Mies's part to adapt them to his visionary postwar concepts.

Another project further illustrates this lesson. The Municipal Housing Development on Afrikanischestrasse in Berlin-Wedding, a rather dreary working-class district, is reliably dated to 1926–27, but probably was commissioned the year before (Fig. 33).[105] Ninety apartments for low-income families, including a small cooperative store, were to be provided in four separate buildings. Three identical blocks are lined up in a row parallel to Afrikanischestrasse with lateral wings facing side streets. Each of them actually consists of three independent units loosely attached at the corners and in a slightly oblique position, since the streets do not meet exactly at right angles. The shift might almost pass unnoticed, except for the irregular shape of the balconies that clamp them together. With their rounded corners these balconies resemble hinges, so that the whole arrangement appears somewhat flexible.

The fourth block, occupying the corner site at Afrikanischestrasse and Tangostrasse, serves as a kind of overture to the row. In spite of its rather different appearance, it is essentially a variation on the general theme of the lateral wings of the main blocks (Fig. 34). It was at this point that Mies decided to place a grocery store, its windows forming a markedly asymmetrical caesura within the repetitive rhythm of the facades.

The apartments are not ample, nor are the individual rooms. But they do provide decent living space, which is all that could be expected in a time when municipal or nonprofit housing societies still had to contend with the abuses of the prewar period. Next to the provision of a bathroom for each apartment, the biggest luxury of the housing at Afrikanischestrasse are the balconies. Those on the three-story facades of the main blocks are oriented toward the communal garden at the rear, looking southwest, while the lateral wings feature loggias with slightly projecting parapets that face the smaller side streets in front of them.

While Mies's housing development at Afrikanischestrasse stands between the traditional closed-block system of planning and the more advanced ribbon development, it displays more of the latter, as is evident in his use of a standard unit allowing numerous variations and combinations. The ribbon or row-house type (Zeilenbau) had several advantages. For example, all blocks could be given a similar orientation, thereby assuring each apartment a maximum amount of sunlight. For the sake of a uniform design, Mies was inconsistent in following

33. *Municipal Housing Development, Afrikanischestrasse, Berlin-Wedding.*
1926–27. Early view

34. *Municipal Housing Development, Afrikanischestrasse, Berlin-Wedding.*
1926–27. Housing block at corner of Tangostrasse, as it appeared in 1986

this possibility, since some of the loggias and balconies face almost north. A
second advantage of the row-house arrangement was that it removed the need
for a special type of corner apartment, which would otherwise have suffered
from a lack of cross-ventilation as well as an awkward layout difficult to connect
to the staircases. On the other hand, in failing to define the space between its
isolated blocks, the *Zeilenbau* was essentially anti-urban. The street, consequently, lost its former function as a public space and became a mere thor-
oughfare for which even the most generous provision of communal green could
not compensate.

Some of this vagueness in respect to urban space may already be perceived
in the negative corners of the blocks at Afrikanischestrasse. No doubt Mies
tried his best to relieve an overall monotony of proportions by a complex pattern
of differently sized windows (nonetheless, all were keyed to the same module).
But apart from this, not much is left that catches the viewer's attention: the
plain-cut loggias and balconies already mentioned, some unpretentious entrances with slightly projecting canopies, a low clinker-brick base and a corresponding molding at the top, and a subtle overall color scheme.[106]

Mies had of course been subject to an extremely tight budget, but so were
Bruno Taut, Ernst May, and J. J. P. Oud when they undertook projects of comparable character. Unlike these three architects, Mies had designed several
elegant country houses while accumulating virtually no experience in low-
income apartment buildings. In any case, the Afrikanischestrasse project fell
considerably short of *Onkel Toms Hütte* or the *Hufeisensiedlung* in Britz, to name
just two of Bruno Taut's outstanding Berlin housing developments begun at
almost the same time. Mies himself seems to have held a low opinion of what
was his largest commission up to that time. When the Royal Institute of British
Architects solicited material for an exhibition on modern architecture, Mies
replied that he would rather not include the Afrikanischestrasse project, since
it did not seem important enough for the purpose.[107]

Some common features notwithstanding, there is a perceptible separation between the visionary projects of the early 1920s and the buildings Mies conceived about 1925. The lack of ease, occasionally bordering on clumsiness, of

65

the latter bespeaks a creative crisis of which he himself must have been aware. Obviously the technical and structural means at his disposal proved disconcertingly inappropriate to what he intended to say in architecture. It does not take much to guess that solid masonry walls formed the biggest obstacle by far. Admittedly he handled them well in the Wolf House and still better in the Lange and Esters houses of 1927–28 (although only by wasting energy on concealed construction devices at the expense of structural consistency).[108] By then, however, he must have realized that conventional building methods had led him into a deadlock. As matters turned out, a solution to his problems was already available and he shortly took advantage of it.

His Apartment Building at the Weissenhof settlement, based on a skeleton system with bricked-up nonbearing walls, must be regarded as marking a second turning point in Mies's career. He was able to build his apartment house using light steel construction with few fixed internal walls, and although the apartments were too small to permit the flexibility Mies desired, the new structural system opened up possibilities for the future execution of the free plan. It is unlikely that he started work on the project before late 1926, when, as director of the Werkbund housing exhibition in Stuttgart, he had completed his second development plan for the project. Construction began only the following spring, yet, thanks to more efficient building methods at Weissenhof, the completion of the building more or less coincided with that of the blocks in Berlin-Wedding, although the latter were conceived about two years earlier. Subsidies for the Werkbund settlement were certainly less rigidly administered than they had been in Berlin, but they could hardly have been called excessive.

In any case, it could not have been budget alone that made the difference in the quality of the later work. Once asked to name a year he considered of particular importance in the development of the modern world, Mies offered a reply obviously related to his own career: "I would say that 1926 was the most significant year. Looking back it seems that it was not just a year in the sense of time. It was a year of great realization or awareness. It seems to me that at certain times of the history of man the understanding of certain situations ripens. Putting it another way, it seems that a particular situation will be ripe at a certain time and will be understood."[109]

The reference to 1926 as "a year of great realization and awareness" would suggest that Mies considered his concept of the Stuttgart Werkbund exhibition a definite personal breakthrough. The practical application of his own architectural principles had proven more complicated than Mies himself might have anticipated; and although his route had essentially been defined by 1923, a good many technical problems still awaited solutions.[110]

Weissenhof: Modern Architecture Becomes International

The Stuttgart *Werkbundsiedlung "Am Weissenhof"* of 1927 is customarily regarded as the event that consolidated and identified the modern movement in architecture (Fig. 35).

Until 1927, the term *modern architecture* was claimed by a heterogeneous group of movements and artists—German Expressionism as well as Russian Constructivism, de Stijl as well as the Amsterdam and the Rotterdam schools, individuals like Le Corbusier and Frank Lloyd Wright as well as the far-flung

35. *Weissenhofsiedlung, Stuttgart. 1925–27. Aerial view*

adherents of an assortment of dynamic, organic, or functional theories. Within this context Gropius's 1923 *International Architecture Exhibition,* subsequently published in the first Bauhaus book, is worth citing. In making a narrow and deliberately one-sided selection from among the various trends and schools available, Gropius no longer was arguing for quality alone. Instead, he was attempting to classify his subject on stylistic grounds. "I have wanted to keep to a very specific line at this exhibition," he wrote to Mies in 1923.[111] "It has been my definite intention not to show the other discernible trend in today's architecture—Finsterlin, Scharoun, Häring, that is, for example—but only to present this very particular cubo-dynamical kind of architecture which is based on construction, and judging from your own oeuvre, and from what you have written to me today, I assume we share opinion on that."[112] In fact, his "very specific line" was not so carefully drawn as he may have thought, for he made room for formal manner ("cubo-dynamical") and functional purpose ("based on construction") without showing their logical link. The examples he selected included purely constructivist skeleton structures, most of which lacked a compact stereometric shape, as well as blocklike assemblages of clear-cut cubes and planes that gave no direct hint of the structural system behind them. In the end, Gropius's endeavor failed to mount an argument strong enough to demonstrate the existence of a uniform modern style, although to the general public almost all the exhibits appeared radical and even irritating.

Such was the situation by 1925, when the Werkbund entrusted a little-known and relatively inexperienced Berlin architect with the conception of a model housing development in Stuttgart. It eventually achieved what Gropius's exhibition had failed at—a powerful demonstration of a strikingly unified architectural avant-garde—although it began as quite an amateurish undertaking and more than once came close to being abandoned. Apart from its two main participants, Gustav Stotz, the secretary of the Werkbund's Württemberg committee, and Mies himself—both backed by a small group of faithful supporters within the Werkbund administration—none of the parties involved seemed to have had any notion of how far-reaching an experiment they were embarking upon.

The initiative for an exhibition in Stuttgart came from the Werkbund's Württemberg branch, and was first discussed by the board in March 1925.[113] Following unanimous affirmation, the event, initially scheduled for 1926, grew to be regarded as a means of repeating the success of the Werkbund's Cologne exhibition of 1914. On this occasion, however, the Werkbund's executives decided to proceed with a distinct theme for the exhibition, which they hoped would achieve a stronger impact. The crucial decision to focus on the dwelling must have been reached by early summer, when the *Bau- und Heimstättenverein* (a co-operative Stuttgart housing society) offered to provide a site and to take charge of the projected buildings once the exhibition was over.[114] Thus, unlike the temporary structures in Cologne, the model houses to be erected were meant for permanent occupation. Mies was officially installed as director of the exhibition at the board's meeting of June 26.[115] Meanwhile, Peter Bruckmann had used his personal influence and party connections to win over the deputy mayor of Stuttgart, Daniel Sigloch,[116] and on July 13, Stotz reported that the local building authorities had consented to the erection of forty housing units on sites not yet decided upon.[117] By early September, the Weissenhof area overlooking Stuttgart was under consideration, and Sigloch had instructed the department of city planning to provide all topographical information to Mies. Still, Sigloch had hesitated to take the decisive step and approach the municipal council,[118] although, as it turned out, he was quite fortunate in having created a delay at this stage of the project.

While keeping the Stuttgart city authorities in suspense about the Werkbund's preliminary proposals for the model development, Mies and Stotz, together with Hugo Häring (who used an office in Mies's Berlin studio, and who as secretary of the modernist architects' group, the Ring, was not uninterested in the project) were already thinking far beyond a master plan. On August 14, Stotz proposed to Häring *Die Wohnung der Neuzeit* (*The Modern Dwelling*) as the title for the exhibition. To some observers this seemed too narrow a focus, and the name was later changed to the simple, but no less ambitious, *Die Wohnung* (*The Dwelling*). In his same message to Häring, Stotz remarked: "I have received word from Oud again suggesting that Corbusier and he be entrusted with a commission, too, even if only a minor one. I, for my part, would honestly welcome the collaboration of these two gentlemen."[119] Mies also favored the proposal, and the exhibition gradually took on an international aspect. Mies turned in his master plan four weeks later, by which time, as the following letter reveals, he aspired to nothing less than the consolidation of the modern movement—or at least that section of it which a few years later—in due reference to 1927—Henry-Russell Hitchcock and Philip Johnson were to formalize as the International Style. Mies's letter to Stotz was obviously meant to be confidential: "Under separate cover I send you, as promised, the master plan in the scale of 1:200. May I ask you to look through it with *Oberbaurat* Dr. Otto so that he knows about it. I hope he will not object to the plan in principle, since we used it to go ahead with our concept. I have planned an interlinking layout of the buildings; first of all, because this seemed of artistic value to me, and last but not least, because we would not depend too much on individual colleagues in such a case. *I have the bold idea to call upon all the left-wing architects*—I think, for the technical part of the exhibition, this may turn out tremendously well. *Thereby, this housing development might gain a similar importance to that of the Mathildenhöhe* [artists' colony] *in Darmstadt of former days.* I only hope we get the necessary support from the city. By no means should the master plan, as it is now, be considered final, since it will largely depend on the individual floor plans; it does show, however, what we are aiming at, and I think it will do perfectly well for the purpose of negotiations."[120]

Mies's first master plan is well documented by a blueprint and photographs of a clay model (Figs. 36, 37). The plaster base of the model, which is faithful to the topography, had been prepared by the city planning department, and Mies was expected to go to Stuttgart by September 30 to take care of the final modeling himself.[121] On October 16 the model was presented by Sigloch to the city council's building committee.[122] It won wholehearted support from several members, but the Social Democrats, who were affiliated with the *Bau- und Heimstättenverein*—owner of the Weissenhof property—were reluctant to give their consent before the site had been decided upon. Meanwhile the representatives of the right-wing German National Party expressed opposition to the participation of architects from abroad (they called them the *Internationale* to imply a Communist plot).[123] Sigloch, seeking to prevent an early defeat, adjourned the meeting without putting the concept to a vote (with municipal elections close at hand, chances for a majority became increasingly unlikely). Sigloch repeatedly engineered a delay in the decision, until finally, by the end of November, a postponement of the exhibition was no longer avoidable.[124]

Mies's preliminary master plan concerned only the general disposition and massing of the projected housing development. Even so, it constituted a noteworthy achievement, in certain ways superior to his final scheme. What he himself described as an "interlinking layout" consisted of a dense grouping of cubic, flat-roofed buildings and terraces, closely interlocked and decidedly sculptural in quality. Situated on one of the heights that border the city to the north and offering an unobstructed view of the valley below, the settlement was given the compact shape and contour of a small medieval town reminiscent of the clustered villages in Mediterranean mountain areas. However, it is not its romantic aspect, later assailed in a polemic by Paul Schmitthenner,[125] that is its most striking quality but, rather, its exceptional urban character and successful adjustment to the topography. Its outlines follow the gentle curve of the Weissenhof ridge, while the staggered buildings and terraces gradually ascend to the three-story structures at its crest. More detached than the smaller houses below, which they dominate like a citadel, these apartment blocks frame a rectilinear public space. Access to the individual buildings is provided by footpaths and stairs winding through and across the terraces on various levels.

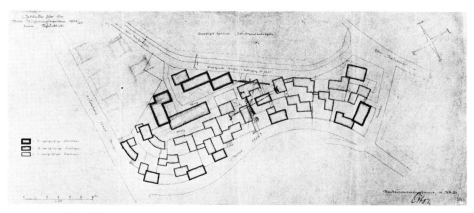

36. *Weissenhofsiedlung, Stuttgart. 1925–27. Preliminary site plan (1925). Red pencil and charcoal on print. The Museum of Modern Art, New York, Mies van der Rohe Archive. Gift of the architect*

37. *Weissenhofsiedlung, Stuttgart. 1925–27. Preliminary site plan (1925). Model. Whereabouts unknown*

At the narrowest point of the development, the ridge is lower than elsewhere, and the terraces reach almost to street level. By contrast, the outer ends of its sweeping curve look rather forbidding because of their heavy substructures. Moreover, the northern end of the settlement has again been emphasized by larger housing blocks, so as to give it a firm termination as well as to counterbalance the central group of buildings.

Mies's first master plan encountered strong opposition once it came up for public discussion. With Stotz and Sigloch having acted secretively to avoid an early defeat, it is no wonder that the majority of the city council were caught by surprise when finally confronted with Mies's concept and a preliminary list of participating architects. The Stuttgart councilmen may have heard of Gropius and Hans Poelzig; names like Mies van der Rohe, Mart Stam, or even J. J. P. Oud were unlikely to be known to the average German citizen in 1926.

With almost 1.2 million marks at stake (or about ten times that much in current value) for which the council had to assume responsibility,[126] it is curious that hardly any of its members took an interest in the affair prior to the crucial meeting in May 1926. The Werkbund's reputation must have offered enough of a guarantee for the council to leave the preliminaries entirely to Sigloch and the building committee. Ironically, this confidence must have been based largely on the personal reputations of two of the Werkbund's local members, Paul Bonatz and Paul Schmitthenner, the men who would become Mies's most fervent adversaries in the ensuing dispute. Their personal styles—in spite of Bonatz's early commitment to the reform movement in architecture—revealed increasingly conservative traits, with a strong leaning toward the vernacular and occasionally toward the monumental effects of a stripped neoclassicism, sufficiently modern to look contemporary, though conventional enough to appear familiar and inoffensive to the general public. This, in all likelihood, was what the average Stuttgart citizen expected of the Werkbund exhibition.

The bombshell exploded on the evening of May 5, 1926, when Bonatz and Schmitthenner simultaneously published heated attacks on Mies's first master plan in the leading local papers.[127] Both articles, aggressively polemical in tone, amount to a devastating judgment of Mies's concept, Bonatz calling it "unrealistic, arty [kunstgewerblich], and dilettantish," Schmitthenner condemning it as formalistic and romanticizing, and bluntly questioning its author's maturity and qualifications.

Both Bonatz and Schmitthenner were well prepared for the ensuing battle. Objections to Mies's concept had been voiced in the building committee several days earlier, and not all of the arguments brought forward against it could be easily dismissed. Its division into irregular plots with frequent overlaps and a complex network of pathways and approaches to the individual houses was bound to cause legal problems, while the complicated system of terraces, requiring massive substructures and extensive movement of soil, would have entailed a disproportionate increase in the total cost.

At this point, trying to prevent the worst, Stotz consented to the compromise of requesting alternative proposals from Bonatz, Gropius, and Oud.[128] Mies, however, having arrived in Stuttgart on May 4, talked the matter over with Stotz, and refused to accept this decision. Another meeting was fixed for the next morning, which Bruckmann attended. While categorically pleading Mies's cause, he left no doubt that he was prepared to recommend to the Werkbund's executive board that the exhibition be withdrawn from Stuttgart and moved to another city. On the strength of this threat the municipal building committee gave in, and Mies was asked to prepare a revised version of his master plan. It was further agreed that he and Bruckmann would arrange a meeting with Bonatz to discuss his possible collaboration. Even this last attempt at cooperation collapsed when the Bonatz and Schmitthenner articles appeared a few hours later. Mies was left with no choice but to insist on his exclusive responsibility or to resign altogether, whereupon (the threat of the Werkbund's withdrawal still pending) his reappointment was formally confirmed on May 8.[129]

Mies's second master plan (Fig. 38), developed during the following months, shows a comparatively open scheme with most of the buildings lined up discretely in a strictly rectilinear pattern. Only the northern extension of the development was turned diagonally, and the buildings in between were shifted slightly in a curve to provide a smooth transition.

The revised project and Sigloch's accompanying petition of July 23 were presented by the mayor to the city council at its meeting of July 29. The concept received a majority of votes, this despite a negative statement by the building committee rejecting the project's architectural aspects and the invitation of foreign participants.[130] The first list of architects was approved on August 24, but it included two local candidates, Hans Herkommer and Heinz Wetzel, not originally nominated by the Werkbund which, therefore, withheld its consent.[131] Almost three more months passed before a final list of architects was approved and the last contracts were signed.

All planning and architectural correspondence was handled by Mies's Berlin office. The city had reserved the right to assign the actual construction of the exhibition to a local architect, and Richard Döcker was installed as building supervisor in early October.[132] However, excavation did not begin before March 1, 1927, less than five months before the exhibition's opening on July 23.[133]

In Mies's final scheme of 1927 (Fig. 39) the smooth transition toward the northern extension of the development was given up, since the architects in charge of two of the buildings in that area (Josef Frank and Mart Stam) preferred an orthogonal plan. Thus, nothing remained of the original curved layout, although the general massing of Behrens's tall terraced house counter-

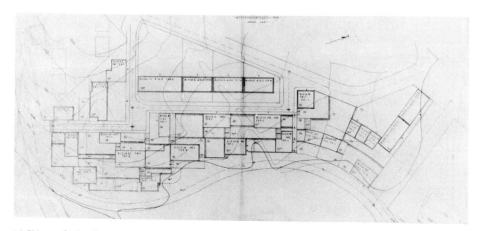

38. *Weissenhofsiedlung, Stuttgart. 1925–27. Site plan with topographic curves. Pencil on tracing paper. The Museum of Modern Art, New York, Mies van der Rohe Archive. Gift of the architect*

39. *Weissenhofsiedlung, Stuttgart. 1925–27. Elevation. Pencil on tracing paper. The Museum of Modern Art, New York, Mies van der Rohe Archive. Gift of the architect*

poised with Mies's dominant apartment block (Fig. 40) betrays a vestige of the early master plan.

Construction must have proceeded at terrific speed, even though work was still in progress as late as September. Some critical voices notwithstanding, the event was a resounding success. The number of visitors from Germany and abroad exceeded even the most optimistic expectations, and the exhibition was extended twice before it finally closed on October 31. Its exemplary character inspired a number of similar events on both a national and an international scale. The most important were the Breslau Werkbund exhibition *Dwelling and Workplace (Wohnung und Werkraum)* of 1929, the Baba settlement in Prague-Dejvice of 1928–32, the housing developments of the Swiss Werkbund in Zurich-Neubühl (1929–32) and of the Austrian Werkbund in Vienna (1930–32), and, to some extent, the Berlin Building Exposition of 1931. None of these, however, came close to matching the Stuttgart exhibition, the impact of which was due less to chronological priority than to the unique combination of first-rank European modern architects.

These designers were invited by Mies himself in consultation with Stotz, and possibly with Häring, although officially the final selection was left to the municipal authorities. Almost all the leading figures of modern architecture were included as well as some marginal ones, although several familiar names were conspicuously absent, among them Erich Mendelsohn, the Luckhardt brothers, and Häring himself. Russia and Czechoslovakia were not represented, but were assigned appropriate sections in the accompanying *Interna-*

40. Weissenhofsiedlung, Stuttgart. 1925–27. View of Apartment Building by Mies van der Rohe

tional Plan and Model Exhibition (Internationale Plan- und Modellausstellung).[134]

How, then, was the list arrived at, and how did its members unite to create the extraordinarily uniform character of the Weissenhof exhibition? Was Mies's effort a deliberate and inspired attempt to enforce the cohesive tendencies that he perceived within the architectural avant-garde? Or was it just a happy chain of coincidences? A consideration of the evolution of the list of architects sheds some light on the unfolding preferences of those involved in the selection process.[135]

Although the Württemberg Werkbund committee had originally meant to promote the cause of the local avant-garde, Mies had always thought of his assignment as having national, even international implications. His marginal notes on the third proposed list named Oud, Le Corbusier, Loos, Mendelsohn, Häring, Gropius, Hilberseimer, and himself, and thus may identify those whom he considered the principal members of the movement. Surprisingly, Adolf Loos's name does not appear in later lists, and both Häring and Mendelsohn, although again suggested by Stotz on October 16, 1926, did not receive commissions. Loos was dropped for unknown reasons, but there can be no question that his importance had slackened by the mid-1920s. Häring withdrew after quarreling with Mies about the architect's fee offered by the city, the conditions of which he was unwilling to accept. Mendelsohn's participation was never questioned either, until he was rejected by the city council for unknown reasons. Even then, Mies and Stotz were working in his favor, and they might have succeeded had he himself not decided otherwise and resigned,[136] as did Heinrich Tessenow, for personal reasons.[137]

The final list was published by the Werkbund's journal *Die Form* in December 1926 and included the following names: Peter Behrens, Le Corbusier, Richard Döcker, Josef Frank, Walter Gropius, Ludwig Hilberseimer, Ludwig Mies van der Rohe, J. J. P. Oud, Hans Poelzig, Adolf Rading, Hans Scharoun, Adolf Schneck, Mart Stam, Bruno Taut, and Max Taut. Among these, Le Corbusier, Gropius, Mies, Oud, and Bruno Taut can easily be identified as leading figures of the movement. In the view of contemporary critics, they would have been joined by Hilberseimer and Stam.

Rading and Döcker fall somewhat short of this standard, as does Frank, his central role in the Austrian avant-garde notwithstanding. Döcker and Schneck stood for Stuttgart, and both of them benefited from the challenge of working with modern architects of the first rank. This holds true especially for Döcker, who had started his career as a home-bred descendant of the regional school but quickly broadened his horizons, his district hospital in Waiblingen being hardly inferior to the highest standard of the day. Schneck had organized the 1924 Stuttgart Werkbund exhibition *Die Form ohne Ornament (Form without Ornament)*. As a teacher at the local arts-and-crafts school, he was more at home with furniture and interior design; nevertheless, his two houses at Weissenhof—one of them a private commission—adapted successfully to the underlying spirit of the exposition. So did Poelzig's.

Poelzig and Behrens were the only representatives of the first generation of Germany's modern architects who were invited to Stuttgart. Behrens's contribution is more urban in scale than the residential character of Weissenhof would seem to have demanded, and in detail as well, with vertical window formats and towering blocks still somewhat reminiscent of neoclassicism. Behrens's inclusion was a form of tribute to the one-time pioneer and former master of both Gropius and Mies, and the latter's endorsement of his nomination helped to restore the amity lost in the Kröller-Müller affair of 1912. Poelzig's influential position on the Werkbund's executive board and his membership in the Ring were factors favorable to his inclusion[138]—especially since he apparently had a tendency to drift to conservatism. (In fact, he later affiliated himself with the Block, a group founded in 1928 by Bonatz and others in reaction to the Ring.)[139] The loss of Häring, Mendelsohn, and Tessenow led to the nomination of Scharoun, who had been discussed during the preliminary phases,[140] and Max Taut, a last-minute choice.[141]

The importance of the Weissenhof exhibition to the consolidation of modern architecture was perceived almost immediately by supporters and opponents alike. As editor of the Werkbund periodical *Die Form,* Walter Riezler was naturally sympathetic to the moderns' objectives. Echoing Mies in his letter of September 1925,[142] Riezler invoked the memory of the Darmstadt *Mathildenhöhe* development of 1901, contrasting Joseph Maria Olbrich's highly individualistic attitude to the collective spirit of 1927: "In spite of the cramped arrangement, making it almost impossible to gain an isolated impression of a particular building, the general effect in Stuttgart is very harmonious. This has not been achieved by artificial adjustment, but is based on the common perceptiveness and sense of style (*gemeinsame Formempfindung*) of the various architects. We do not agree with a Swiss critic's prediction that the housing development, as far as its formal appearance is concerned, will suffer the fate of the Darmstadt settlement. On the contrary! We believe the common element will come to the fore even more clearly in time."[143]

While making a distinction between Darmstadt and Weissenhof, Riezler considered both events as part of one movement. Appearing as it did at the threshold of the twentieth century, the Darmstadt exhibition seemed to him a departure from the past activated by isolated achievements and led by a select circle of bohemian artists and patrons. In 1927, by contrast, the initiative had passed from individual personalities to a collective effort, with public bodies and communities now assuming the responsibilities of the client.[144] Modern architecture, as may be deduced from Riezler's argument, had entered a second stage, a phase of maturity and accord in which a real style had begun to emerge.

As early as 1925, while inveighing against Mies's first master plan, Paul Schmitthenner also acknowledged the existence of an "international style" based on the "everlasting principles of building," which he defined as "form follows construction, construction is determined by materials."[145] However, having claimed the superiority of the artist's personality, his perception of internationalism took an inconsistent turn as he made a special plea for the Germanic aspect. One of his major objections to the Weissenhof exhibition was Mies's apparent intention to restrict the international style of the twentieth century to what Schmitthenner saw as recipes. Yet the argument raises a crucial question: was the homogeneity of the Werkbund exhibition indeed deliberately enforced by a set of rules and principles, or did it derive from what the Austrian art historian Alois Riegl had tried to express by a general *Kunstwollen*—a partly instinctive, partly conscious will to style that characterizes the art of a given epoch?

According to the correspondence on record, the only requirement imposed

41. *Weissenhofsiedlung, Stuttgart. 1925–27. View toward the south with house by Max Taut in center*

42. *Weissenhofsiedlung, Stuttgart. 1925–27. View toward the east with house by Walter Gropius in center*

on the participants was the use of the flat roof,[146] and even so, some of the structures, like Scharoun's, show slightly sloping eaves. A light tone for the external plastering had been originally recommended by Mies, and thus off-white was mutually agreed upon, while the architects were free to accent individual surfaces with different colors.[147] Max Taut preferred one of his two houses gaily patterned, and no one prevented him from doing so (Fig. 41). The one little building that Mies referred to in an interview as "painted blue on one side, red on one side, yellow on one side, and black on the other side"[148] was by Bruno Taut. Le Corbusier used gradations of tone on the exterior as well as extremely rich coloring inside, and during the recent restoration of Stam's row houses some of the original plaster work turned out to be a bright blue. The general massing of the master plan allowed for occasional alterations, too. At Le Corbusier's request, the outline, volume, and orientation of the two buildings assigned to him were changed considerably.[149] The budget as well as the specific requirements of the city's housing plan prompted restrictions with respect to the size, cost, and prospective clientele of the individual houses, and likewise affected the total number of rooms to be provided for. These regulations, however, had also not been binding, since several smaller rooms could be combined to make a larger one.[150]

Apart from all this, an open agreement by the architects to contribute to the uniform effect of the Werkbund exhibition (Fig. 42) was further enforced by a common task and the general limits implicit in Mies's master plan. But what is style if not a tacit consent to the general form and objective of artistic production? Moreover, the majority of the participants were more or less the same age. They shared similar backgrounds, read the same periodicals and books, knew and learned from each other, and faced the same antagonists. Those who were of an older generation, like Behrens and Poelzig, born in 1868 and 1869, respectively, had once been their mentors. The Werkbund exhibition and the supplementary *International Plan and Model Exhibition,* as documented by the publications of Ludwig Hilberseimer,[151] fostered the notion that a modern architectural style had crystallized in about 1927. Walter Curt Behrendt's pamphlet *Der Sieg des neuen Baustils* (*The Triumph of the Modern Style*), which appeared in Stuttgart the same year, was the first publication to speak expressly of modern architecture as a style. Its cover illustration showed a view of Weissenhof with a triumphant row of flags in the foreground (Fig. 43). Five years later The Museum of Modern Art in New York held its famous show *Modern Architecture: International Exhibition*. Coinciding with this event the curators, Henry-Russell Hitchcock and Philip Johnson, published *The International Style,* which coined the term by which modern architecture came to be known in the Anglo-American world.[152] The obvious reference to the Weissenhof event has never been denied by the authors. If, then, the Werkbund exhibition must be seen as the climax of modern architecture (or of the International Style), it must be regarded as a turning point as well. So long as artists are united by a common condemnation by the establishment, their identity as a group is assured; but once a breakthrough has been achieved, disintegration usually follows, and did so in the case of modern architecture.

43. *Cover of* Der Sieg des neuen Baustils *by Walter Curt Behrendt (Stuttgart, 1927)*

For one thing, the degree of consensus reached at Weissenhof is confirmed by the polarization it engendered within the German architectural profession. The confrontation of the Ring by the Block was one direct consequence.[153] While the moderns were still enjoying their triumph, the conservatives began to unite for what became the final defeat of modernism, which indeed occurred in Germany in 1933. The ranks of the Werkbund itself were split, although for the moment the moderns seemed to have won the battle. For that matter, Paul Schultze-Naumburg, propagator of a racist "blood and soil culture," was a founding member of the Werkbund, and not all of his former companions may have been relieved by his withdrawal from the organization. When Bonatz and Schmitthenner left its ranks in the wake of the Weissenhof dispute, the Werkbund lost an important stronghold in one of the leading German architecture schools.

The rift that was to end in a deep gulf separating the moderns from the subsequently politically sanctioned neoconservatives of the 1930s had begun as early as 1925, when both Bonatz and Schmitthenner had in their Weissenhof polemics made faintly xenophobic references to some of the invited architects as "Frenchmen and Dutch and [even] Berliners." Schmitthenner spoke affirmatively of *völkisch* architecture. Similarly, while Bonatz's likening of a Jerusalem suburb with Mies's master plan was not necessarily an anti-Semitic reference, considering the general tenor of the time it may as well have been. Several years later it definitely was. The famous postcard transforming the Weissenhof exhibition into an Arab village was not an invention of Nazi propaganda; it was already in circulation in 1928 (Fig. 44). Thus the fatal alliance of conservative German architecture with National Socialism had roots in the Stuttgart dispute of the summer of 1926, even before fascism became an alarming political presence. If Weissenhof may be called the ultimate triumph of modern architecture as well as a key event in the career of Mies, it must also be seen as a major cause of the conflict that led to modernism's early defeat in Germany, resulting in the enforced emigration of most of its proponents—Mies being one of the last to leave his native country, in 1938.

For all of that, modernism's major figures continued in one way or another. Individual chapters of the catalogue of The Museum of Modern Art's 1932 exhibition (as distinguished from the simultaneously published book titled *The*

44. *"Arab Village" postcard. c. 1928. Anonymous photograph of the Weissenhofsiedlung, Stuttgart, altered to include Arab figures, lions, and a camel*

International Style) were devoted to Frank Lloyd Wright, Walter Gropius, Le Corbusier, J. J. P. Oud, and Ludwig Mies van der Rohe (in that order), the purported heroes of the movement.[154] However, neither Gropius nor Oud made significant contributions to the history of modern architecture after about 1930; and Wright's work, while approximating the look of the International Style during the 1930s, was soon to take off again in its own individual direction. Thus further advancement in the field was left to Mies and Le Corbusier; and for a while there appeared to be certain similarities in their work—the Tugendhat House, for example, seems to have been inspired in part by the Stein–La Monzie House in Garches (Figs. 45, 46).[155] By 1930, however, both were about to take different directions architecturally.

In Le Corbusier's oeuvre, sculptural qualities took on increasing priority, as is borne out in his telling demand for "strong objectivity of forms, under the intense light of a Mediterranean sun."[156] Mies, on the other hand, headed toward a metaphysical understanding of space that entailed the gradual reduction of architectural volume to its structural core.

For Le Corbusier architecture was an achievement in its own right, an outgrowth of artistic creativity which needed no vindication beyond a standard of quality.[157] With Mies, creative spontaneity and formal inventiveness were not ends in themselves. For him, architecture had to have meaning. Almost all of his buildings, except some purely utilitarian structures, appear to mark out a place in space or, rather, to define their environment by establishing a fixed point of orientation. Mies's approach amounts to a definition of man's position relative to the outside world; and since this definition, in spite of his yearning for "universal truth," had by its very nature to be an extremely personal one (as was Le Corbusier's self-image of the creative artist), the Weissenhof consensus was apt to remain a transitory phenomenon, an experiment, as Mies himself preferred to call it.[158]

Long before, Adolf Behne had pointed out the basic incompatibility of the

45. *Tugendhat House, Brno, Czechoslovakia. 1928–30. Garden facade*

46. *Le Corbusier and Pierre Jeanneret: Stein–La Monzie House, Garches, France. 1927–28.*
Garden facade

two positions by contrasting Le Corbusier's expressive point of departure with those of the Berlin functionalists and constructivists.[159] In 1932, even Hitch-cock and Johnson, when trying to establish the criteria for the so-called In-ternational Style, acknowledged that neither Mies nor Le Corbusier had completely adhered to what they identified as its principles.[160] This distinction seems all the more intriguing in the case of the Barcelona Pavilion, since there was no doubt, even in 1932, that it was one of Mies's most masterly accomplish-ments as well as a landmark of twentieth-century architecture. Had it featured only some formal peculiarities, the Pavilion might indeed have been little more

79

than the exception that proved the elasticity of what Hitchcock and Johnson's principles established as the general rule.[161] The question is, therefore, how far Mies had already deviated in substance from the objectives of the movement by then. His infrequent public comments of about 1930 betray a gradual shift in emphasis and a growing concern for the spiritual aspects of architecture.[162]

The Barcelona Pavilion

The literary reputation of the German Pavilion at the Barcelona International Exposition of 1929 (Fig. 47) greatly exceeded its own brief material existence. Inaugurated one week after the official opening of the exposition on May 19, it was completely dismantled after the closing in January 1930. With evidence based exclusively on photographs, a limited number of eyewitness reports,[163] and a single publication plan of rather doubtful reliability, the Pavilion quickly became an object of legend and speculation. A set of original plans and drawings only recently rediscovered, with some of the sheets showing preliminary stages, has helped to settle many misunderstandings. Further valuable information may be drawn from the fragmentary office correspondence as well as from other contemporary sources of rather remote provenance that have not been previously taken into consideration.[164]

47. German Pavilion, International Exposition, Barcelona. 1929. View from the street

Approached by the commissioner general of the Reich, Georg von Schnitzler, in early summer 1928, Mies was approved as artistic supervisor of the design of all the German sections in Barcelona. Chief among his responsibilities was the creation of a prestigious structure that would represent the Weimar Republic. Customary as such a commission might seem, in this case it touched upon some delicate political issues. For the first time since the First World War, Germany had been officially invited as an equal partner in the community of nations (on previous occasions participation had been restricted to private economic or cultural delegations). Von Schnitzler's choice of Mies, although motivated to a degree by the latter's successful management of the Weissenhof exhibition, must have been affected as well by Mies's relationship to the politics of the Pavilion.

The Weimar Republic's affiliation with modern architecture has commonly been associated with the large number of publicly funded housing developments by Bruno Taut, Martin Wagner, Ernst May, Walter Gropius, and a couple of others in major German cities. However, these were municipal commissions often delegated to union-controlled cooperative housing societies. Only twice in its short history (leaving aside some unexecuted projects, like the extension to the Reichstag building) did the Weimar Republic become directly involved in establishing its own national architectural image: first at the Barcelona International Exposition of 1929, and then in the following year when Karl Friedrich Schinkel's Neue Wache (New Guardhouse) at Unter den Linden in Berlin (Fig. 48) was transformed into a Tomb of the Unknown Soldier to commemorate the victims of the First World War. But while in the latter instance the jury's decision to award the commission to Heinrich Tessenow may

PERSPECTIVISCHE ANSICHT DES NEUEN WACHT-GEBÄUDES IN BERLIN.

48. *Karl Friedrich Schinkel: Neue Wache (New Guardhouse), Berlin. 1816–18. Perspective*

indeed be taken as representative of a politically ambivalent position, the former must be attributed to the personal initiative of a few professional people in charge, if not to the commissioner general himself. Contemporary commentaries, including an article initialed by Mrs. Lilly von Schnitzler, explicitly refer to the German section as a characteristic reflection of the positive and radical changes the nation had recently undergone.[165] "We wished here to show what we can do, what we are, what we feel today, and see. We want nothing else but clarity, simplicity, honesty." [166]

These words were doubtless calculated to evoke the image of a democratic and peaceable Germany, a nation as remote from former imperial megalomania as the "clarity, simplicity, and honesty" of Mies's eventual design for the Pavilion appeared to be from the bombastic pathos that had dominated public commissions of the prewar period. [167] While historical fact defies a simple identification of ideological conviction with a preference for a certain kind of architectural style, there must have been some recognized relationship between modernism's objectives and a liberal and democratic attitude, which—in consideration of the anticipated response from abroad—evidently prompted Mies's nomination as architect in charge.

Once he was installed, Mies's first official act was to determine the site of the future Pavilion. The exposition grounds occupied the northern slope of Montjuich Park to the west of the old city center of Barcelona (Fig. 49). Their strictly axial disposition was dominated by a broad avenue that led up a mon-

49. *International Exposition, Barcelona. 1929. Aerial view (Mies's German Pavilion is circled at upper right)*

umental flight of stairs and finally to the crowning structure, the National Palace. A squarelike concourse crossing the avenue perpendicularly contributed a subordinate axis. Two exhibition halls started in 1923 by the former architect in charge, Puig i Cadafalch—the palaces of Alfonso XIII and of Victoria Eugenia—were arranged symmetrically at the junction of the two axes, on either side of the great stairs.

It had been suggested that the German Pavilion occupy the vacant corner adjacent to the Palace of Victoria Eugenia, opposite its French counterpart, which was located in the corresponding corner of the site of the Palace of Alfonso XIII. What might have been meant as a diplomatic move by the local officials was likely to stir old sentiments of national rivalry; Mies was thus well advised to reject the initial proposal and to choose a less prominent, although artistically more challenging site at the western end of the perpendicular axis. As a consequence, the Pavilion came to cut across a footpath leading up the hill to the so-called *Pueblo español*, a kind of Disneyland mock-up composed of traditional housing types from various regions of Spain and, indeed, one of the exposition's most popular attractions.[168]

Both a *point de vue* closing the narrow end of the perpendicular concourse as well as an object athwart the route to the Spanish Village, the Pavilion took full advantage of its site. Off the main traffic route, its elevated platform offered a resting place from which an attractive view of the square, with its fountains and trees, could be enjoyed. At the same time, the building's open structure provided a passageway leading to a small semicircular garden area, thence to an easy flight of stairs at its rear, by which the visitor was able to resume his route to the Spanish Village beyond.

The Pavilion is set upon a narrow podium 185 feet (56.5 meters) long (Fig. 50), which is clamped between rectangular end walls and visible only on its eastern side facing the square. Since the ground rises toward the Village, the podium at its rear is level with the garden. Much of the surface of the Pavilion is occupied by a shallow pool that captures the visitor's attention as soon as he has climbed the podium via the flight of steps at the recessed northeastern corner. By then he has had to pass by the glazed front wall of the roofed

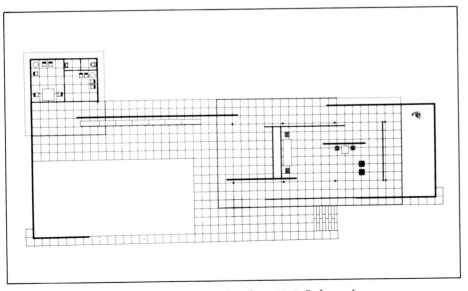

50. *German Pavilion, International Exposition, Barcelona. 1929. Redrawn plan*

51. *German Pavilion, International Exposition, Barcelona. 1929. Interior view*

section to his right, and he thus may already have caught a glimpse of the interior (Fig. 51). He also will have detected one or two of the eight freestanding columns that carry the roof slab (Fig. 52). These slender cruciform shafts belie their actual function, as they seem to pierce, rather than physically support, the ceiling. The mirroring effect of their chrome sheathing further obscures their actual strength. The regular bays of the double row of columns that forms the structural system can only be appreciated in plan and, therefore, will likely escape the attention of the visitor, whose sense of order is constantly confused by the asymmetrical placement of the intersecting partition walls.

Thanks to the freestanding columns, all wall elements (except those of the small office annex at the opposite end of the platform) have been relieved of any load-bearing function and thus Mies gave them a minimum thickness of only 7 inches (18 cm) in section. Like the glass panes that shield most of the roofed part of the structure, the walls are held up by metal frames covered on both sides with thin marble slabs, although again, their solid end pieces create a different illusion. The delicate profiles and free arrangement of the walls give the impression of movable screens that appear to slide along parallel lines into and out from under the horizontal slab that hovers above. The effect is one of weightlessness and poise, faintly reminiscent of the floating rectangular planes in the paintings of El Lissitzky and, especially, Kasimir Malevich. At the same time, the podium and clamplike end walls diminish any Constructivist spatial ambiguity: they act to stabilize both the position and complex structure of the spaces in between. (By contrast, the asymmetrically balanced layout of the plan that has been occasionally compared to Piet Mondrian's de Stijl paintings must be regarded as common property by 1929.)

The staggered sequence of longitudinal wall elements that blocks the perpendicular axis of the square in front and the footpath and stairs beyond diverts the approaching visitor to the right, where a broad open passageway leads

52. *German Pavilion, International Exposition, Barcelona. 1929. Entry*

straight into the interior of the building. The lure of precious marble, glistening chrome, and a selective display of colored fabrics exerts an additional pull. (This may still be experienced in the recent reconstruction of the building, although it uses steel sheathing for the columns and glass walls of a much lighter tint.) In spite of its apparent openness, the interior remains largely obscure and only gradually reveals itself to the amazed visitor. Inside, the central section is dominated by a freestanding wall of onyx doré. Directly in front of it stands one **X**-legged coffee table and several ottomans. Two Barcelona Chairs are placed at a right angle to the onyx wall (Fig. 53). The sitting area, whose general layout was repeated almost unaltered in Mies's later residential projects, is given further prominence by a black wool carpet that stretches all the way from the onyx wall to the glazed front on the east, where a deep red velvet curtain can be drawn to keep out the sun.

The combination of black, red, and gold suggests the colors of the German Republic, although in an unobtrusive way that renders an additional national emblem in the interior superfluous. The reading of the Barcelona Chair as "a modern version of the royal throne"[169] seems far-fetched considering its low seat, the tilted curve of its back, and the lack of armrests. In any case, neither Alfonso XIII nor his queen, Victoria Eugenia, felt any inclination to be seated at the official reception on May 19, 1929. What remains is a serene place in which to relax while enjoying an architectural interior of luxurious materials and a pleasant view of a spacious square.

For all that, a certain mystic and ethereal quality about the Pavilion befalls the observer as he proceeds to the heart of the building. Resuming his path along the direction of the frontal passageway he arrives at a kind of atrium, screened off from the central area by a perpendicular partition wall of bottle-green, semitransparent glass. (Due to changes in manufacturing, green glass of a comparably dark tint is no longer available today. Thus, the corresponding wall of the reconstructed Pavilion appears to be almost completely transparent

53. *German Pavilion, International Exposition, Barcelona. 1929. Interior view*

*54. German Pavilion, International Exposition, Barcelona. 1929. View of pool with sculpture
by Georg Kolbe*

when seen from the inside—with the fatal consequence of destroying the central space's integrity and generating a different kind of atmosphere.) Otherwise, the atrium is completely closed in on three sides by the northern end wall of Tinian marble (Fig. 54). Although open to the sky, this is the most introverted part of the Pavilion, where all visual relationship to the outside world has been masked off. The edge of the platform continues some 8 feet, 2 inches (2.5 meters) beyond the tinted glass wall, as does the roof, with the remaining space occupied by a small pool. While the larger pool on the outside terrace is exposed to the wind, the smaller one is totally sheltered from breezes and drafts and thus lies almost motionless. In addition, its bottom and sides have been clad in black glass tiles (in contrast to the greenish paint applied to those of the larger pool). The overall effect is that of a dark, reflecting mirror forming the surface of some seemingly crystalline substance of unknown depth beneath.

I would not go so far as to claim a deliberate inspiration from architectural fantasies of ancient legends, such as Albrecht von Scharfenberg's medieval description of the temple of the Holy Grail, which was said to be raised upon an enormous podium of solid black obsidian.[170] The fact that this was located by some medieval authors on the Montserrat, not far from Barcelona, suggests a tempting coincidence, as does Sergius Ruegenberg's recollection of the extensive talks about Gothic architecture that Mies carried on in those days with the Catholic priest Carl Sonnenschein.[171] According to Ruegenberg, Mies once even remarked upon the vertical pane format of some of the Pavilion's glass walls as being decisively Gothic in spirit. Was there more here than just an accidental formal analogy?

At the west end of the inner pool, lined up with the axis of the rear passageway, rises a nude female figure. Early sketches as well as the only elaborate

55. *German Pavilion, International Exposition, Barcelona. 1929. View of pool with Kolbe sculpture reflected on marble walls*

representation drawing of the Pavilion show a reclining sculpture in that place; but there is reason to believe that the final selection of Georg Kolbe's *Der Morgen* (*Morning*) was really a matter of choice. Levitated above the blackness of the water and shielding her eyes against the brilliant sun (Fig. 55), the figure imparts a quality of innocence and birth. Is it conceivable that Mies intended the whole arrangement as a kind of allegory? The release associated with the Holy Grail; the purgatorial effect of war and defeat, in the wake of which the peaceable and democratic forces of the nation had come forth to replace a suppressive and violent political system?

There is no hard evidence to support such a notion, and if there lurked any deeper meaning behind the obvious facts, Mies was careful not to talk of it. Nor has any visitor been reported to have offered a similar interpretation. What appears in tune with the eschatological, almost messianic spirit of Mies's formative years following the turn of the century, and consonant with the associational thinking of the utopians of about 1919,[172] would seem utterly out of place in the rationalistic climate that dominated the second half of the 1920s.

And yet, this was exactly the time when Mies's plea for an architecture that also appeals to the spirit began to be enunciated.[173] It is, in fact, this spiritual aspect that distinguishes the Pavilion from most of the architecture of its day, a disjunction that seems to have escaped most historians' attention.

The Barcelona Pavilion rightly deserves to be called a key work of modern architecture: its elegance, poise, and perfect detailing have been rarely if ever surpassed. The skeleton frame with its freestanding columns and nonbearing walls, which allowed for a continuous sequence of spaces, provided the grammar for many of Mies's subsequent projects, including the Tugendhat House and the Court House projects of the mid-1930s. Even the New National Gallery, completed shortly before Mies's death, betrays a subtle indebtedness to his early masterpiece. No longer a mere legend since its reconstruction in 1986, the Pavilion may now be appreciated again as a genuine example of "pure" architecture. On the other hand, does it disclose more than that; can it yield a deeper understanding where the original escaped a coherent interpretation?

In his excellent study, *Architecture and Its Interpretation,*[174] Juan Pablo Bonta has cited the Barcelona Pavilion to demonstrate how scholarly criticism is bound up with the changing context of architectural thinking. In every decade following the Pavilion's inauguration (and dismantling) new and unfamiliar aspects of the building have been deemed worthy of examination. Such discussions may reveal more about their participants' own respective times than about the architect's actual original intention.

Nevertheless, the Barcelona Pavilion presents uncommonly complex issues. While it was conceived in a peaceful period of economic and political stability, its completion was quickly overshadowed by a depression that changed the course of history, bearing heavily on the future development of modern architecture. As a signpost of the Weimar Republic and the positive values it intended to represent, the Pavilion was bound to fail in its message once the republic became identified with the desperate conditions that marked the beginning of the next decade for the majority of the German people. Toward the end of the exhibition, Mies himself seems to have seen the Pavilion with different eyes than those that served him at the beginning, which may explain his evasiveness when asked to think about the building's possible preservation once the exhibition closed down.[175] Even more telling is the cursory way in which he later, after the Second World War, tried to play down the role of his former public clients, hardly crediting them with even the vaguest notion of what they had expected of his services.[176]

Nevertheless, it was this official commission that once and for all established Mies van der Rohe's international reputation. During the latter part of the 1930s, under the strain of a totalitarian regime aggressively hostile to the objectives of modern architecture and its proponents, the inviting openness and unobtrusive elegance of the Pavilion gave way to an introverted, occasionally forbidding temper in his buildings and projects. Still the basic elements of his architecture remained essentially unaltered. In Barcelona, Mies set a standard whose impact can be felt throughout the major part of his later oeuvre, although it was only in his Farnsworth House of 1946–51 that the Pavilion's lyric and almost arcadian atmosphere reappeared for another time.

Notes

The following abbreviations are used throughout these notes:

BA: Bauhaus-Archiv, Berlin
LC: Mies Collection, Library of Congress, Washington, D.C.
MoMA: Mies van der Rohe Archive, The Museum of Modern Art, New York
OMH: Karl - Ernst - Osthaus - Museum, Hagen, Germany

No work of art can be said to have been conceived out of the blue; this of course is also true of research and writing. I am deeply indebted to those friends and colleagues who contributed to this essay by readily sharing their knowledge and advice on the subject. My special thanks go to Franz Schulze for his helpful comments and constant support. Winfried Nerdinger kindly drew my attention to the rare photograph of the 1923 Bauhaus exhibition, which shows the previously unknown model of the Concrete Office Building next to that of the Glass Skyscraper of 1922. Thanks also go to Ludwig Glaeser, who years ago introduced me to the Mies van der Rohe Archive at The Museum of Modern Art, and particularly to Pierre Adler and Robert Coates, on whose friendship and helpfulness I have relied. Harriet Schoenholz Bee, Hartmut Hansen, and Alfred Willis deserve my warmest gratitude for turning my queer notion of English into a language I hope is not offensive to the native reader. The essay is dedicated to the memory of Arthur Drexler, and this speaks for itself.

1. "No Dogma" (Interview, London, May 29, 1959), *Interbuild*, vol. 6, no. 6 (1959), p. 10.
2. Mies exhibited with the Novembergruppe for the first time in summer 1922 (*see below*, n. 45). Together with Wassili Luckhardt and Walter Kampmann he was elected treasurer and given a chair on the working committee at its general meeting on January 17, 1923 ("Bericht über die Generalversammlung der Novembergruppe," February 2, 1923, LC). The next year saw him in charge of organizing the group's section at the annual *Berlin Art Exhibition* (*see* his letter to Peter Behrens of May 1, 1924, asking him to participate, LC). For the Novembergruppe in general, *see* Helga Kliemann, *Die Novembergruppe* (Berlin, 1969); for the *Arbeitsrat für Kunst*, *see* the catalogue of the Akademie der Künste (Berlin, 1980).

3. *See* Mies's letters to the BDA, Landesbezirk Brandenburg, of August 13, 1923, and January 30, 1926 (LC).
4. Letter of Otto Baur, executive secretary of the Werkbund, to Mies (LC).
5. The official version is given by Joan Campbell, *The German Werkbund: The Politics of Reform in the Applied Arts.* (Princeton, 1978); cf. the Gropius correspondence in OMH.
6. Cf. Gropius's letters to Osthaus of April 11, July 10, and July 20, 1914 (OMH: Kü 339/210, Kü 385/33, and Kü 385/45). A brief but excellent account of the issue is given by Peter Stressig in *Karl Ernst Osthaus: Leben und Werk* (Recklinghausen, 1971), pp. 466ff.
7. Cf. Campbell, *German Werkbund*, pp. 141–170; for Gropius's attitude toward the Werkbund in 1918–19, *see* his letters to Osthaus of December 23, 1918, February 2, 1919, and August 3, 1919 (OMH: Kü 346/282, Kü 347/290, and Kü 347/302)—the last one openly calling the Werkbund a danger to German culture—and, finally, his declaration at the meeting on June 30, 1919 ("Protokoll der Vorstandssitzung des DWB," OMH: DWB 270). The relevant passages are quoted by Stressig, *Osthaus*, pp. 471–473.
8. Mies to Kiesler, March 22, 1924 (LC). Translations throughout this essay are mine unless otherwise credited.
9. Henning failed, however, to secure for himself a lasting influence on the organization's future policy. Ibid.; cf. Campbell, *German Werkbund*, p. 181.
10. Stotz to Mies, October 26, 1925 (MoMA); Mies's nomination to be supervisor of the Stuttgart exhibition took place at the committee meeting of June 20, 1925 ("Protokoll der Vorstandssitzung des DWB," June 26, LC). (The Berlin exhibition referred to in Stotz's letter is the Berlin Building Exposition of 1931, which was then planned as a Werkbund exhibition.)
11. "Mitteilungen des DWB," *Die Form*, vol. 1, no. 10 (1926), following p. 228.
12. Campbell, *German Werkbund*, p. 181.
13. The story was reported by Ruegenberg himself, who had been working in Mies's office from November 1925 to July 1926, and again from September 1928 to February 1931 (undated letter of reference by Mies on Ruegenberg, probably of 1931, in the possession of the latter with copy in MoMA, and recent letter to the author).
14. Paul Westheim, "Mies van der Rohe: Entwicklung eines Architekten," *Das*

Kunstblatt, vol. 11, no. 2 (1927), pp. 55–62, ill. p. 59 (according to the caption, the house was planned for Neubabelsberg, near Potsdam).
15. Ibid., p. 57.
16. *See* Fritz Neumeyer, *Mies van der Rohe. Das kunstlose Wort, Gedanken zur Baukunst* (Berlin, 1986), ills. p. 118; Neumeyer also tracked down the contemporary Feldmann House in Berlin-Grunewald: ibid., ills. pp. 114ff.
17. The Bauhaus-Archiv in Berlin has a complete set of blueprints for the Eichstaedt House, while a small number of detail drawings is in MoMA. For the recently restored Perls House, *see* Dietrich von Beulwitz, "The Perls House by Ludwig Mies van der Rohe," *Architectural Design*, vol. 53, nos. 11–12 (1983), pp. 62–71.
18. The official publication of the monument commission: Max Schmid, ed., *Hundert Entwürfe aus dem Wettbewerb für das Bismarck-National-Denkmal auf der Elisenhöhe bei Bingerbrück-Bingen* (Düsseldorf, 1911), gives a view of the forecourt toward the exedra enclosing a statue of Bismarck. The entry is titled "Deutschlands Dank" (Germany's Gratitude) and signed by E[wald] and L[udwig] Mies—Aachen. (Ewald, Ludwig's older brother, carried on their father's business in Aachen.) A draft from the local records of 1937 (MoMA) reveals that Mies, between July 1910 and May 1911 (on temporary leave from the Behrens office), again took up residence in his home town.
19. Franz Schulze, *Mies van der Rohe: A Critical Biography* (Chicago and London, 1985), p. 52; Schulze gives no source for his claim that Ewald was listed as responsible for the design of the Bismarck sculpture (ibid., p. 51), but he may be right.
20. Salomon van Deventer, *Aus Liebe zur Kunst: Das Museum Kröller-Müller* (Cologne, 1958), p. 70. In a letter of September 23, 1959 (LC), van Deventer feels compelled to explain the issue once more to Mies. His consoling statement: "Maybe the great disappointment has been helpful to your future development," confirms my understanding that the Kröller-Müller affair was crucial to Mies's later career.
21. Meier-Graefe's letter (MoMA) is dated November 18, 1912. The matching correspondence is lost, but there can be little doubt that it was intended for Mies personally, not the clients.
22. Mies to Gropius, February 11, 1919

(BA); the preceding letter by Gropius has not been located.

23. Sandra Honey, "Who and What Inspired Mies van der Rohe in Germany," *Architectural Design*, vol. 49, nos. 3–4 (1979), pp. 99–102, esp. p. 99; no sources given.

24. Max Berg, "Die formale Auffassung des Hochhausgedankens: Charakteristische Entwürfe des Berliner Wettbewerbs," *Die Bauwelt*, vol. 13, no. 21 (1922), pp. 359–363, esp. p. 363.

25. According to Renate Petras, the interior of the house at Karl-Marx-Strasse 28–29 in Potsdam-Neubabelsberg, now a pediatric clinic, was completely changed in 1933. Excavation on the site had begun in September 1924. Rough construction was completed by the end of February 1925 (letter in MoMA), but it was not ready for occupancy before April 1926 (Petras). Local building authorities in Potsdam hold a complete set of drawings signed by Mies and dated August 23/24, 1924, as well as an extensive file of correspondence with client and architect. *See* Renate Petras, "Drei Arbeiten Mies van der Rohes in Potsdam-Babelsberg," *Deutsche Architektur*, vol. 23, no. 2 (1924), pp. 120ff., including a recent photograph.

26. Florian Zimmermann, ed., *Der Schrei nach dem Turmhaus: Der Ideenwettbewerb Hochhaus am Bahnhof Friedrichstrasse Berlin 1921/22* (Berlin, 1988). This Bauhaus-Archiv catalogue gives a detailed account of the Friedrichstrasse competition and the contemporary discussion of it in Germany. For a summary, *see also* Rainer Stommer, "Germanisierung des Wolkenkratzers—Die Hochhausdebatte in Deutschland bis 1921," *Kritische Berichte*, vol. 10, no. 3 (1982), pp. 36–53; Josef Ponten, *Architektur die nicht gebaut wurde* (Stuttgart, Berlin, and Leipzig, 1925), vol. 1, pp. 117–133; Walter Curt Behrendt, "Skyscrapers in Germany," *Journal of the AIA*, vol. 11, no. 9 (1923), pp. 365–370.

27. With war loans having absorbed most of the capital that had been invested in real estate, the housing shortage was one of the major challenges facing the country and one of the only problems the young Weimar Republic finally succeeded in bringing under control after inflation had halted almost all private building activities. For the economic situation during the time of the Weimar Republic, *see* Dietmar Petzina, *Die deutsche Wirtschaft in der Zwischenkriegszeit*, edited by Hans Pohl (Wiesbaden, 1977). Barbara Miller Lane, *Architecture and Politics in Germany, 1918–1945* (Cambridge, Mass., 1968), ch. 4, concentrates on the mass-housing developments initiated after 1924 without mentioning the skyscraper debate of about 1921.

28. For Adolf Behne, the American skyscraper—in spite of architects' frequent recourse to Gothic or Renaissance ornament—represents the most advanced solution of its kind (Adolf Behne, "Wolkenkratzer," *Sozialistische Monatshefte*, vol. 58, no. 29 (1922), pp. 147ff.); while Peter Behrens insisted that "even artistically, there is a good deal to learn in New York" ("Zur Frage des Hochhauses," *Stadtbaukunst alter und neuer Zeit*, vol. 3, no. 24 [1922], pp. 369–371).

29. *See* Stommer, "Germanisierung des Wolkenkratzers," pp. 40–43; Möhring's project of 1914 (ill. 2, p. 41) is erroneously dated 1915.

30. Bruno Möhring, "Über die Vorzüge der Turmhäuser und die Voraussetzungen, unter denen sie in Berlin gebaut werden können," *Stadtbaukunst alter und neuer Zeit*, vol. 1, nos. 22–24 (1920), pp. 353–357, 370–376, and 385–391.

31. "Erlass des preuss. Ministers für Volkswohlfahrt vom 3.1.1921 über die Genehmigung vielgeschossiger Häuser (Hochhäuser) in Ausnahmefällen," in *Zentralblatt der Bauverwaltung*, vol. 39, no. 7 (1921), p. 48.

32. *See* the competition requirements discussed below.

33. The announcement of the competition was published in *Zentralblatt der Bauverwaltung*, vol. 39, no. 89 (November 5, 1921), p. 552. Unless otherwise stated, all background information derives from Friedrich Paulsen, "Ideenwettbewerb Hochhaus Bahnhof Friedrichstrasse," *Stadtbaukunst alter und neuer Zeit*, second special issue (1922), and Renschmidt, "Das Hochhaus am Bahnhof Friedrichstrasse," *Wochenschrift des Architekten-Vereins zu Berlin*, vol. 17, nos. 9–10 (1922), pp. 29–31, 34ff.; both sources quote literally from the original text giving the specified conditions.

34. *Mies in Berlin*. Record based on an interview by RIAS Berlin, October 1964: *Bauwelt Archiv*, I (Berlin, 1966).

35. First published by Berg, "Die formale Auffassung des Hochhausgedankens" (p. 363), in May 1922. The floor plans, some of them rendered in ink on heavy tracing paper, conform in medium and paper quality to those of the curvilinear Glass Skyscraper, and thus may date from about the same time, early 1922.

36. Philip Johnson, *Mies van der Rohe* (New York, 1947), p. 26; Ludwig Glaeser, *Mies van der Rohe: Drawings in the Collection of The Museum of Modern Art* (New York, 1969), pl. 2, shows the present state of the drawing now cropped and mounted on board.

37. Ludwig Mies van der Rohe, "Hochhäuser," *Frühlicht*, vol. 1, no. 1 (1922), pp. 122–124.

38. Ibid., p. 124.

39. Ibid.

40. Arthur Drexler, *Ludwig Mies van der Rohe* (New York, 1960), p. 14.

41. Johnson, *Mies van der Rohe*, p. 26.

42. Graeff to Ludwig Glaeser, letter (in English) of July 6, 1968 (MoMA).

43. Mies van der Rohe, "Hochhäuser," p. 124.

44. Carl Gotfrid, "Hochhäuser," *Qualität*, vol. 3, nos. 5–12 (August 1922–March 1923), pp. 63–66, esp. p. 65.

45. *Grosse Berliner Kunstausstellung 1922: Verzeichnis der ausgestellten Kunstwerke* (Berlin, 1922), p. 64, cat. nos. 1385–1387; a brief commentary is given in the special guide to the section on the Novembergruppe (*Grosse Berliner Kunstausstellung 1922: Führer durch die Abteilung der Novembergruppe*, p. 9). On the Marine-Panorama, *see* Stephan Oettermann, *Das Panorama: Die Geschichte eines Massenmediums* (Frankfurt-am-Main, 1980), pp. 212–214.

46. Ill. in Irmgard Wirth, ed., *Die Bauwerke und Kunstdenkmäler von Berlin: Bezirk Tiergarten* (Berlin, 1955), p. 324.

47. *See*, e.g., the ill. in Mies van der Rohe, "Hochhäuser," p. 122.

48. Graeff to Ludwig Glaeser (*see* n. 42); the importance that Mies attached to the small clay models surrounding the skyscraper model is emphasized in his draft of a letter to Gropius of September 6, 1923 (LC): "On this occasion, I once again would like to draw your attention to the small plaster models which seem to me absolutely necessary additions to my work, since I intend . . . with my project." Unfortunately, the missing passage in this sentence, evidently meant for later insertion, was never added.

49. *Prinzipien der Baukunst* (*Principles of the Art of Building*). Watercolor and pencil, 13⅝ × 9⅞" (34.4 × 25.1 cm). Unsigned, undated. Akademie der Künste, West Berlin.

50. Sehring's Tietz Department Store is amply illustrated in *Berliner Architekturwelt*, vol. 3, no. 9 (1901), ills. 417–421, pp. 312–317.

51. Kenneth Frampton, *Modern Architecture: A Critical History* (New York and Toronto, 1980), pp. 114ff., refers to Gropius's "nostalgia for the classical" and the strong impact of Behrens's AEG Turbine Factory on Gropius's Fagus Factory.

52. Mies to Werner Jakstein, November 14, 1923 (LC).

53. At the invitation of Gropius, Mies had contributed models of the curvilinear Glass Skyscraper and the Concrete Office Building, as well as a drawing of the Concrete Country House. For reasons unknown, a drawing of the Friedrichstrasse skyscraper, which Mies also sent to Weimar, was not exhibited (*see* Mies's letters to Gropius of June 14 and September 26, 1923, LC). There was no catalogue for the architecture section, but Walter Gropius, *Internationale Architektur*, Bauhausbücher, no. 1 (Munich, 1925), gives a fairly good selection of the material on display.

54. Letter to Werner Jakstein of September 13, 1923 (LC).

55. *See* his reply to Walter Riezler in *Die Form*, vol. 2, no. 2 (1927), p. 59, which starts: "I do not object to form, but only to form as an end in itself."

56. Otto Wagner, *Die Baukunst unserer Zeit* (Vienna, 1914), pp. 135–136. (4th ed. of *Moderne Architektur*, first published in 1896.)

57. *See*, e.g., the heavy critique that Behrens had to face because of the fake corner pylons of his AEG Turbine Factory.

58. Ludwig Mies van der Rohe, "Bürohaus," *G*, no. 1 (July 1923), p. 3.

59. Listed as cat. no. 1271 in the catalogue to the *Grosse Berliner Kunstausstellung 1923* (*see above*, n. 45); an extremely poor photo of the model appears at the lower margin of a contemporary collage showing architectural models that were displayed at the 1923 Bauhaus exhibition; *see* Karl-Heinz Hüter, *Das Bauhaus in Weimar: Studie zur gesellschaftspolitischen Geschichte einer deutschen Kunstschule* (East Berlin, 1976), ill. 17.

60. Werner Graeff, in a tape-recorded interview by Ludwig Glaeser, September 17, 1972 (MoMA).

61. "Les Architectes du Groupe 'de Style,'" October 15–November 15, 1923; Mies was the only nonmember of the group to be personally invited to participate by van Doesburg (cf. Mies correspondence in LC).

62. *See* shipping list and Mies's letter of confirmation to van Doesburg, October 8, 1923 (LC).

63. Glaeser, *Mies van der Rohe: Drawings.*

64. Interview, September 17, 1972 (*see above*, n. 60).

65. Note the similar arrangement of the basement floor at the Architecture, City Planning, and Design Building (S. R. Crown Hall), at IIT.

66. For the entry solution, *see* Wolf Tegethoff, *Mies van der Rohe: The Villas and Country Houses* (New York, 1985), p. 22.

67. *See*, e.g., Konrad Werner Schulze, *Glas in der Architektur der Gegenwart* (Stuttgart, 1929), p. 25; Ludwig Hilberseimer, *Groszstadtarchitektur*, Die Baubücher, III (Stuttgart, 1927), p. 54, arrives at a similar conclusion when commenting on the early country house projects.

68. Tegethoff, *Villas and Country Houses*, chs. 1, 3.

69. Ill. in Westheim, "Mies van der Rohe," pp. 60, 61.

70. Letter of application to Albrecht, February 14, 1923 (LC).

71. *Magistrat der Residenzstadt*, Potsdam, to Mies, March 31, 1923 (LC), referring to his request of March 11.

72. Mies to Albrecht, April 30, 1923 (LC).

73. Mies to Deutsche Bank, July 18, 1923 (LC); the purchase order was for 5,000 marks in stocks (*Lingel Schuhfabrik*) and 100,000 marks in bonds (*Bergius Obligationen*). If Mies was serious about his intention, the time was well chosen: from January to November 1923 the mark had decreased in value from 17,172 to 2,194 billion per dollar, and chances could hardly have been better.

74. Hans Richter, *Begegnungen von Dada bis heute: Briefe, Dokumente, Erinnerungen* (Cologne, 1973); Richter recalled that it had been van Doesburg who introduced him to Mies in 1921 (p. 53).

75. Ibid., p. 55.

76. This location has also been referred to in some of the reviews of the annual *Berlin Art Exhibition*, where the project was first on display in May 1924; cf. Tegethoff, *Villas and Country Houses*, pp. 40ff.

77. These were the Riehl House (1907), the Urbig House (1914–17), and the Mosler House, then under construction. The Petermann and Lessing houses of 1921 and 1923 had been planned for Neubabelsberg as well, but were never built.

78. *Das Kunstblatt*, vol. 9, no. 4 (1925), ill. p. 110.

79. Cf. Westheim, "Mies van der Rohe."

80. *Ausgeführte Bauten und Projekte von Frank Lloyd Wright* (Berlin, 1910), and *Frank Lloyd Wright: Ausgeführte Bauten*, intro. by C. R. Ashbee (Berlin, 1911); a compilation of Mies's personal comments regarding his early encounter with Wright's oeuvre is given in Tegethoff, *Villas and Country Houses*, p. 57, n. 16.

81. Glaeser, *Mies van der Rohe: Drawings*; the introverted spaces of the Concrete Office Building, presumably oriented toward an inner court, also strongly recall the Larkin Building; cf. Schulze, *Critical Biography*, p. 108.

82. Frank Lloyd Wright, *An Autobiography*. 3rd, rev. ed. (New York, 1977), p. 165.

83. Henry-Russell Hitchcock, *In the Nature of Materials: The Buildings of Frank Lloyd Wright, 1887–1941* (New York, 1942), p. 30.

84. Cf. Wolf Tegethoff, "On the Development of the Conception of Space in the Works of Mies van der Rohe," *Daidalos*, vol. 4, no. 13 (1984), pp. 114–123.

85. Conversation with the author in Berlin, December 1979.

86. Vincent Scully, Jr., *Frank Lloyd Wright* (New York, 1960), p. 17.

87. Cf. Tegethoff, "Space in the Works of Mies van der Rohe," p. 115.

88. Ludwig Glaeser, in discussions with the author, 1979. This may explain the absence of human figures in Mies's drawings, which thus identify the observer exclusively with the inhabitant of the house.

89. Mies was never actually divorced, but continued to see his wife and daughters from time to time, and occasionally even spent a couple of weeks with them on holiday in the Alps; cf. Schulze, *Critical Biography*, pp. 94ff., 128ff.

90. Illustrations appeared in many leading architectural periodicals and avant-garde journals, including *Die Bauwelt* (vol. 13, no. 21, 1922), *Qualität* (vol. 3, nos. 5–12, 1922–23, and vol. 4, nos. 1–2, 1925), *Wendingen* (vol. 5, no. 3, 1923), *Der Neubau* (vol. 6, no. 13, 1924), *Merz* (vol. 2, nos. 8–9, 1924), *Das Kunstblatt* (vol. 9, no. 4, 1925), *La Cité* (vol. 6, no. 4, 1926), *Bouwbedrijf* (vol. 3, no. 2, 1926), *Das Werk* (vol. 13, no. 7, 1926, and vol. 14, no. 9, 1927), *Cahiers d'Art* (vol. 3, no. 1, 1928), *L'Architecture Vivante* (vol. 5, no. 21, 1928), *L'Amour de l'Art* (vol. 10, no. 9, 1929), *Architectural Record* (vol. 68, no. 4, 1930). Plans, drawings, and sometimes even models of Mies's early projects appeared in at least the following exhibitions: *Grosse Berliner Kunstausstellung* (1922, 1923, 1924), *Internationale*

Architekturausstellung, Bauhaus, Weimar (1923), "*Les Architectes du Groupe 'de Style*,'" Galerie L'Effort Moderne, Paris (1923), *Neue deutsche Baukunst*, Kunstverein, Jena (1924), *Architecture et Arts qui s'y rattachent*, Ecole Spéciale d'Architecture, Paris (1924), *Neuzeitliche Geschäftshaus- und Fabrikbauten*, Kunstverein, Gera (1925), *Der gute Industriebau*, Museumsverein, Duisburg (1925), *Typen neuer Baukunst*, Städtische Kunsthalle, Mannheim (1925), *Internationale Plan- und Modellausstellung*, Stuttgart (1927).

91. Cf. Petras, "Drei Arbeiten in Potsdam-Babelsberg."

92. Walter Vitt, ed., *Homage à Dexel (1890–1973): Contributions to Celebrate the Artist's 90th Birthday* (Starnberg, 1980), p. 74, n. 12.

93. Tegethoff, *Villas and Country Houses*, ch. 4.

94. Quoted in Vitt, *Homage à Dexel*, p. 93.

95. Mies to Walter Dexel, January 24, 1925 (letter in the possession of the artist's son, Bernhard Dexel).

96. The building was denied a permit in spite of formal intervention on the part of the Werkbund (drafted by Behrens, Mies, and Poelzig) to which Meyer had applied for support. Executive board of the Werkbund to Meyer, December 22, 1925 (LC).

97. Tape-recorded interview by Ludwig Glaeser, February 4, 1974 (MoMA); for a more detailed discussion of the project, *see* Tegethoff, *Villas and Country Houses*, ch. 5.

98. Specific information and necessary documents were sent to Mies on March 17 by the architect Werner March, whom Eliat seems to have entrusted with the management of his project.

99. *See* Tegethoff, *Villas and Country Houses*, pp. 26–28.

100. Ibid., pp. 38ff.

101. Ibid., ch. 2; the floor plan illustrated in Westheim, "Mies van der Rohe," p. 59, is all that is left of this early commission.

102. Tegethoff, *Villas and Country Houses*, ch. 6.

103. This information was kindly provided by Paul Young, who attempted to visit the site in 1984.

104. The corrections have been entered in hasty pencil strokes—apparently in Mies's hand—on one of the blueprints of the final version (Tegethoff, *Villas and Country Houses*, ill. 6.7).

105. Illustrated in Wolfgang Hermann, "Neue Berliner Baukunst," *Kunst und Künstler*, vol. 26, no. 1 (1927), p. 34; [Christian Zervos], "Mies van der Rohe," *Cahiers d'Art*, vol. 3, no. 1 (1928), p. 35; Walter Müller-Wulckow, *Deutsche Baukunst der Gegenwart: Wohnbauten und Siedlungen* (Königstein, 1928), p. 110; E. M. Hajos and L. Zahn, *Berliner Architektur der Nachkriegszeit* (Berlin, 1928), p. 33; Heinz Johannes, *Neues Bauen in Berlin* (Berlin, 1931), p. 84. Both Hajos and Zahn, and Johannes give the date 1926–27, while Philip Johnson, in Henry-Russell Hitchcock, Johnson, and Lewis Mumford, *Modern Architecture: International Exhibition* (New York, 1932), p. 129, refers to it as 1925. Fritz Neumeyer, "Neues Bauen im Wedding," *Der Wedding im Wandel der Zeit* (Berlin, 1985), pp. 26–34, came to my attention only recently; according to Neumeyer, plans are dated November 18, 1925, and a building permit was granted on April 19, 1926.

106. Judging from contemporary photographs, the rough-cast plaster has always had a kind of yellow-gray tint (it was definitely not white, as Sandra Honey has argued in her brochure for the Mies exhibition at the Building Centre Trust, London, 1978). Accordingly, the white paint of the window frames must be original, as is the red clinker-brick cladding of base and eaves. That the loggias and balconies were always set off in a different color, as they are now, seems rather doubtful to me.

107. Mies to Royal Institute of British Architects, October 6, 1934 (LC).

108. Ernst Walther, Sr., to Ernst Walther, Jr., October 1, 1928 (MoMA, Lange/Esters file).

109. "No Dogma" (*see above*, n. 1).

110. Neither the Karl Liebknecht–Rosa Luxemburg Monument of 1926 nor the proposal for a Berlin Traffic Tower of 1925, two minor projects preceding the second Weissenhof master plan, partook of that process, and should be dealt with in a different context. For the Liebknecht–Luxemburg Monument, *see* Schulze, *Critical Biography*, pp. 125–128, and Rolf-Peter Baacke and Michael Nungesser, "Ich bin, ich war, ich werde sein!" in *Wem gehört die Welt—Kunst und Gesellschaft in der Weimarer Republik* (Berlin: Neue Gesellschaft für bildende Kunst, 1977), pp. 280–298 (exhibition catalogue). The Traffic Tower (*Verkehrsturm*) was a joint competition entry by Mies, Paul Mahlberg, and Heinrich Kosina for a prototype to be erected at the crossing of Friedrichstrasse and Leipzigerstrasse in Berlin; cf. correspondence of February to June 1925 in MoMA, and reviews in *Berliner Tageblatt* (evening edition, June 3, 1925); *Vossische Zeitung* (June 4, 1925); *Berliner Börsen-Courier* (morning edition, June 4, 1925); the model ill. in Hilberseimer, *Groszstadtarchitektur*, p. 83, ill. 194, Heinz and Bodo Rasch, *Wie Bauen?* (Stuttgart, 1927), p. 129, ill. 295, and Hermann Gescheit and Karl Otto Wittmann, *Neuzeutlicher Verkehrsbau* (Potsdam, 1931), p. 172.

111. Gropius to Mies, October 15, 1923 (LC).

112. Gropius to Mies, October 6, 1923 (LC). The reason for both letters was an unauthorized initiative by Hugo Häring: under the pretense of having Gropius's consent to show an expanded version of the *Internationale Architekturausstellung* in Berlin, he had solicited the cooperation of Mies and Adolf Behne.

Mies's judgment of Gropius's Bauhaus exhibition was withering, as can be read in his letter to Theo van Doesburg of August 27, 1923 (LC): "Through Richter you may already have heard about Weimar. I fear that from there a constructivist vogue will sweep all over Germany. This I really regret, since work will become very difficult for the true constructivist artist because of it. One should realize in Weimar how easy it is to juggle constructivist shapes, as long as one only strives for the formal aspect." *See also* Mies's letter to Jakstein, September 13 (n. 54 *above*).

113. *See: Vorläufiger Plan zur Durchführung der Werkbundausstellung "Die Wohnung" Stuttgart 1926.* Preliminary program for the exhibition, June 27, 1925, MoMA; and minutes of the meeting of the board of the Deutsche Werkbund, March 30, 1925 (LC). For a recent comprehensive study of the history of the Weissenhof exhibition, *see* Karin Kirsch, *Die Weissenhofsiedlung: Werkbund-Ausstellung "Die Wohnung"—Stuttgart, 1927* (Stuttgart, 1987); cf. also Wolf Tegethoff, "Weissenhof, 1927—Der Sieg des neuen Baustils?" *Jahrbuch des Zentralinstituts für Kunstgeschichte*, vol. 3 (1987), pp. 195–228. Furthermore, two eyewitness reports deserve mentioning: Heinz Rasch, "Aus den zwanziger Jahren," *Werk und Zeit*, vol. 9, no. 11 (November 1960), pp. 1–3, and Werner Graeff, "Aus den zwanziger Jahren," *Werk und Zeit*, vol. 17, nos. 2–5 (February–May 1968).

114. Stotz to Mies, June 3, 1925 (MoMA).

115. Minutes of the meeting of the board, June 26, 1925 (LC).

116. Cf. Jürgen Joedicke and Christian Plath, *Die Weissenhofsiedlung* (Stuttgart, 1977) (1st ed., 1968), p. 10. The early history of the Werkbund settlement was not fully documented, and so Bruckmann's share in it is not altogether clear. His contribution must have been considerable, since one of the streets on the Weissenhof site—the one in front of Mies's block—was named after him. On Bruckmann's support of the Mies group within the Werkbund's executive board, *see* the letter by Stotz of October 29, 1925 (MoMA).

117. Stotz to Mies, July 13, 1925 (MoMA).

118. *Stadterweiterungsamt* (Department of City Planning), Stuttgart, by Dr. Otto, to Mies, September 2, 1925 (MoMA).

119. Stotz to Häring, August 14, 1925 (MoMA).

120. Mies to Stotz, September 11, 1925 (MoMA) [italics mine]; "left-wing" was rather a common label for progressive or radical architects until the mid-1920s, without necessarily implying an extreme political inclination, since even a democrat was called a leftist at the time.

121. Stotz to Mies, September 24, 1925 (MoMA).

122. Stotz to Mies, October 20, 1925 (MoMA); *see also* Sigloch's petition to the city council of July 23, 1926 (MoMA): ". . . the original concept [of Mies van der Rohe], as it has been transferred to the site plan enclosed by the department of city planning on October 14, 1925 . . ."

123. Stotz to Mies, October 20, 1925 (MoMA).

124. Ibid.; and Mies to Otto Ernst Sutter, November 13, 1925 (MoMA): No decision yet, "since the municipal elections should first be awaited." On December 1, 1925, Stotz reported to Mies (MoMA) that a decision would not be taken before 1926, "because the present council does not have the courage any more." The postponement to 1927 was officially announced at the meeting of the Werkbund's executive board on November 29 (minutes in LC); the minutes of the press conference on January 22, 1926 (MoMA), rather unconvincingly refer to the aggravated economical situation as the actual reason for the delay, which was probably meant not to compromise Sigloch in his actions on the council.

125. Paul Schmitthenner, "Die Werkbundsiedlung," *Süddeutsche Zeitung* (May 5, 1926).

126. Sigloch's petition concerning the "*Werkbundsiedlung auf dem Weissenhof*," July 23, 1926 (MoMA); item b) reads as follows:
"At a flat-rate basis of 35 marks per cubic meter the architect of the Werkbund will calculate the cost of construction at:
926,000 M
in addition, there must be designated:
architects' fees   50,000 M
fees for retaining walls   60,000 M
expenses for developing the site
                          127,000 M
in total: 1,163,000 M
or approximately 1.2 million.
Consequently, an allowance of about 15,200 marks for net construction costs (without additional facilities) goes to each individual housing unit."
For the actual expenses finally allocated to the various buildings, see the official catalogue and guide book: *Werkbund-Ausstellung "Die Wohnung,"* Stuttgart 1927, 23.*Juli*–9.*Okt.*, published by the exhibition management.

127. Schmitthenner, "Werkbundsiedlung;" Paul Bonatz, "Noch einmal die Werkbundsiedlung," *Schwäbischer Merkur* (May 5, 1926).

128. A detailed account of this and the following events has been given in Stotz's letter to Richard Riemerschmid of May 8, 1926 (MoMA).

129. Sigloch, petition of July 23 (*see* n. 126).

130. "Mitteilungen des DWB," *Die Form*, vol. 1, no. 11 (1926).

131. *Stadtschultheissenamt* to *Württembergische Arbeitsgemeinschaft*, August 24, 1926 (MoMA).

132. Stotz to Mies, October 8, 1926 (MoMA).

133. *Die Form*, vol. 2, no. 7 (1927), p. 213, and Ludwig Mies van der Rohe, [introduction] *Die Form*, vol. 2, no. 9 (1927), p. 257.

134. Selectively published as: Ludwig Hilberseimer, *Internationale neue Baukunst*, Die Baubücher, II (Stuttgart, 1927), and idem, "Internationale neue Baukunst," *Moderne Bauformen*, vol. 26, no. 9 (1927), pp. 325–364.

135. *List A*: architects recommended by Stotz in his letter to Mies of September 24, 1925 (MoMA): Peter Behrens, Paul Bonatz, Le Corbusier, Richard Döcker, Theo van Doesburg, Josef Frank, Walter Gropius, Hugo Häring, Richard Herre, Ludwig Hilberseimer, Hugo Keuerleber, Ferdinand Kramer, Adolf Loos, Erich Mendelsohn, Ludwig Mies van der Rohe, J. J. P. Oud, Hans Poelzig, Adolf Schneck, Mart Stam, [Bruno?] Taut, Heinrich Tessenow. *Bonatz* and *Loos* are crossed out in ink (by Stotz?); *van de Velde* is added in Mies's handwriting.
List B: agreed upon by Mies, compiled in his office (by Häring?), and sent to Stotz on September 26, 1925 (MoMA) [Names in italics have been marked with pencil strokes (by Mies?)]: Otto Bartning, *Behrens*, H. P. Berlage, *Le Corbusier*, *Döcker*, *Doesburg*, Alfred Gelhorn, *Gropius*, *Häring*, *Herre*, *Hilberseimer*, Arthur Korn, *Kramer*, [Hans?] Luckhardt, *Mendelsohn*, *Mies*, *Oud*, *Poelzig*, Hans Scharoun, *Schneck*, *Stam*, [Bruno?] *Taut*, *Tessenow*, Henry van de Velde.
List C: undated list (by the Württemberg committee?), addressed to the *Stadtschultheissenamt* (town official's office) in Stuttgart, with corrections in Mies's handwriting (MoMA); this list may have preceded the Werkbund's second official proposal of July 20, 1926 (now lost), mentioned in Stotz's letter of October 8, 1926 (MoMA): Bartning, Le Corbusier, Döcker, Gropius, Häring, Hilberseimer, Mendelsohn, Mies, Oud, Rading, Schneck, Taut, Ernst Wagner, group of young Stuttgart architects; alternate candidates: Frank, Scharoun, Tessenow, Kramer, Hannes Meyer, Herre. Alternate candidates were named in the event of rejections; the margin bears a list of names in Mies's handwriting: *Oud, Corbusier, Loos, Mendelsohn, M[ies], Häring, Gropius, Hilberseimer*; Rading is crossed out on the main list and replaced by Tessenow; Hannes Meyer is crossed out on the alternate list and Herre is advanced to the fifth position.
List D: approved by the city council on August 24, 1926 (*Stadtschultheissenamt* to *Württembergische Arbeitsgemeinschaft* [MoMA]): Bartning, Döcker, Frank, Gropius, Häring, Hans Herkommer, Hilberseimer, Mies, Oud, Rading, Schneck, Taut, Tessenow, Heinz Wezel [Wetzel].
List E: alternate proposal presented by Stotz to the Werkbund's executive board on October 16, 1926 ("Mitteilungen des DWB," *Die Form*, vol. 1, no. 14 [November 1926]): Le Corbusier, Döcker, Frank, Gropius, Häring, Hilberseimer, Mendelsohn, Mies, Oud, Rading, Schneck, Stam, Taut, Tessenow.

136. In the case of Häring and Mendelsohn, cf. the correspondence in MoMA, Weissenhof file; Mies's letter to Mendelsohn, October 9, 1926, and the latter's reply of October 13 are of particular

interest. According to Mendelsohn, there seems to have been some kind of intrigue against him (by Häring?) in the Berlin Ring circle.

137. Tessenow to Mies on September 16, 1926 (MoMA).

138. Richard Riemerschmid (who held the chair before Bruckmann's and Mies's election), Poelzig, and some of the older Werkbund members resigned from the executive board at its fifteenth annual meeting in June 1926, "to give younger forces a chance to try their strength at important tasks" ("Mitteilungen des DWB," [see above, n. 11]).

The Zwölfer-Ring Berliner Architekten originally constituted an informal association of progressive Berlin architects within the local BDA, and centered around Mies and Häring. Its founding manifesto of April 26, 1924 (LC), signed by Jürgen Bachmann, Otto Bartning, Peter Behrens, Otto Firle, Hugo Häring, Erich Mendelsohn, Mies van der Rohe, Hans Poelzig, Otto Rudolf Salvisberger, Emil Schaudt, Walther Schilbach, and Bruno Taut—was primarily directed against the conservative Berlin building authorities of the Ludwig Hoffmann era. In a letter to Otto Haesler of March 26, 1926 (LC), Mies justifies his withdrawal from the BDA (cf. above n. 3); his prime argument was that the association's left-wing architects affiliated with the Zehner-Ring or the Novembergruppe had been passed over during the recent election of the BDA board. By then, the Zehner-Ring included the following members: Otto Bartning, Peter Behrens, Hugo Häring, Erich Mendelsohn, Hans and Wassili Luckhardt, Hans Poelzig, Walther Schilbach, Bruno and Max Taut, and Mies van der Rohe (letter by Hans and Wassili Luckhardt to the Zehner-Ring, c/o Mies van der Rohe, April 27, 1926 [LC]). Its official consolidation at its Berlin meeting of May 29–30, 1926, may well have been connected with the Stuttgart exhibition, inasmuch as all German participants (excepting Schneck) became members (the founding was announced in Die Form, vol. 1, no. 10 [1926], p. 225).

139. Poelzig's affiliation with the Block has been mentioned by Döcker in Joedicke and Plath, Weissenhofsiedlung, p. 20. On the founding of the Block, in which Paul Schultze-Naumburg was to take an active part, see Campbell, German Werkbund, pp. 212ff., and Lane, Architecture and Politics, p. 140. There is no question

about its ardent hostility to the Ring, which it was intended to counter, and Bonatz's and Schmitthenner's participation again suggests the crucial impact of the Weissenhof affair.

140. See above, lists of architects (n. 135).

141. Ibid. The lists usually give only the architects' surnames. I would assume, though, that "Taut" usually refers to Bruno Taut, whose reputation far exceeded his brother's. Cf., however, Kirsch (Weissenhofsiedlung, p. 57), who is inclined to think of Max Taut instead.

142. See above, n. 120.

143. Walter Riezler, "Die Wohnung," Die Form, vol. 2, no. 9 (1927), pp. 258–259.

144. Ibid.

145. Schmitthenner, "Werkbundsiedlung."

146. Cf. Mies's introduction to Bau und Wohnung, published by the Werkbund (Stuttgart, 1927), p. 7, and his foreword to the special issue of Die Form (vol. 2, no. 9 [1927], p. 257) claiming he had refrained from imposing any kind of guidelines on the architects. For another reference, see Riezler, "Die Wohnung," p. 259.

147. Mies to Gropius, May 30 and June 4, 1927, and Gropius's reply of June 6 (MoMA).

148. H. T. Cadbury-Brown, "Ludwig Mies van der Rohe: An Address of Appreciation" [Interview], Architectural Association Journal, vol. 75, no. 834 (1959), p. 31; Mies's comment is revealing, indeed: "I said, 'For Heaven's sake, can you not do better than that?' He said, 'You are afraid of color.' I said, 'No. You are color blind.'" (Ibid.)

149. Le Corbusier to Mies, December 15, 1926 (MoMA).

150. Mies to Le Corbusier, November 10, 1926 (MoMA).

151. See above, n. 134.

152. Henry-Russell Hitchcock and Philip Johnson, The International Style: Architecture since 1922 (New York, 1932). For Mies's attitude, see Cadbury-Brown, "Address of Appreciation," p. 30: "At that time many people were working together. I think it was unfortunate, in a way, to call it the international style, but we laughed over it."

153. See above, n. 138 and n. 139.

154. Hitchcock, Johnson, and Mumford, Modern Architecture; the chapters on Hood, Howe & Lescaze, Neutra, and the Bowman brothers barely compete with those devoted to Wright, Gropius, Le Corbusier, Oud, and Mies. Cf. Hitchcock and Johnson, International Style, p. 33: "The four leaders of modern

architecture are Le Corbusier, Oud, Gropius, and Mies van der Rohe."

155. See Tegethoff, Villas and Country Houses, p. 95.

156. Le Corbusier, The Modulor (Cambridge, Mass., 1958), p. 224. The conception of architecture showing the graceful play of volumes under the impact of light does, of course, already occur in his Vers une Architecture of 1920–22.

157. The judgment on his German colleagues given by Le Corbusier at a Stuttgart work conference (with Mies, Stam, and himself) on November 11, 1926, may help to clarify the difference in mentality: "People are working hard in Berlin. The German is a glutton for work but he has not mastered the art of hiding his effort. With him, everything is pensive and laborious. In Paris, one is working hard also, but the stranger does not notice." (Heinz Rasch, in Stuttgarter Neues Tageblatt [November 29, 1926]; reprinted in Werk und Zeit, see above, n. 113).

158. Mies in Bau und Wohnung (see above, n. 146); the context leaves no doubt that it is the spiritual aspect of architecture he has in mind and not the numerous technical innovations usually referred to by his contemporaries.

159. Adolf Behne, Der moderne Zweckbau (Munich, 1926); for a short history of the book and its competitive relation to Gropius's Internationale Architektur, see Ulrich Conrads's introduction to the reprint edition (Berlin, Frankfurt, and Vienna, 1964), pp. 6–10.

160. Hitchcock and Johnson, International Style, pp. 47ff.

161. Ibid., p. 49; cf. Hitchcock's introduction to the 1966 Norton Library edition, pp. ixff.

162. See Neumeyer, Mies van der Rohe, pp. 196ff.

163. On how the pavilion was seen and interpreted at different times, see Juan Pablo Bonta, Mies van der Rohe, Barcelona 1929: Anatomy of Architectural Interpretation (Barcelona, 1975), as well as his Architecture and Its Interpretation: A Study of Expressive Systems in Architecture (London, 1979).

164. See Tegethoff, Villas and Country Houses, ch. 10, pp. 69–89.

165. Ibid., p. 73, n. 15.

166. Georg von Schnitzler, quoted in L. S. M. [Lilly von Schnitzler], "Die Weltausstellung Barcelona 1929," Der Querschnitt, vol. 9, no. 8 (1929), p. 583.

167. Four years later, the same Georg von Schnitzler who had appointed Mies van der Rohe and who had made the preced-

ing statement in his opening speech at the Pavilion, felt no scruples about coming to terms with the republic's enemies. Like many a captain of German industry, von Schnitzler, a leading manager of I. G. Farben, changed sides after the Nazis' rise to power—apparently without bothering to alter his artistic predilections accordingly. On von Schnitzler's involvement with I. G. Farben politics, *see* Josef Borkin, *The Crime and Punishment of I. G. Farben* (New York, 1978).

168. On the importance of the topography for the Pavilion's layout, *see* Tegethoff, *Villas and Country Houses,* pp. 83–86.

169. Ludwig Glaeser, *Mies van der Rohe: The Barcelona Pavilion, 50th Anniversary* (New York, 1979).

170. On the description of the temple of the Holy Grail in *Younger Titurel, see* Blanca Röthlisberger, "Die Architektur des Graltempels im Jüngeren Titurel," in *Sprache und Dichtung,* vol. 18 (Bern, 1917); and Gudula Trendelenburg, *Studien zum Gralraum im "Jüngeren Titurel"* (Göppingen, 1972).

171. Conversation with the author in Berlin, December 1979; Carl Sonnenschein, born 1876 in Düsseldorf and thus like Mies a native of the Rhineland, was an outstanding representative of the Catholic social movement and a founder of the Berlin *Kreis katholischer Künstler* (Circle of Catholic Artists). Sonnenschein died in February 1929.

172. *See* Rosemarie Bletter, "The Interpretation of the Glass Dream—Expressionist Architecture and the History of the Crystal Metaphor," *Journal of the Society of Architectural Historians,* vol. 40, no. 1 (1981), pp. 20–43.

173. At the Vienna Werkbund Conference in June 1930, Mies declared categorically: "We have to impose new values and to show ultimate purposes, in order to achieve standards. For every time's significance and claim, including the new one's, rest in its ability to provide the precondition and the possibility for the spirit to exist" (Ludwig Mies van der Rohe, "Die neue Zeit," *Die Form,* vol. 7, no. 10 [1932], p. 306).

174. Bonta, *Architecture and Its Interpretation.*

175. Kettler to Lilly Reich, October 29, 1929; letters of Lilly Reich and Gabriele Seeger, December 29, 1929, and January 5, 1930.

176. *See* his interview by Katharine Kuh of December 1964: "Mies van der Rohe: Modern Classicist," *Saturday Review,* vol. 48, no. 4 (January 23, 1965), pp. 22–23, 61.

RICHARD POMMER

Mies van der Rohe and the Political Ideology of the Modern Movement in Architecture

Politically, Mies was the Talleyrand of modern architecture: in less than ten years, he designed the Karl Liebknecht–Rosa Luxemburg Monument for the Communist Party in Germany (Fig. 1), the Barcelona Pavilion for the Weimar Republic, a monument to the war dead for the Socialist-led government of Prussia (Fig. 2), and a competition project for the German Pavilion at the Brussels World's Fair of 1935 (Fig. 3), which, had it been built, would have been the first Nazi monument of international significance. Mies defined his true aims quite clearly in a letter of the mid-1920s in which he turned down a post as municipal architect because it was dependent on party politics. In his work, Mies wrote: "I pursue very specific spiritual-political goals [*geistig-politische Ziele*]."[1]

Not only was Mies monumentally indifferent to the formal politics of parties and governments: even more significant of his ideological position was his attitude toward social reform as manifested in his commissions and projects. He designed no theoretical housing projects and built only one typical development in his German years, a group of four small blocks on Afrikanischestrasse in Berlin (Fig. 4). They are perfectly sound, economical buildings, which should have won Mies a share in the vast projects for the building societies that constituted the largest part of building activity in Berlin and elsewhere; but nothing came of it.

Yet it is widely believed that the modern movement was committed to some form of socialist ideology. As the historian John Willett wrote of the modern artists of the Weimar years: "Nothing emerges more clearly from a study of their achievement than that it was founded on a broadly socialist, and in many cases communist ideology."[2] The critic Colin Rowe similarly wrote: "It is possible to argue that modern architecture was conceived as an adjunct of socialism and probably sprang from approximately the same ideological roots as Marxism."[3]

Nevertheless, the modernists repeatedly named Mies to central positions within the modern movement—as chairman and director of architectural exhibitions for the Novembergruppe, the main outlet of the avant-garde in Berlin; a founding member in 1924 of the Ring, the elite cell of Berlin architects who helped to establish the postwar modern movement; vice president in the late 1920s of the Deutsche Werkbund, and artistic director of its Weissenhof exhibition; and the last director of the Bauhaus in Germany. Only Walter Gropius achieved a position of equal prestige and power in the modern movement in Germany.

Three explanations of this anomaly have been advanced. Donald Drew Egbert has argued that Mies's commission from the Communists for the Liebknecht-Luxemburg monument supported "the view that—other things being equal—political radicals are more inclined than conservatives to be sympathetic to radicalism in other fields, including the radicalism of artists," and

1. *Monument to the November Revolution (Karl Liebknecht–Rosa Luxemburg Monument), cemetery, Berlin-Friedrichsfelde (destroyed). 1926*

that "the belief in progress so characteristic of socialism in general and of Marxian socialism in particular, usually leads the Marxian to be sympathetic to the most advanced forms of art, unless there are special reasons . . . for attacking such art."[4] But this argument cannot survive a glance at Stalinist Russia on the one hand or the Rockefellers' patronage of modern art on the other. Joan Campbell, developing the idea of "the politics of cultural reform"

2. *War Memorial, Berlin (Remodeling of Karl Friedrich Schinkel's Neue Wache, 1816–18). Competition project, 1930. Interior perspective. Whereabouts unknown*

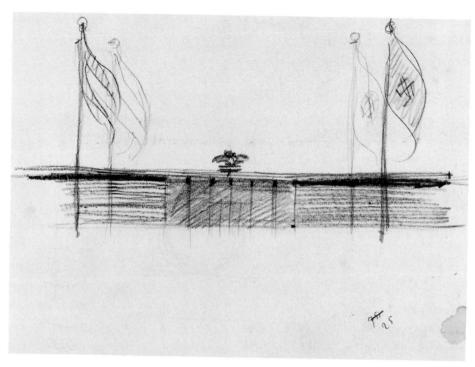

3. *German Pavilion, 1935 World's Fair, Brussels. Competition project, 1934. Sketch of central portion of facade. Collection Dirk Lohan*

from her book on the Werkbund,[5] proposed that Mies "was inclined to define 'cultural reform' in aesthetic and spiritual rather than material or social terms, in this differing from Gropius," and that "for them, as for most members of the Werkbund, the 'politics of cultural reform' came to represent a *surrogate* for political involvement in the usual sense."[6] There is ample evidence for both statements, but the notion of cultural reform fails to deal with the differences

4. *Municipal Housing Development, Afrikanischestrasse, Berlin-Wedding. 1926–27*

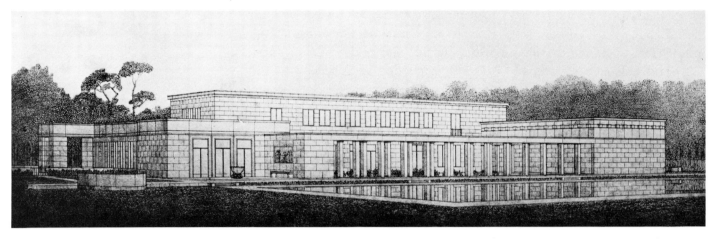

5. *Kröller-Müller House, Wassenaar, The Netherlands. Project, 1912. Perspective. Whereabouts unknown*

of political ideology between Mies and the more committed architects, which in turn, as will be seen, led to conflicts between them in the last troubled years of the Weimar Republic and threatened to split the movement in the early years of the Nazi regime. Recently, the Italian Marxist historian Manfredo Tafuri has argued that the group of artists and architects with which Mies was associated in the early 1920s, including Theo van Doesburg, Hans Richter, and El Lissitzky, "declared its own non-political nature."[7] But while some of these artists and Mies himself did just that, it does not follow that they were in fact apolitical or without political ideologies.

6. *Hermann Finsterlin: Observation Tower (Fernsehturm). 1919. Whereabouts unknown*

My intention in what follows is to demonstrate that Mies did indeed have a political ideology of his own, both in the Marxian sense of a disguised or implicit system of beliefs, and in more explicit formulations; that these political convictions cannot be consistently separated from his philosophical statements and architectural production; that he shared some of his most fundamental political and social beliefs with many modernists but held to other ideals that brought him into direct conflict with them; and that the beliefs of the modernists were too diverse to be characterized as socialist, often too political to be seen only as cultural reform or dismissed as a retreat into utopia or aesthetics, and yet were coherent enough to justify the conception of the modern movement as an ideologically defined development which had a place at its center for Mies.

The first indication of the position Mies was to take after the First World War was his submission of the project he had made in 1912 for the Kröller-Müller House in Wassenaar, near The Hague, to the *Exhibition of Unknown Architects* (*Ausstellung für unbekannte Architekten*) in Berlin held by the Work Council for Art (*Arbeitsrat für Kunst*) in 1919 (Fig. 5).[8] The jury, led by Gropius, chose "fantastic images" similar to Hermann Finsterlin's Observation Tower (*Fernsehturm*) (Fig. 6) as signs of "a longing for a world of beauty built anew from the ground up, and for a rebirth of that spiritual unity which led up to the miraculous making of the Gothic cathedral."[9] But Mies's project in its amplitude and neoclassical forms closely recalls the architecture of Peter Behrens, whose design of 1911 for the Kröller-Müller project Mies had been asked to execute (Fig. 7). Understandably, Gropius turned down Mies's luxurious and classicizing submission, which harked back to prewar ideals.

Not only artistically but also in his political attitudes, Mies had moved very little from Behrens's position within the prewar Werkbund. Organized in 1907 to bring artists and industrialists together for the reform of German products, the Werkbund had been conceived by one of its founders, Friedrich Naumann, as an instrument for heading off Marxist revolution by assimilating socialist reform to nationalist fervor in the domain of cultural reform through the agency of an educated middle class.[10] Such a policy based on contradictory aims obviously allowed a good deal of latitude left and right. On the right stood another founder of the organization, Hermann Muthesius, who took an aggressively nationalistic line aimed at increasing German exports and raising the taste of the middle class, but seldom at improving the lot of the working class.[11] At the other extreme was Henry van de Velde, an idealistic socialist (of a Nietz-

7. *Peter Behrens: Kröller-Müller House, Wassenaar, The Netherlands. Project, 1911. Perspective. Whereabouts unknown*

schean bent) more occupied with the fate of the workers and less with production for export.[12]

Between these poles stood Behrens, the designer in charge for the AEG (*Allgemeine Elektricitäts Gesellschaft*), the German electric company. Although Behrens's designs may have increased domestic and foreign sales and eased the discontent of the workers for the AEG, he paid rather limited and conventional attention in his writings before the war to the social and economic justifications of his work.[13] Instead he concentrated on aesthetic issues in order to assure the elevation of art over mere technique, material, and use, and of the artist over the engineer in the competition for the direction of modern industry.

The chief aesthetic instrument of these reforms was the doctrine of Form. The earlier Werkbund ideal of Quality, inspired by the moral and social dicta of John Ruskin and William Morris, was a virtue attributable to craftsmen and workers. But the idea of Form that soon rose alongside it, from sources in the idealizing aesthetics of Konrad Fiedler, Adolf von Hildebrand, Heinrich Wölfflin, and Alois Riegl,[14] could be recognized and conferred upon industrial products only by artists, that is, by the special representatives of the educated middle class. From Form the craftsman could learn joy in work and the entrepreneur take the measure of his social responsibility. Form could guide middle-class consumers to educated acquisitions. It was the perfect emblem of the cultural reform of industrial society from on high, allowing some architects, such as Muthesius, to emphasize its social functions, and others, like Behrens, its aesthetic implications.

Toward the end of the First World War, however, a socialist position came to the fore in the nascent modern movement. Bruno Taut was able to reconcile the socialist and Nietzschean components evident in van de Velde's approach

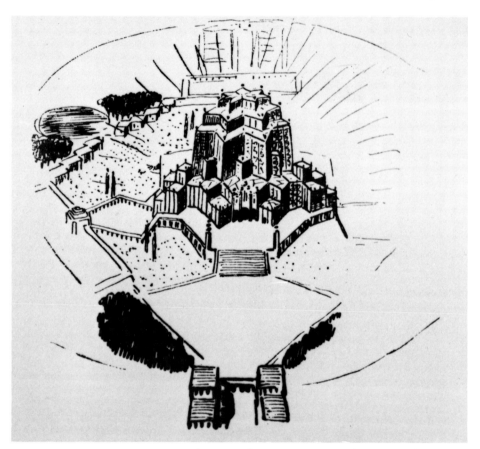

8. *Bruno Taut: House of Heaven* (Haus des Himmels). *1920. Drawing. Whereabouts unknown*

by calling upon the artistic elite to lead the people *spiritually* to a new sense of community.[15] The result would be a purified society, free of class conflict, whole once again as in primitive or medieval times. Taut gave form to his ideas in visionary projects such as his House of Heaven (*Haus des Himmels*) of 1920 (Fig. 8), a communal hall of glass for the artists, prophets, and children who were to create the new society.[16] As Rosemarie Bletter has explained, such glass structures represented the crystal, an ancient symbol of spiritual purification,[17] which here becomes a metaphor for the transformation of society made believable by an ecstatic appeal to the senses through sharp, aspiring forms, a rainbow of colors, and the sounds of a Bruckner symphony! The pallid remedies of the prewar Werkbund had been left far behind.

To support his cause, Taut organized the Work Council for Art and the more informal *Gläserne Kette* (Glass, or Crystal, Chain), in 1918 and 1919. He was joined in these organizations by some of the more influential Berlin architects and critics who were to represent themselves as socialist in their sympathies, including Gropius, Adolf Behne, the Luckhardt brothers, Ludwig Hilberseimer, and Hans Scharoun. But Mies, when he came back from the army late in 1918, did not join either. He did become a member of the Novembergruppe in 1922, and its chairman in 1923–25,[18] but by that time this organization had lost its social and political ambitions and had become no more than a loose association of aesthetically radical artists without a clear political direction.

Thus Mies bypassed the center of the socially oriented movement in Berlin during its peak years, 1918–19. When he did commit himself to the new architecture a few years later, he went out of his way to demonstrate his distance from the ideals of the *Arbeitsrat* circle by publishing his glass skyscraper projects of 1921 and 1922 for the first time in Bruno Taut's magazine *Frühlicht* (Fig. 9),[19] thereby paying homage to Taut's glass structures, such as the House of Heaven, while at the same time shedding all the social functions, ecstatic overtones, symbolic forms, and strains of Bruckner symphonies in order to fix on the steel framework and the play of reflections in the faceted glass. Mies had chosen the most charged symbols as models in order to bring out by contrast his reduction of the building to its structural and material elements.

In returning to the *sachlich,* or objective, steel-and-glass architecture given prominence by Behrens before the war, Mies once again proclaimed his deep and enduring affinity with his old master. Like Behrens, Mies was to devote himself primarily to aesthetic issues (although insisting that they were objective ones), to welcome modern technology but only on a highly idealized plane, and to offer his services to any client who did not interfere with his artistic judgment.

But in his extreme depoliticization of architecture, Mies had also moved away from Behrens, who for all his aesthetic idealism was still rooted in the prewar Werkbund's expectations of social reform. Nothing makes this clearer than Mies's new idea of Form, the old Werkbund doctrine inherited from Muthesius and Behrens. In a well-known statement of 1923, whose contextual implications have gone unrecognized, Mies said: "We refuse to recognize problems of Form, but only problems of building. Form is not the aim of our work, but only the result. Form as an aim is formalism, and that we reject. Architecture instead is: The will of the epoch translated into space, living, changing, new."[20]

By rejecting Form in favor of building, Mies also dismissed the implications of social reform that clung to the old doctrine. The difference between Mies and Behrens was apparent also in their work. Whereas Behrens concerned himself chiefly with what Mies called his "grand form,"[21] that is to say, monumental form created by means of illusion and symbolic references, as in the AEG Turbine Factory, Mies saw his own work as fulfilling the demand of the Dutch architect Hendrik Berlage for "clear construction."[22] For Mies, the ideal of objectivity precluded *any* reference outside the work itself.

Instead of Form, Mies echoed the idea referred to in his circle as *elementare Gestaltung,* an act of primary creation, of forming prior to form. It had been advanced in 1923 by van Doesburg, the apostle of de Stijl to the German architects, in the first issue of Richter's new publication, G, to which Mies also contributed.[23] Mies probably met van Doesburg late in 1920 or early in 1921 in Richter's circle in Berlin;[24] by 1923 they were corresponding about Mies's inclusion in van Doesburg's exhibition in Paris,[25] and Mies had designed the first of his projects to show the influence of de Stijl, the so-called Concrete Country House.

Van Doesburg has often been lumped together with other de Stijl or Constructivist artists who saw their work as advancing the utopian cause of world harmony. But in the early 1920s he felt it necessary to defend his beliefs, which were much more about elementary purity than world harmony, against the politicized and functional approach of the European modernists. He wrote in 1923: "A form of art which is directed to one specific social class does not exist. An art produced by proletarians does not exist because the proletarian, in creating art, ceases to be a proletarian and becomes an artist instead. . . . Art . . . is tied to its own laws *and nothing but its own laws.*"[26]

Another member of the G group, El Lissitzky, wrote that his magazine, *Veshch/Gegenstand/Objet,* "stands equally aloof from all political parties, because it is not occupied with the problems of politics but of art. This does not mean, however, that we are in favor of an art that stands outside of life and is apolitical on principle. On the contrary, *we cannot imagine a creation of new forms in art unrelated to the change in social form.*"[27] On the other hand, Richter, who had fought for the revolution in Munich in 1919, continued to be active in film productions and organizations that had support from the far left.[28]

Thus it is clear that Mies's detachment was not a personal aberration, but a position shared with some of the other artists and architects who had committed themselves to a more abstract and objective art in Berlin c. 1922–23. Within the G group this commitment was large enough to embrace politically neutral architects such as Mies, socially more dedicated if not revolutionary artists such as El Lissitzky, and activists on the left like Richter.

An even greater diversity characterized the Ring, which unlike the G circle was formally organized and soon became a more influential avant-garde architectural organization. The Ring was established in April 1924 by a nucleus of reform architects from Berlin within the *Bund Deutscher Architekten* (BDA), the German architects' professional association, in order to free themselves from aesthetic restrictions imposed by the old guard through the municipal administration of Berlin.[29] They were particularly incensed by the outcome of several competitions, among them the Friedrichstrasse skyscraper competition, which had rejected Mies's project.[30] At stake were many commissions controlled financially as well as artistically by the city, particularly the settlements (*Siedlungen*), which were to be the major architectural tasks of the Weimar period.

Mies and Hugo Häring seem to have been the originators of the group,[31] which met in Mies's office and elected Häring secretary when it expanded in 1926.[32] The Ring, at its founding, called for "freedom for all artistically creative architects of whatever direction,"[33] and succeeded in representing many of the stylistic currents of the new architecture in Berlin. Varying from nine to twelve members during 1924–25, the original Ring included Behrens and Hans Poelzig from among the prewar founders of the new architecture; Bruno Taut, Erich Mendelsohn, Otto Bartning, and Häring, then identified as Expressionists or the equivalent; Otto Firle and Otto Rudolph Salvisberg, who worked in

9. *Friedrichstrasse Office Building, Berlin. Competition project, 1921. Perspective, north and east sides. Charcoal and pencil on brown paper. The Museum of Modern Art, New York, Mies van der Rohe Archive. Gift of the architect*

derivatives of the rural nativist *Heimatstil* or the turn-of-the-century *Jugend-stil*; and Max Taut and Mies, leaders of the emerging trend toward a new "objectivity."[34] Politically they ranged from Bruno Taut, who advocated "socialism in an unpolitical, suprapolitical sense,"[35] and Bartning, one of the founding members of the *Arbeitsrat*,[36] to Mendelsohn, Häring, and Mies, who were all conspicuously apolitical. Häring was later to write, when attempting to defend the Ring from Nazi attacks: "For membership in the Ring, what mattered above all was personal and distinctive purity, then a certain level of professional competence, and last but not least, a fundamental agreement with a renewal of architecture on the basis of modern social, technical, and economic conditions. . . . The Ring never had anything to do with politics."[37]

From these small elites dedicated to an ideal of abstract form or to "personal and distinctive purity" the emerging avant-garde of the modern movement received its structure, which diverged both from the looser framework of the earlier Werkbund, held together only by the vague ideal of cultural reform, and from the closer one of the *Arbeitsrat,* united by a utopian political faith.

Mies was never closer to the mainstream of the modern movement than at this moment, when the disruptions of war, revolution, and inflation were coming to an end, and hopes for building again were rising. The standard of objectivity brought with it a faith in the efficacy of technology that Mies fully shared—for a short while. In 1924 he wrote his only unqualified paean to industrialization: "I consider the industrialization of building methods the key problem of the day for architects and builders; once we succeed in this, our social, economic, technical, and even artistic problems will be easy to solve;" and he concluded that the solution was the invention of a light, weatherproof, soundproof, insulating, and industrially processed material.[38] His unbuilt projects of the time, particularly his Concrete Office Building of 1922–23 (Fig. 10), are the toughest, barest structures of his career in Germany.[39] Mies shared this faith in technology not only with Gropius and Ernst May, but also with van Doesburg, who despite his dreams of pure planes of color in space believed that the "striving for an elementary style based on elementary means runs parallel to a progressive form of technology. . . . When these two developments, in art and technology, meet, mechanical form will lend itself automatically to the new style."[40]

Mies also became interested in housing in the winter of 1923–24[41]—just when it was emerging as the central opportunity of the Weimar architects for construction and social reform. Early in 1924, in the only contemporary record we have of his attitude toward the politics and financing of housing, Mies published a brief review in *Die Baugilde,* the journal of the BDA, of a book by Paul Tropp, an architect and Berlin city councilman, about regulating rents and financing new housing.[42] The book was written as the German government was considering the extension of controls imposed on the housing market during the war, and the development of taxes to build more dwellings.

Tropp argued for a return to a free housing market, for taxes that with the end of rent control would have put the main burden on tenants rather than landlords, and for subsidized mortgages for individuals rather than for the building societies (which were often affiliated with the Socialist Party).[43] His position on rent control mirrored that of the conservatives, including the Nationalists (DNVP), the People's Party, and the right wing of the Democratic Party (DDP), who had voted against the federal law supported by the Socialist Party (SPD),[44] Independent Socialist Party, part of the Catholic Center Party, and the left wing of the democrats.[45] The politics of the tax on rents (*Hauszinssteuer*) were not clearly divided between left and right in the winter of 1923–24;[46] but in favoring landlords over tenants, Tropp placed himself unmistakably on the far right of the political spectrum, close to the DNVP.[47]

Mies had nothing but praise for Tropp's discussion: "For the first time our housing economy is here clearly illuminated from the specialist's viewpoint. Tropp shows what it is and what it could be." By subscribing to Tropp's presentation, Mies identified himself with those who wished to return to the prewar economy, before governmental controls had been imposed.

In Berlin, with its Socialist city government and housing societies, Mies had effectively talked himself out of any major housing job, although late in 1925 he received the Afrikanischestrasse commission in the Wedding district of Berlin (*see* Fig. 4).[48] The only other housing commission he received in the Weimar years was the apartment house block he built as part of the Weissenhof settlement (*Weissenhofsiedlung*), a commission given to him by the Werkbund for his skills as a publicist of modernism rather than as a proponent of housing.[49]

Nevertheless, Mies's views did not estrange him at this time from the socially concerned architects further to the political left in the movement, judging from the following incident. Late in 1925, an industrialist in Magdeburg, G. W. Farenholtz, wrote to Mies about the vacant position of chief municipal architect,[50] which had earlier been held by Bruno Taut with the support of the Socialist Party.[51] When it appeared that the Socialists wanted to reject the list of candidates, Taut was asked to look for a suitable architect for the job. Mies then wrote the industrialist: "Taut and I shared the opinion that it is of greatest importance to the modern movement not to let this position be filled again with a mediocrity. Taut believes that a candidate who would be proposed by the Democrats can get the support of the Socialists. I would like to trouble you now once again in this matter and ask you to let me know if you believe that the Democrats might be won over to my candidacy. The Socialists, as Taut believes, would probably not raise anything against me."[52]

But shortly afterwards, Mies wrote to Farenholtz to withdraw his candi-

10. Concrete Office Building. Project, 1922–23. Perspective. Charcoal and crayon on tan paper. The Museum of Modern Art, New York, Mies van der Rohe Archive. Gift of the architect

dacy: "I myself would never have considered accepting such a position if I were not anxious to prepare the grounds somewhere for a new attitude to building [*Baugesinnung*], since I can't imagine for what other reason I should give up my artistically free and materially far better position. Since I pursue very specific spiritual-political goals in my work, I don't find it difficult to decide whether or not I can assume such a post. If the possibility of achieving the goal of my work does not exist in such a position, then I must forego it; therefore Magdeburg must decide whether it will entrust this job to a functionary or to a spiritual man."[53]

In short, the ideological differences between Mies and Taut mattered little if at all; their only concern was to further the cause of the modern movement.

Nor was Mies as indifferent to the political beliefs of his fellow modernists as he liked to profess and often seemed to appear. His conflicting and probably self-serving recollections of the commission for the Liebknecht-Luxemburg monument provide a more ambiguous measure of his position (*see* Fig. 1).[54] As Mies recounted the story to Egbert in a letter of 1951, at the beginning of the McCarthy era, "everything was accidental from the beginning to the end." He had been invited to meet Eduard Fuchs, the Socialist editor, art historian, and collector, who had purchased the house he had designed for Hugo Perls, and wanted him to do an addition. Fuchs, who was acting as the Communist Party's agent in the search for an architect of the monument, showed Mies a project with Doric columns and medallions of Liebknecht and Luxemburg. Then, Mies recalled, "I started to laugh and told him it would be a fine monument for a banker. . . . I told him I hadn't the slightest idea what I would do in his place, but as most of these people were shot in front of a wall, a brick wall would be what I would build as a monument."[55]

His cynicism, or realism, might be compared with Gropius's more self-righteous recollection of his intentions in building his memorial to workers slain at the time of the *Kapp Putsch,* a monument dedicated in 1922 in Weimar (Fig. 11). Gropius said in 1968: "I made it with a true feeling for the progressive act of the workers, who wished to defend the new thinking of the time."[56]

But Mies gave an account with different overtones in Aachen in 1968, in the midst of the student revolts. He said at that time: "Yes [I built it] in squared form. Clarity and truth were to join against the fog that had arisen and killed off hopes—the hopes, as we quite rightly saw at the time, for an enduring German republic. That would have had to be a thoroughgoing democracy. Everything else led back to the black-white-red reaction, for which we Aacheners in any case had no use. We were of course Rhenish revolutionaries."[57]

He was referring to the flag under the Kaiser, replaced by the black, red, and gold of the Weimar Republic; and, it would seem, to those who had fought for the freedom of the Rhineland in the wake of the French Revolution. To have been a supporter of the Weimar Republic was not, however, a routine position in that torn nation, and was uncommon in right-wing circles. Despite the inconsistencies in his recollections,[58] it is not unreasonable to assume that Mies for all his calculated appearance of neutrality did indeed support the Weimar Republic along with the great majority of his fellow modern architects in Germany.

From these accounts of Mies's social and political actions in the mid-1920s, a shadowy portrait emerges of a republican with laissez-faire views. It was a

11. Walter Gropius: Monument to the Kapp Putsch Victims (Denkmal der Märzgefallenen), *Friedhof Weimar (destroyed). 1922*

position close to the right wing of the new Democratic Party.[59] One of the three parties of the so-called Weimar coalition, collaborating with the Socialist Party and the Catholic Center Party, the Democratic Party had been organized after the war with the support of, among others, Naumann and some of his followers. The party was strongly committed to the new constitution and the republic.[60] But as a party of civil servants and administrators, businessmen and independent industrialists, teachers and intellectuals,[61] it soon began to retreat from the objectives of social reform inherited from Naumann and his circle.[62] The smaller group of left-wing members continued to vote for some of these social programs, but the right wing hoped for a return to laissez-faire policies, as seen in its stance on rent control.[63] Some of these differences were covered over as the Democratic Party tended increasingly to emphasize cultural reform[64] over social and economic measures such as housing, particularly at the municipal level where German social policies were normally implemented—a shift congenial to Mies's elevation of what Germans called spiritual matters over mere material ones. This became the party of such key supporters of the modernists as the mayors of Frankfurt-am-Main and Dessau, who invited May and Gropius to take over all or part of their building and housing programs;[65] of the most consistent advocates in the Stuttgart city council of the Weissenhof exhibition and of Mies's project for it;[66] and of some of the major figures in the Werkbund during much of the late 1920s.[67] The party often expressed as much interest in the cultural significance as in the socio-economic advantages of the new housing, offices, and schools,[68] whereas the socialists in Weimar, Dessau, and Stuttgart gave or withdrew their support over the political and economic issues of housing, not over issues of *Kultur* or style to which they paid only sporadic attention.[69]

Nevertheless, it is clear from the correspondence with Farenholtz that Mies had joined neither the Democratic Party nor any other party, and had little interest in the differences between them. In this refusal of party affiliation in order to pursue "spiritual-political goals" Mies was at one with most of the architects further to his left. Behne, although himself a member of the Socialist Party, wrote to Gropius in 1920 that the *Arbeitsrat* stood "far from party politics, on Socialist grounds, of course, but independent of any party connection."[70] This was Gropius's policy at the Bauhaus in Weimar and in Dessau, anxious as he was to protect it from attacks by the right;[71] and it was equally the position of Bruno Taut, despite all his work for Socialist building societies.[72] It was a stance derived from the utopian socialism of the *Arbeitsrat*, strengthened by the increasingly bourgeois policies of the Socialist Party during the Weimar Republic. Among the few modernists clearly identified with political parties were two municipal architects in cities with powerful Socialist parties: Martin Wagner, the chief architect of Berlin, though even he distanced himself from official socialism,[73] and Ernst May, who held a similar but more powerful position in Frankfurt-am-Main.[74] Of the "free architects," as Germans called those without governmental positions, Ludwig Hilberseimer, a friend and ally of Mies in the late 1920s, stands out for his identification with the Socialists.[75] Until the late 1920s, no major modern architect in Germany was openly identified with the Communist Party, to my knowledge.[76]

Because the modernists played down party politics in favor of their mutual support of the modern movement itself, the underlying ideological differences between them remained hidden during the mid-1920s as the movement struggled to consolidate its successes. Similarly the collaboration of the Socialists and the Democrats in the support of many of the modernist programs disguised the real differences between their programs as the Democrats retreated into cultural reform.

By 1927 Mies began to move away from the ground he held in common with the main group of the other modernists.[77] He chose the most conspicuous moment for a shift, the opening of the Weissenhof exhibition in June 1927. There he told the assembled leaders of the Werkbund: "The problem of the modern dwelling is primarily architectural, in spite of its technical and economic aspects. It can be solved only by creative minds, not by calculation or organization, despite the current talk of 'rationalization and standardization.'"[78]

Not only did this turn against Mies's own call of 1924 for the industrialization of building methods to solve "our social, economic, technical, and even artistic problems," but it directly contradicted the express purpose of the Weissenhof settlement, which the Werkbund on planning it in 1925 said was to demonstrate the standardization and rationalization of the construction and planning of housing for the lower and middle classes.[79]

Mies was not alone in his disappointment following the hopes for the rationalization of industry that had swept Germany in the aftermath of the war.[80] Standardization and rationalization had some success during the 1920s, which stirred up increasing resistance to both.[81] From the beginning of its wider application in the war, standardization had been attacked as a threat to the creative, individualistic German soul;[82] and even at the height of its vogue it had prominent opponents who saw it, for example, as contrary to the "spiritual differentiation" of the Germans.[83] By the late 1920s, continuing unemployment had led workers and their unions to turn more sharply against labor-saving methods.[84] As Germany became less dependent on American financing, more

Germans became skeptical of "American" methods such as rationalization.[85] Resistance was particularly strong in the building industries, where skilled craftsmen predominated and industrialization had far to go. Stonemasons, bricklayers, and roofers spoke through their professional journals against the concrete structures and tar-papered flat roofs of the new architecture.[86] By the late 1920s, it had become apparent that rationalization was not reducing costs or improving quality significantly, if at all, and that rents in most housing projects remained too high for the working class.[87]

Disillusionment soon led Mies to his most sustained attempt to spell out a rationale for his architecture, recorded in a sheaf of notes and the manuscript for a lecture probably written late in 1927 or early in 1928.[88] Mies argued here that the coherence of Antiquity and the Middle Ages had been destroyed by nominalism, the new science of the Renaissance, and the technological instrumentalism of the Industrial Revolution. This had brought about the rise of hyperindividualism, on the one hand, and the masses, on the other, as well as the preeminence of abstract economic and technological forces independent of human considerations and control. In current architecture, which Mies illustrated with a wide range of examples from the past two decades,[89] the result was chaos. Reacting to these changes, Mies noted, some wanted to return to the past, which he thought a commendable effort to preserve values and insights that should not be lost. But Mies believed that there was no choice except to affirm one's own time. The answer, he concluded, was not less but more technology and knowledge; more control of nature, but also more freedom; and greater power over their lives for the masses as well as for the individual through a more human and spiritual technology based on "life." "We must master the unchained forces and build them into a new order, an order, to be sure, that leaves life free play for its development."[90] Only this could bring an end to the chaos of modern architecture.

His ideas and often his words came largely from a 1927 book by Romano Guardini, a Catholic theologian at the University of Berlin, whose book, *Briefe vom Comer See* (*Letters from Lake Como*),[91] deplored the domination of nature by modern technique and the destruction of the ancient Mediterranean harmony between man and landscape. Guardini insisted that the solution was to master the new forces of industry, not to run from them. Before the war, German writers on the "philosophy of technology" (*Philosophie der Technik*)[92] had asserted that technology was the chief modern agent of human freedom and spiritual development, and, like the early Werkbund,[93] had called for the "spiritualization" of technology and production. The reformers of the *Heimatschutz* movement for the preservation of the landscape had already advocated a reconciliation of industry with nature and the past, but they usually meant by this less technology, or more concealment of it.[94] To have seen both the spiritual and cultural advantages and the dangers of technology was Guardini's exceptional contribution and his legacy to Mies.[95] For Mies to talk of extending technology to control nature while preserving freedom, and to express sympathy with the values of the past while resolving to face the present, represented a departure from both avant-garde and conservative attitudes in the late 1920s.

In effect, Mies here fashioned his own explicit credo for the reform of architecture in capitalist society, directed not toward changing that society but toward the symbolic control of its exploitation of nature, its blindness to the

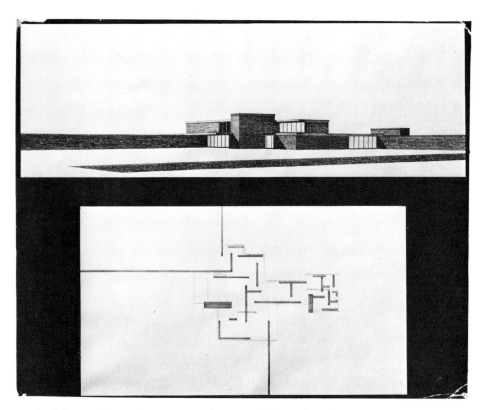

12. Brick Country House. Project, 1924. Elevation and plan. Whereabouts unknown

past, and its destruction of freedom through unrestrained mechanization. It was a viewpoint equally removed from the abstract aesthetics of van Doesburg, the mechanistic dreams of the Constructivists, the antitraditionalism of the avant-garde, and the sociopolitical interventionism of Gropius and May, which was directed not toward human liberty but to social justice.

The results can be read in Mies's architecture. The Barcelona Pavilion of late 1928–29 returns suddenly to classical tradition, to Karl Friedrich Schinkel and the Erechtheum, befitting its Mediterranean site, but reconciles it with steel, glass, and open interior spaces. The Tugendhat House of almost the same time sets the new architecture in harmony with nature by opening the living room to a winter garden, which belongs both to nature and to architecture, and directly to the field below through windows that could be lowered into the basement: the house is a machine for the exploration of nature—nature controlled but not dominated. The passage through deep space to nature, the disappearance of the enclosing wall, and the disengagement of the supporting frame from the walls all serve to liberate sight and movement as, simultaneously, a metaphor and an experience of freedom.[96] Mies's earlier houses also opened visually to the exterior, but more to built-up terraces, or to abstract planes in models and drawings, as in the Brick Country House of 1924 (Fig. 12), among others, rather than to trees and grass, which appear conspicuously in the drawings of the late 1920s and 1930s (Fig. 13).[97] Nor do his earlier villas offer an equal sense of escape into nature, for despite their large windows they are enclosed by sheer, impenetrable, and often supporting walls. At the same time, the exposed frames could impose a clearer visual module of order on space than freestanding walls alone did in the Brick Country House. Only in the contemporary work of Le Corbusier, notably in the Villa Savoye,

113

01

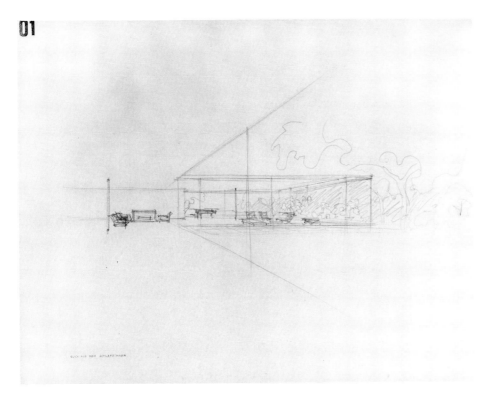

13. *Gericke House, Berlin-Wannsee. Project, 1932. Interior perspective of living room. Pencil on illustration board. The Museum of Modern Art, New York, Mies van der Rohe Archive. Gift of the architect*

with its reference to the Parthenon and its aloneness in a field at the edge of a forest, do we find a comparable hope of reuniting modernity with the past and with nature, but not with an equivalent representation of freedom (Fig. 14).[98]

The new abstract classicism, with its potential signification of freedom and order and of tradition and modernity, was well matched to the tendency of the liberal supporters of the Weimar Republic to withdraw into cultural neutralism, removed from open provocation of the extreme right or left.[99] At the opening of the Barcelona Pavilion, the German commissioner for the exhibition said

14. *Le Corbusier and Pierre Jeanneret: Villa Savoye, Poissy-sur-Seine, France. 1929–30*

"we want nothing else but clarity, simplicity, honesty;"[100] and although little documentation survives to explain the commission, it is remarkable that Mies was allowed to eliminate all the signs and symbols usual in such exhibition buildings.[101]

The retreat from political statement and controversy was more clearly documented in the competition of 1930 for the reconstruction of the interior of Schinkel's Neue Wache (New Guardhouse) as a memorial to the German soldiers killed in the First World War.[102] The controversial project had been initiated by Otto Braun, the powerful Socialist president—"the Red Czar"—of Prussia, who wished to have it built in Berlin.[103] But German provincial and military groups wanted it on the Rhine or in the Thuringian forest—where German national monuments had been constructed before the war, and nationalistic groups had more power than they did in proletarian and socialist Berlin—and this had been agreed to by the government and Paul von Hindenburg, the president of the Reich. Therefore Braun turned around and made the project a memorial to Prussian soldiers, and proposed that it be set within the Neue Wache,[104] which had sufficient ties to the monarchy and the army to win the approval of the right. But for Braun its appropriation by the republic had turned it into "the tomb of the Prussian monarchy and its militaristic attributes." His fait accompli preempted the project of the nationalists, and the monument became the memorial to all the soldiers of the Reich.

The competition brief did not specify any references to the republic or the nation, but called for the interior to create "a simple, solemn impression" in harmony with Schinkel's exterior and "the seriousness of the times;"[105] the jury was agreed that all "unrestrained sentimentality, excessive mysticism, or even the expressive symbolism of a sculpture" should be avoided.[106] The *Frankfurter Zeitung*, a journal close to the Democratic Party, praised the absence of symbols "because we are far too disunited to come again to an understanding that would be common to all," and asked rhetorically, "Haven't we had enough of our Bismarck towers?"[107] But a right-wing architectural journal complained that the Neue Wache could only become a popular national (*volkstümlich*) monument if the greatness of the events of the war were made evident in signs and carvings.[108]

The judges were carefully balanced between advocates of the *Neue Bauen* (new architecture) and defenders of prewar reform ideals who increasingly were becoming identified with nationalistic and politically more conservative factions. Among the former were Martin Kiessling, chief of building in the Prussian Finance Ministry, the main sponsor of the exhibition together with the Defense Ministry; Walter Curt Behrendt, another Finance Ministry official; Martin Wagner, the chief municipal planner and architect of Berlin; and Edwin Redslob, curator of art for the republic. The conservatives included Wilhelm Kreis, designer of many prewar monuments to Bismarck, and Karl Scheffler, the art critic.[109] Similarly, the invited architects included Mies, Behrens, and Poelzig, but also the more conservative reform architects, Erich Blunck and Heinrich Tessenow, both of whom had joined the opposition to the architects of the Ring.[110]

Mies chose to present a cuboidal interior, roofed over instead of open to the sky in the "atriumlike arrangement" specified by the competition brief (*see* Fig. 2); he said this would be quieter, more suited to reflection, and more con-

15. Heinrich Tessenow: War Memorial, Berlin (Remodeling of Karl Friedrich Schinkel's Neue Wache, 1816–18). Competition project, 1930. Interior perspective. Whereabouts unknown

sonant with the closed and cubic form of Schinkel's exterior.[111] The walls were faced with a veneer of green Tinian marble, and a low altarlike granite monolith, carved on top with the eagle of the Reich, sat just to the rear of center; the only light came through large windows of gray glass on the facade, but a door opened to the stand of trees in the rear, allowing even in this shut-in space the freer connection with nature of Mies's new approach.

The classicism announced in the Barcelona Pavilion thus became much more explicit because the special site obviously ruled out bare steel or de Stijl asymmetries; indeed, it recalls Mies's prewar project for a monument to Bismarck, which itself owed much to Schinkel's architecture.[112] Mies's project received second prize, and the strong support of Kiessling, Wagner, and Redslob. But the interior had too little light for most of the jurors, so the first prize went to a project by Tessenow with an oculus in the center (Fig. 15).[113] Tessenow, an opponent of the Ring, had as his ideal the simple German architecture of about 1800. Yet Mies's design bore a striking resemblance to Tessenow's reductively classicizing interior—an indication of the distance Mies had traveled from the center of the modern movement.

In the face of the same difficulties with rationalization and standardization, other German architects reacted in exactly the opposite way, looking to even wider and more intensive use of prefabrication, mass-production methods, and rationalization to lower costs and improve quality in housing. This was particularly true of Walter Gropius and Ernst May. In 1926 they were instrumental in working out a plan for a federal subsidy of ten million marks to develop housing settlements as large-scale experiments in standardization and rationalization.[114] The largest grant went to Gropius's Törten housing in Dessau, constructed with the help of cranes traveling on rails; another grant to a study of concrete plates for May's Praunheim housing settlement in Frankfurt-am-

Main; and a small one for observation of the efficiency of planning and building materials at Weissenhof.[115] Gropius erected at Weissenhof the houses most conspicuously directed toward the study of prefabrication; May set up, on the adjacent hilltop site reserved for experimental methods, a demonstration of his concrete plate structures that stood almost as a rebuke to the conventional methods used in much of the Weissenhof settlement itself (Fig. 16).[116] By 1928 or 1929, both architects had abandoned their earlier site plans, which were fitted to the landscape in the tradition of garden-city suburbs, for the strict straight-row (*Zeilenbau*) system that was intended to provide maximum sunlight, air, and equality[117]—an image of standardization in housing.

16. *Ernst May: Concrete Plate House under construction, Weissenhof Exhibition, Stuttgart. 1925–27*

In short, a split had arisen in the ranks of the modernists between those who asserted its positivist and materialistic tenets more strongly in the face of difficult times, and those who, like Mies, turned back more and more to its idealist and formalist underpinnings. Mies summed up this division succinctly early in 1929 in a letter to Le Corbusier: "Especially in Germany, the land of the organizers, it seems to me necessary to emphasize with special clarity that architecture is something other than raw functionalism. In Germany the fight against the rationalists will be harder than against the academicians."[118]

Meanwhile, others further to the left began to withdraw almost entirely from the consensus that had permitted Mies, Gropius, May, and Taut to work harmoniously together into the late 1920s. Some younger architects whose politics had been formed after the years of war and revolution now took a more explicitly Marxist approach, free of the idealistic assumptions of harmony between the classes or universal brotherhood. There were few of them in Germany, and fewer still who were acknowledged Communists. But when they rose to influence within the modern movement, the conflict between their views and the earlier utopian socialism or democratic liberalism came into the open.

The most conspicuous break with the political consensus was made by Hannes Meyer, who succeeded Gropius as head of the Bauhaus in 1928. Meyer had come from Basel and the far left circle of *ABC*, the architectural journal founded by Mart Stam, Hans Schmidt, El Lissitzky, and others to propagate (in Meyer's words) a "functionalist-collectivist-constructivist" line.[119] Although Meyer's espousal of that line at the Bauhaus could be seen as a rebuke to the more idealistic and formalistic approach of Gropius, it was only in 1930 when Meyer's politics began to threaten the position of the Bauhaus in the political councils of Dessau that he was forced out of the directorship.[120] Mies was then brought in to clean up the school, and his swift and ruthless purge of the Communists among the student body opened him to attacks from the extreme left in the modern movement[121] (even though Mies himself continued to support avant-garde artists and organizations on this end of the political spectrum).[122]

The following year, in the deepening depression, the first major critical attacks were launched against Mies's work. His ample house at the Berlin Building Exposition of 1931, spreading out before the minimal dwellings of the other architects, was "disliked by many architects and critics, especially the Communists," or so Philip Johnson reported at the time.[123] The leftist Czech critic Karel Teige wrote: "The most remarkable architectonic structures of this exhibition are the most reactionary as far as social content is concerned, for example, the house of Mies van der Rohe, which is not even a villa. It is a mere irrational application of the maker's German Pavilion in the Barcelona exhibition. The difference is limited to the insertion of a toilet and bath into the pavilion, which was a fantastic architectonic and plastic play, somewhat similar to Wright, where space was capriciously divided by several partitions—and thus a villa of the future is created. It is a useless abstract space composition, *Raumkunst,* determined solely by creative intentions, and built of luxurious materials."[124] A short while later, Walter Riezler, the editor of the Werkbund journal *Die Form,* defensively praised the recently completed and far more costly Tugendhat House in distinctly anti-Marxist and antifunctionalist terms.[125] This was not the architecture of Le Corbusier's machine for living, Riezler wrote, but of a new feeling of spatial connection with nature, a new spirit that united the individual with the larger realm, all of which was beyond Marxist sociology to understand, as Riezler put it, in terms that reflected Mies's own new approach.

Roger Ginsburger, a German architectural writer in France and a Marxist, replied to this with an attack on the costliness of the materials and technical features of the villa.[126] Although he accepted the argument that the villa's openness to light, air, and nature fulfilled basic needs of modern man, he rejected Riezler's idealistic arguments for this in favor of a positivist one based on measurable psychological reactions to light and air.

The overtly political and the deeper ideological distance that had developed between Mies and the other leaders of the movement increased almost to the breaking point in the early years of the Nazi regime. The bitterness of those years erupted publicly as late as 1965 when Sibyl Moholy-Nagy, the widow of the leftist Bauhaus artist László Moholy-Nagy, charged that Mies had repeatedly sought the favor of the Nazis and that the style of his projects for the Nazis proved that "he who lies down with dogs gets up with fleas."[127] No other leader of the modern movement was subjected to such attacks, although others also attempted to collaborate with the Nazis. Why then was Mies singled out for his political stance?

The nature of Mies's connection with the Nazis was pointed out as early as 1933 by Philip Johnson, who wrote of "the young men in the Nazi party, the students and revolutionaries who are ready to fight for modern art. . . . In architecture there is only one man whom even they can defend and this is Mies van der Rohe. Mies has always kept out of politics and has always taken his stand against functionalism."[128]

Led by the young painter Otto Andreas Schreiber, these pro-modern artists sought the protection of Joseph Goebbels, the head of the Propaganda Ministry, who was thought to favor modern art in opposition to Alfred Rosenberg, the leader of the Strike Force for German Culture (*Kampfbund für deutsche Kultur*) and the chief advocate of a nativist (*völkisch*) art.[129] The young artists promoted exhibitions of older Expressionists such as Emil Nolde (who was particularly admired by Goebbels and some of his underlings), Erich Heckel, Max Pechstein, and Karl Schmidt-Rottluff.[130]

Through Goebbels's influence, the group was able to organize the fine arts section of the Strength through Joy (*Kraft durch Freude*) group, an offshoot of Robert Ley's German Labor Front (*Deutsche Arbeitsfront*), organizations which were to be open for a short while to the modernists.[131] The section then scheduled a competition for December 1933 to be juried by Mies, Heckel, Paul Hindemith, and Richard Strauss,[132] both Hindemith and Strauss being leaders of Goebbels's organization of German composers, the *Fachschaft I des Berufstandes der deutschen Komponisten*.[133] According to one of Mies's Bauhaus students, "the head of the Chamber of Arts and Culture announced in public that he expected Mies to some day build a palace of culture for Hitler"[134]—apparently referring to Eugen Hönig, president of the National Chamber of Fine Arts (*Reichskammer der bildenden Künste*), an organization established by Goebbels's National Chamber of Culture (*Reichskulturkammer*). The modernists were effective enough to provoke the right-wing artists of the German Artists League of 1933 (*Deutscher Künstlerbund 1933*), a Munich group which included Paul Troost, Hitler's favorite architect, to attack the "tendencies that demoralized personalities such as Nolde, Klee, Schmidt-Rottluff, and Mies van der Rohe now attempt to smuggle into the National Socialist state as the real new German art."[135]

During this period, Mies joined a number of Nazi organizations and remained in others that had been taken over by the Nazis.[136] In February 1934 he was granted membership in the *Reichsluftschutzbund*, a Nazi-sponsored organization for home air defense,[137] and in October he joined the *National-Sozialistische Volkswohlfahrt* (NSV), the Nazi social welfare organization.[138] The significance of these moves may be judged by the pleas of Max Pechstein, when under pressure to leave the Prussian *Akademie der Künste,* that his membership in the NSV and the Nazi air sports union had earned him the right to remain.[139] Like Pechstein, Mies refused to resign from the *Akademie* when it asked him to in May 1933. He said it would lead to "misunderstandings," i.e., would mark him as an opponent of the regime.[140]

After the Nazis closed the Bauhaus in April 1933, Mies attempted to negotiate its reopening, first with Rosenberg and then with the Gestapo.[141] According to a student then at the Bauhaus, a group of faculty members and students met with Mies to discuss a transfer of the Bauhaus to another country: "Mies himself was very much against emigration; he had hoped, as all of us did, for a better understanding of the cultural questions in the NSDAP [the National Socialist Party] after the party came to power."[142] The Nazis agreed to let it reopen with certain restrictions, but the following day at Mies's request the faculty dissolved the Bauhaus because of financial and political pressure. Mies was later to say that this last-minute maneuver enabled him to have the closing celebrated with champagne, implying that he wished to make a show of spurning the Nazis' offer.[143] But more significant was his willingness to try for an agreement with Rosenberg, the opponent of all that Mies stood for in architecture.[144] Little more than a year later, just after Hitler had abolished the title of president of the Reich and designated himself Führer and chancellor, Mies signed a petition in his support sponsored by Goebbels in an effort to bring together under his (Goebbels's) wing, with the new Führer's blessing, his own coterie of modernists and some of Rosenberg's following among the antimodernists.[145]

The first of Mies's attempts to adapt modern architecture for Nazi patronage was his competition project for an addition to the Reichsbank.[146] When the competition originated in February 1933, however, it was still rooted in the policies and personalities of the Weimar Republic. Hitler had just been made chancellor, and the Finance Ministry was still directed by Hans Luther, a supporter of the Weimar Republic. Like the competition for the Neue Wache, the one for the Reichsbank was organized by the Finance Ministry, and once again Kiessling and Wagner served as jurors, this time along with Behrens and the architecturally more conservative Fritz Schumacher and Paul Bonatz. Kiessling invited thirty architects,[147] who again ranged from modernists such as Mies, Gropius, Richard Döcker, and Otto Haesler—which occasioned an attack from Rosenberg's *Völkischer Beobachter*, the official party newspaper[148]—to more conservative architects such as Blunck, Kreis, and Tessenow. Kiessling did, however, want to accommodate the Nazis,[149] and some of the competitors were (or soon became) members of the party.[150] A more ominous indication of kowtowing to Nazi pressure was the exclusion of Jews such as Erich Mendelsohn from the list (as he himself remarked).[151] Jews, not socialists or modernists, were the first to be banned from the new state organization and patronage lists. Nevertheless, the chosen competitors as a group were aligned neither with the right nor the left, politically or stylistically.

Immediately after the Nazis won the election in March, enabling Hitler to begin to consolidate his regime, the new government began to influence the outcome of the competition more decisively. Hjalmar Schacht assumed the directorship of the Finance Ministry in March and took part through his representatives in the final deliberations of the jury.[152] Wagner was forced out of his municipal office, and his replacement took over his seat on the jury.[153] It was in this period that Mies prepared his designs.[154]

In July, six of the competitors—including Mies—were awarded prizes of money for their projects, though none was chosen as the winner.[155] Two of them, Pinno and Grund from Dortmund and Kurt Frick from Königsberg, were members of the Nazi party and of Alfred Rosenberg's Strike Force of German Architects and Engineers (*Kampfbund deutscher Architekten und Ingenieure*);[156] their projects and that of Pfeiffer and Grossman of Mülheim were in the stripped-down, faintly classicizing style developed before the war by Behrens and other Werkbund architects and used during the Weimar period by architects such as Bonatz.[157] This style was to become one of the most common for larger buildings under the Nazis, as in Werner March's Olympic Stadium. Paul Mebes, who had been a member of the *Arbeitsrat* and had built housing projects in Berlin with flat International Style surfaces,[158] submitted a conservative version of Bauhaus modern, and Fritz Becker of Düsseldorf a somewhat more up-to-date one. The indecisive variety of the solutions and the mixture of political backgrounds was characteristic of early Nazi competitions,[159] carried over in this instance from the Weimar competition for the Neue Wache. Nevertheless, the premiated architects were architecturally and politically conservative enough to lend some substance to Sibyl Moholy-Nagy's charge that Mies's participation was taken as a "terrible stab in the back for us [in the modern movement]." Hitler himself was reported to have ordered the construction of the project by the bank's building director, Heinrich Wolff, whose building, designed in a stripped-down classicizing style, still stands (although used for other purposes) near Unter den Linden in East Berlin.[160]

For his project, Mies curved the facade along the street facing the old bank, and extended the offices back to the Spree Canal in three ten-story slabs (Figs. 17, 18). The main public feature of his design was the tall lobby, lighted

17. *Reichsbank, Berlin. Competition project, 1933.*
Facade. Drawing. Whereabouts unknown

by a great window wall, raised above ground level, and reached by a grand staircase. The staircase vaguely recalls Schinkel's entrance to the nearby Altes
Museum. But the facade, which received no comment from the jury, reflects
Mendelsohn's Schocken Department Store in Chemnitz of 1928–29
(Fig. 19)—Mies even asked about Mendelsohn's use of proportions, according
to one report.[161] The tall slabs of the rear elevations are derived in their turn
from plans by the architects of the *Neue Bauen* that were intended to maximize
light and air in office buildings, as in Poelzig's new administration building for

18. *Reichsbank, Berlin. Competition project, 1933. Canal elevation. Drawing. Whereabouts*
unknown

19. Erich Mendelsohn: Schocken Department Store, Chemnitz, Germany. 1928–29

I. G. Farben in Frankfurt-am-Main of 1928–30 (Fig. 20), which was also laid out on a curving plan.

The experiments in abstract classicism of the Weimar monuments now took another turn, at once grandiose and symmetrical but sheathed in the steel and glass of modernism. Even at the time this was thought to be an appeal to Nazi taste: Philip Johnson said of Mies's project that "a good modern Reichsbank would satisfy the new craving [of the Nazis] for monumentality."[162] It provoked Sibyl Moholy-Nagy to speak of Mies's "deadly Fascist designs" for the Reichsbank and later for the Silk Industry Administration Building in Krefeld.

20. Hans Poelzig: I. G. Farben Administration Building, Frankfurt-am-Main. 1928–30

In recent years the assumption that Mies's project marked a major shift in his style from "informal asymmetry to symmetrical monumentality"[163]—with the obvious inference that this shift was politically or opportunistically motivated—has become a staple of architectural history.

But the shift was less clear-headed and purposeful than it seems. Although it already appeared that Hitler himself favored a monumental classicizing style for public buildings, as evidenced by his commitment to Troost for refurbishing the Brown House and building the House of German Art (*Haus der deutschen Kunst*) in Munich,[164] Mies was more than a little naive if he thought he was shrewdly catering to the tastes of the new chancellor, for the Schocken store in Chemnitz to which his design referred was not only designed but owned by Jews, and Hitler had specifically inveighed in *Mein Kampf* against "the miserable discrepancy prevailing in a city even such as Berlin between the structures of the Reich and those of finance and commerce," particularly "the department stores of a few Jews."[165] Nor was Mies the only modernist to find it difficult to adapt the language of modernism to monumental governmental buildings. When the younger generation of modernists first had the opportunity to draw up such projects in the late 1920s, they often resorted to blander and more formal and symmetrical designs, especially when the project was for a specific urban site, as for example Le Corbusier's Centrosoyuz Building in Moscow (Fig. 21).[166]

The index of Mies's uncertainty is the discrepancy between his references to factories, office buildings, and department stores and the civic monumentality of his layout. Some of the incongruousness of Mies's project, as measured by conventional standards of monumentality, was mirrored in the jury's critique, which praised Mies's entrance hall as "a particularly grandiose solution from an architectonic viewpoint," but judged that the elevation on the canal "corresponds neither in its height nor in its massing to the character of the appearance of the city"—meaning the lower but more monumental buildings across the canal.[167] By contrast Gropius's project was overtly modern enough to be dismissed, despite the symmetry of its facade (Fig. 22), on the grounds that "the overall impression is that of a great factory more than of a bank building,"[168] while a few others, like Döcker's, were uncompromising in their antimonumentality.[169]

Mies abandoned this formal, symmetrical mode in his next work for the Nazis, the only one of any significance he was able to carry out: it consisted of two exhibits for the *German People/German Labor* (*Deutsches Volk/Deutsche Arbeit*) exhibition held in Berlin from April to June 1934.[170] Intended as propaganda for National Socialist doctrines of race and labor in Germany, the exhibition as a whole was a warning to Germans of the dangers of racial degeneracy, with a display of the countermeasures of the new regime.

Probably through the influence of the *Deutsche Arbeitsfront*, one of the major exhibitors, a conspicuous number of modernists participated.[171] Shortly before, in January 1934, the *Deutsche Arbeitsfront* had sponsored a competition for a House of Labor, a workers' clubhouse similar to the Italian fascist *Casa del Dopolavoro*, which attracted modernist entries from Gropius, Bartning, the Luckhardt brothers, and other members of the modern movement.[172] Gropius, with Joost Schmidt, produced the nonferrous metals exhibit;[173] Herbert Bayer, the Bauhaus typographer who also worked for the so-called "factory exhibi-

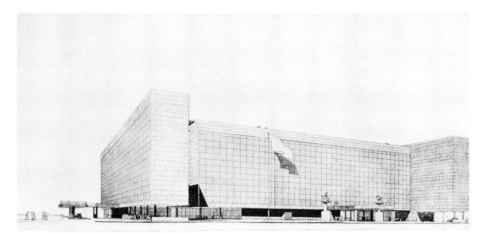

21. *Le Corbusier and Pierre Jeanneret: Centrosoyuz Building, Moscow. Project, 1928–29*

22. *Walter Gropius: Reichsbank, Berlin. Competition project, 1933. Model*

tions" of modern art sponsored by Schreiber's group, designed the exhibition flyer;[174] and Cesar Klein, a founding member of the Novembergruppe and a leader of the *Arbeitsrat,* painted a large mural with a swastika and other Nazi insignia.[175]

According to Sergius Ruegenberg, a sometime assistant of Mies,[176] the gray eminence behind Mies's nomination for the commission was Albert Speer, who certainly was well placed to play this role: in addition to his work for Goebbels and Hitler, he was given charge of the new *Schönheit der Arbeit* (Beauty of Labor) unit in the *Kraft durch Freude* bureau of the *Deutsche Arbeitsfront*—a unit that promoted architectural standards and forms similar to those of the modernists—and had served as a juror on the *Deutsche Arbeitsfront*'s House of Labor competition.[177] Late in life Speer recalled that he had admired Mies because he used "noble materials" and was a "classicist."[178] In fact, the somewhat abstracted classicism of Speer's early work, for example, the Zeppelinfeld in Nuremberg, was not so far from that of Mies's project for the Neue Wache.

23. *Mining Exhibit*, Deutsches Volk/Deutsche Arbeit *exhibition, Berlin. 1934*

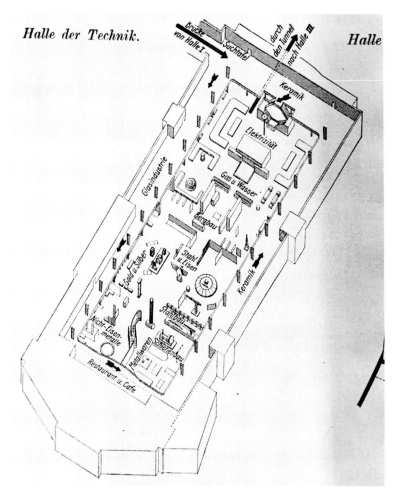

24. *Hall of Technology*, Deutsches Volk/Deutsche Arbeit *exhibition, Berlin. 1934.*
Mies's mining exhibit is toward the center of the hall.

Mies prepared two displays for the *Deutsches Volk/Deutsche Arbeit* exhibition, on the mining of potash and bituminous coal and on the glass and ceramic industries. His layout for the mining industries (*Bergbau*) returns cautiously to the principles of de Stijl for the plan of the walls, exhibition cases, and placards (Fig. 23).[179] It is reminiscent of his plan for the Brick Country House of 1924 (*see* Fig. 12), although it is more symmetrical. But exhibition design escaped the Nazi demands for formal layouts in public buildings, and Mies's exhibit was submerged in the other displays on the open floor of the exhibition hall (Fig. 24).

Soon Mies was to develop his modernist ideas for the Nazis on a more monumental scale in the most extensive and ambitious of his dealings with the regime, his participation on the competition for the German Pavilion at the Brussels World's Fair of 1935. The competition was not made public, and needs going into in some detail. The program for the pavilion was drawn up by the national commissioner for the exhibition in May 1934.[180] It called for a hall of honor for Goebbels's Propaganda Ministry and four major exhibits in addition to the industrial exhibits. The exhibit *Weltanschauung*, or world view, Hitler's slogan for fundamental Nazi principles, was to include the domain of the *Reichskulturkammer*, Goebbels's bureau for the control of the arts. That on "People and Nation" was to range from the Nazi party, the storm troopers, and the *Deutsche Arbeitsfront* and its *Kraft durch Freude* organization to youth and the school, crafts and the middle class, and the landscape. Another section was to be called "Peasant and Soil" (*Baver und Boden*), a variant of the slogan of Nazi racism and expansionism "Blood and Soil" (*Blut und Boden*), because the latter was deemed "not feasible in Brussels." A fourth exhibit was to deal with transportation.

The exhibition building was "to give expression to the will of National Socialist Germany in impressive form and as a symbol for the stance of National Socialism, its aggressive force [*kämpferische Macht*] and heroic will," especially in its external form, "which must stand in contrast to the rather bombastic character of the Belgian buildings,"[181] designed in variations of Art Deco,[182] as it might now be called. The projects were to be ready July 2 to allow for the opening of the pavilion on April 1, 1935.

Early in June, Eugen Hönig, the president of the *Reichskammer der bildenden Künste*, an organization, as noted before, under the control of Goebbels's ministry, invited Mies to prepare a preliminary design for the pavilion and to come to Brussels for that purpose.[183] Again, it is quite possible that Speer, who had just become Hitler's chief architect and who participated in Hitler's judging of the project, was instrumental in Mies's nomination.[184] The other invited architects were Emil Fahrenkamp of Düsseldorf, a prolific architect in a range of styles from diluted modern to medieval;[185] Eckart Muthesius, son of the founder of the Werkbund but young and little known; Ludwig Ruff of Nuremberg, who had been chosen by Hitler to build the Kongresshalle there (Fig. 25) and was thought to be in line to finish Troost's buildings in Munich;[186] Paul Schmitthenner of Stuttgart, a leader of the movement to return to a traditional German architecture, author of *Die Baukunst im neuen Reich* (*Architecture in the New Reich*), and a member of the Nazi Party;[187] and Karl Wach of Düsseldorf, who was also a party member.[188]

The site set aside for the German Pavilion in Brussels was adjacent to the

126

general exhibition halls of the Grand Palais.[189] The other competitors distributed the different exhibits and functions in separate halls, spread around an internal court or forecourt, or lumped together as in Ruff's project (Fig. 26). Mies chose instead to gather the main exhibits into one large hall—116 meters (380.57 feet) square—with a few small appendages and satellite buildings (Fig. 27).[190] He laid out an ample triangular entrance plaza before a long facade of clinker brick that stretched from a small enclosed pool on the left to a café restaurant a short distance to the right of the pavilion (Fig. 28). The main entrance opened through a narrow glazed section in the wall to the right of the central axis of the pavilion. Inside, a hall led to the square Court of Honor, which was enclosed on three sides by "mouse-gray" glass, and decorated with sculpture (Fig. 29). Flanking the hall and extending into the court were two freestanding walls of Silesian marble, similar to the low walls of Mies's exhibit for the *Deutsches Volk/Deutsche Arbeit* exhibition (*see* Fig. 24, under *Bergbau*).[191] A large swastika was carved into one wall; *Deutsches Reich* was inscribed on the other, and a bronze eagle of the Reich stood at the far end of the court. Travertine paved the hall and court, linoleum the rest of the pavilion, and a rug and table provided a focus for ceremonies in the hall, which bore a resemblance to Mies's project for the Neue Wache (*see* Fig. 2). The underlying classicism of the project was made explicit in one telling detail: the altarlike table on two pillars decorated with volutes.[192] Because of the gray glass and the open exhibition space, the hall and court were visible from other areas of the pavilion, with the governmental exhibits grouped closely around this center, and the industrial exhibits arranged around the perimeter.

The structure was carried on cruciform steel columns whose slender cores rose free a short distance to support the superstructure hidden above the flat ceiling, which would have appeared almost to float. Several freestanding walls separated exhibition areas from one another in an echo of Mies's de Stijl arrangements.

25. Ludwig Ruff: Kongresshalle, Nuremberg. Project, 1934. Model

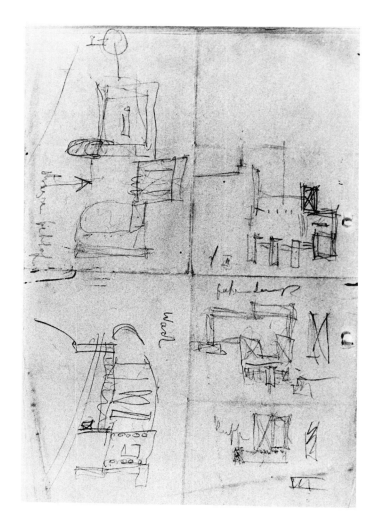

26. Various sketches of competition plans for the German Pavilion, 1935 World's Fair, Brussels. 1934. Pencil and colored pencil on tracing paper. The Museum of Modern Art, New York, Mies van der Rohe Archive. Gift of the architect. Ruff's plan is at the lower right.

In his accompanying brief, Mies explained that Germany in recent years had developed an exhibition technique or format that "is a totality, flows together, is articulated, to be sure, but not chopped up. . . . The building receives through this all-encompassing totality such a grand form, such a colossal volume, that it makes the strongest public effect even with the simplest form."[193] Mies was referring to the open exhibition spaces, subdivided only by thin columns, freestanding walls, and glazed light courts, that he had developed in the Barcelona Pavilion and the Berlin Building Exposition of 1931, which in Brussels he greatly enlarged and adapted to a square format, in line with his increasingly more contained designs of the 1930s and the grandness of the commission. In its union of symmetrical and freer aspects, of openness and containment, the Brussels pavilion was the fullest realization of Mies's efforts to create a monumental modern architecture for the Nazis.

Mies learned late in July that Ruff's project had been chosen.[194] Ruegenberg, who had worked in Mies's office earlier, said years later that Ruff's design was in "Richard Wagner style; his [Mies's] drawings lay on the floor behind Hitler's desk."[195] There is every reason to think that Hitler did make the selection personally, since he later intervened to determine details of form and ma-

128

terials in Ruff's project.[196] Mies was paid 5,500 marks for his design and model in August.[197] Despite his having lost, Mies was entrusted with the exhibit for the chemical industry, and Lilly Reich, his collaborator on many interior designs, especially for textiles, was assigned that for the textile firms.[198] But in November the government abruptly cancelled its participation because of an unfavorable balance of payments with Belgium.[199]

What was most significant in this project was the convergence of ideas expressed by Mies and by the Nazis. The Nazis wanted a building that would be impressive but not bombastic. In his turn, Mies had in mind a building that would make "the strongest public impression even with the simplest form;" he stressed that "this clear and impressive language corresponds to the character of German production."[200]

Hitler himself in his address on culture at the party congress in September 1933 had called "functionalism imbued with crystal clarity" the measure of beauty and had emphasized that "from material and function new forms are

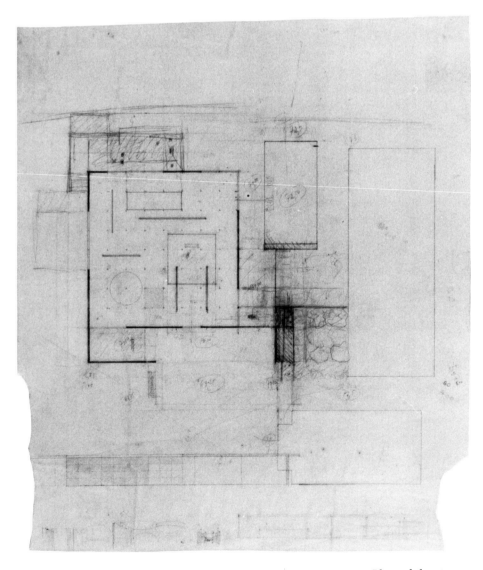

27. *German Pavilion, 1935 World's Fair, Brussels. Competition project, 1934. Plan and elevation.*
Pencil and colored pencil on tracing paper. The Museum of Modern Art, New York,
Mies van der Rohe Archive. Gift of the architect

129

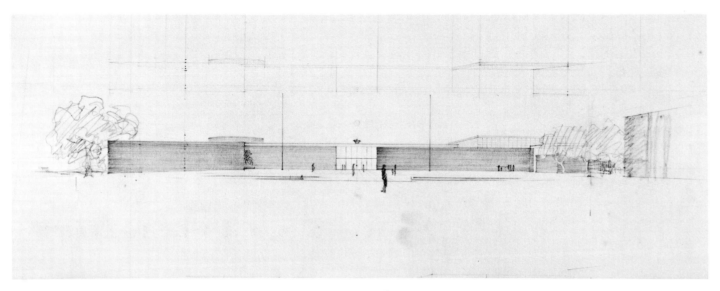

28. *German Pavilion, 1935 World's Fair, Brussels. Competition project, 1934. Preliminary drawing of facade. Collection Dirk Lohan*

found and developed that breathe more of the Greek spirit in the aesthetic of many machines, for example, than in many a poorly conceived building."[201] But he also railed against *Sachlichkeit* and the search for a new style, and insisted that "the future is built only from the past and the present equally." A similar mixture of admiration for modern technology and for tradition colors the writings of an influential line of intellectuals in Germany who have been described as "reactionary modernists."[202] Among them, Goebbels—whose ministry played so large a role in the development of the Brussels pavilion—was particularly strident in his call for a "steely romanticism."[203]

Although Hitler and the "reactionary modernists" insisted upon the importance of both ideals, it was easy in 1933 and 1934 to imagine that a tendency toward one or the other would prevail. To compound the uncertainty, Hitler allowed Goebbels to encourage modern artists and Rosenberg to champion *völkisch* art at one and the same time. But in the fall of 1934, when Hitler had consolidated his leadership of the Nazi Party and the regime, he made it clear in his annual address on culture that neither direction would predominate: from then on the classicism of Troost and Speer, as well as that of Hitler's vision of the Brussels pavilion, became the premier form in the hierarchy of Nazi architecture.[204]

Mies was not alone among the leaders of the modern movement in his hopes of exploiting this brief moment of confusion and seeming opportunity to seek favor among the Nazis. As scholars have known for two decades, Gropius, Wagner, Behrens, and others tried to reach an accommodation with the Nazis.[205] As late as the end of 1936, after he had been appointed to Harvard, Gropius could write to Hönig, who until shortly before was the president of the *Reichskammer der bildenden Künste*: "As I have till now, so will I in the future remain loyal; and I see my mission at Harvard as that of serving German culture."[206] With support from Gropius, Hugo Häring attempted to persuade the Nazis that the new architecture was German rather than international.[207] Wagner, who had resigned from the *Akademie der Künste* in protest against the Nazi takeover of that institution,[208] who spoke up in June 1933 against Nazi attempts to force

130

Jews out of the Werkbund,[209] and who as late as June 1934 described himself to the Nazi architect Schmitthenner as "still a Socialist,"[210] nevertheless, in concert with Gropius, submitted a proposal in February 1934 to the Nazi president of East Prussia for a model town and regional planning policy. The latter was meant to demonstrate the superiority of German technology and organization to that of Russia, Japan, and America.[211] He also tried to sell the *Neue Bauen* to the Nazis as more in keeping than traditional architecture with their ideology.[212] Only a few of the modernists, in fact, chiefly the handful of Communists such as Meyer, or leftists such as May who had worked in Russia—and not all of the latter—made no attempt, so far as is known, to reach an accommodation with the Nazis, who were unlikely in any case to have given them a chance.[213]

But Mies, in contrast to the others in the modern movement, aimed his efforts at those modernists in the Nazi closet, and as Gropius complained, he was preferred by those Nazis willing to accept some form of modernism.[214] Bruno E. Werner, who had been appointed chairman of the Association of German Art Critics (*Verband deutscher Kunstkritiker*) by the Nazis, wrote in the fall of 1933 that Mies, in comparison to Gropius and Poelzig, had, "thanks to his attitude, the best supporters in Munich" (i.e., in Hitler's entourage).[215] Nor is it surprising that Winfried Wendland, a young architect appointed by the Nazis to help reorganize the Werkbund, could write to Walter Riezler: "I personally esteem Mies van der Rohe extraordinarily in contrast to so many other of the modernists" in a context which indicates that he was referring to Mies's architecture rather than his politics.[216]

For it was not only Mies's political neutrality but his more monumental style with its fusion of references to technology and to classicism in the late 1920s—especially in the Barcelona Pavilion—that must have found a sympathetic response among those Nazis trying to reconcile Hitler's obvious preference for classicism with his insistence upon the value of functionalism and modern technology, as well as his supreme ideal of clarity. This may also help to explain why Mies was the only major artist associated with abstract art, as distinct from Expressionism, who found any acceptance among the Nazis, and not simply because abstraction was easier to accept in architecture than in the more representational arts.[217]

Mies's estrangement from the modernists crystallized when he signed the petition for Hitler; even Mies, according to Rosenberg, felt it necessary to apologize to his friends, and Gropius and Sibyl Moholy-Nagy never forgave him for it.[218] But their anger signified a deeper conflict. Gropius, Wagner, and others still clung to the aesthetic and the social ideals of the Weimar years; Wagner wanted to see his old dream of bringing together town and country put into effect under the Nazis, and Gropius employed his factory style in the House of German Labor project, which was meant to serve the workers even if through the Nazis. Mies however could be seen as betraying the movement because he had compromised *both* the social and the aesthetic ideals of the modernists, especially in the Reichsbank project—that "deadly Fascist" design, in Sibyl Moholy-Nagy's doubly significant phrase.

But the end result of all this maneuvering by the modernists was the same for all who had risen to prominence after the First World War: they were excluded from Nazi patronage. Not that the modern style itself was ruled out by

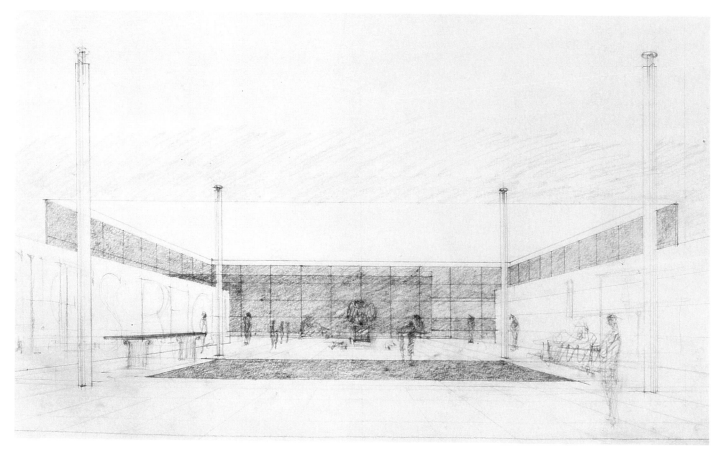

29. *German Pavilion, 1935 World's Fair, Brussels. Competition project, 1934. Sketch of Court of Honor. Collection Dirk Lohan*

the Nazis: in keeping with Hitler's admiration for clarity and directness it was often adopted in simplified form for structures identified with modern technology—among them several major factories by Herbert Rimpl, who, according to Albert Speer, had worked in the office of Mies, and whose work resembles Mies's project of 1937 for the Silk Industry Administration Building in Krefeld.[219] But it was fundamental to the ideology and politics of Hitler's regime to reject its liberal predecessors, and those individuals and institutions prominently identified with the Weimar Republic, whether Mies, Taut, Gropius, or the Bauhaus, were completely unacceptable on this count alone—although outsiders and lesser officials often failed either to understand this or to take it seriously in the early years of Nazi rule.

Because the Nazis rejected all of the Weimar generation of modernist leaders without distinction, the political differences among them were obscured. They were further lost to sight when the architects emigrated to Britain and the United States and left the political and many of the social concerns of the Weimar years behind them. The ideological basis of the modern movement could now be ignored by architects, critics, and scholars, particularly in the United States, where Philip Johnson presented Mies's work as if it had no political, social, or even philosophical foundation, and the modern movement as if it were merely a style.[220]

In light of these shifting attitudes toward society and politics among the modernists from 1918 to 1934, what underlying structure of belief remains that accounts both for the trust they placed in Mies in the earlier years and the conflicts that arose in the early 1930s?

Clearly, the internationalism of the modernists, with its connotations of socialist brotherhood extending across national boundaries, cannot have been the constant force that both opponents and advocates of the new architecture made it out to be in the 1920s. As we have seen, leading German modernists moved from their extremely nationalistic positions before the war, to the internationalism of the Weimar years in the aftermath of the revolutions in Russia and Germany, and back again to a defense of their architecture as Teutonic in response to Nazi policies. While these swings can partly be discounted as opportunism, of course, it follows that the political meanings of nationalism and internationalism were not at the root of the beliefs of the modern movement.

But there was a conviction that all these architects did indeed share: the certainty that the world had moved into an impersonal and collective age, and that the architect had to reveal it. Mies himself wrote in 1924: "We are concerned today with questions of a general nature. The individual is losing significance. The decisive achievements in all fields are impersonal and their authors are mostly unknown. Our engineering structures are examples. Gigantic dams, great industrial installations are built as a matter of course, with no designer's name attached to them. They point to the technology of the future."[221]

Such comments on the collective structure of the modern world were commonplace, needless to say, in leftist publications, including the most extensive Marxist discussion of architecture to appear in Germany, *Das Buch vom Bauen* (*The Book of Building*), published in 1930 by Albert Sigrist under the pen name of Alexander Schwab.[222] This critic had been a leader of left-wing splinter groups of communists after the war, and in the late 1920s was a member of an important socialist discussion group in Berlin.[223] In his book he mentions with approval a few socialist architects such as Hilberseimer, but also some work of Mies's.[224] Schwab's viewpoint was summed up in a chapter called "The Two Faces of Modern Architecture," which, in his words, was at once "upper bourgeois and proletarian, fully capitalist and socialist. One can even say: autocratic and democratic."[225] The resolution of these antitheses in Schwab's thinking came from his conviction that the modern world no longer belonged to the individualistic petty bourgeoisie but rather to the great trusts and the great unions equally—to the new large collective enterprises that had created the great industrial metropolises and an impersonal technology to replace the freewheeling chaos of earlier capitalism.

The belief in the collective and impersonal nature of modern society and economy was not confined in Germany to Marxists and utopian socialists. It had been given a broader impetus by the war, not least by the successes of Walter Rathenau in marshaling Germany's raw materials and by his subsequent writings calling for the "organic unity" of society without communism or socialism.[226] Rathenau, who had been head of the AEG and who became famous as a foreign minister of the Weimar Republic, was widely read in Germany during the 1920s. The Nietzschean faith in the heroic individual, which before the war had dominated the hopes of many artists, even those inclined to socialism, such as van de Velde, now gave way to a general faith in the "totality."

The Nazis, too, believed in a collective society, but of a different order than the socialists: a *Volksgemeinschaft*, based on the mystical entity of the German people, rather than on social class, or the impersonal nature of modern industry and economy.[227] Perhaps this may help to explain why some of the leftists and socialists among the modernists, such as Wagner, could hope that the Nazis might accept the new architecture if it could be sold as a German product—a hope based on a misunderstanding of Nazi ideology as well as of Nazi politics, for it was precisely the Weimar ideals of collectivity that the Nazis opposed with their own.

But there was a fundamental difference of opinion among the modernists about what constituted the new collective age. For Mies it was determined chiefly by the impersonal nature of modern technology itself, even after he had superimposed upon it his new ideals of spirituality and freedom in the later 1920s. By contrast, Gropius, May, Taut, and the main line of modernists in Germany believed that the new collectivity was first and foremost a social reality that had to use technology for the common material good.[228]

These differences remained unexamined, however, and their confusion in the catchall slogans of the period was completed by the chosen language of modern architecture: the abstract planes, volumes, and frames of the new style. Having been sufficiently emptied of received meaning, the bare forms and surfaces could be read equally well as signs for a sociopolitical vision of the collective structure of the modern world, or a technological or mechanistic one (whether or not it might be freighted with idealist meaning as in Mies's work). Thus in the housing projects by Ernst May in Frankfurt-am-Main the unified rows of small town houses behind their smooth walls could be read according to a prescription going back to the socialist architect Berlage as an emblem of working-class unity,[229] whereas in the Tugendhat House the sheer surfaces could only be interpreted as standing for the impersonal precision of the machine.

While the new movement and the new architecture were being formed, therefore, it could easily appear that everyone shared the same goals. Only after the coherence of the new architecture had been publicly affirmed at the Weissenhof exhibition, and the difficulties of changing modern society or just mere housing through technology had become increasingly evident, did the differences between Mies and the others begin to emerge, although without ever coming up for critical examination.

From a Marxist viewpoint, the differences between the social reformers and an idealist like Mies amount to little or nothing, since both served only to dress up capitalism. But the smaller, subtler intentional distinctions of belief about whom and what architecture should serve did make for differences in the meanings of the new architecture, if not in the material conditions of society, differences that I think should not be glossed over.

The most significant ideological differences emerged in Mies's ideas and work of the late 1920s. What was new was his intention of intensifying our understanding of our freedom, allowing us to bring together past and present, nature and the machine, in an experience of unhindered movement in space. His earlier belief in technology as the "will of the time" was not abandoned but, rather, became the foundation of the order upon which the creative spirit of the artist could act—the precondition, in effect, of freedom.[230]

His social and political ideology, as signified by his support of laissez-faire economic policy and of the Weimar Republic, was the analogue of his belief in freedom in architecture. For the other modernists, who were devoted above all to social justice, freedom was seldom an issue. But Mies's idea of freedom had to be largely metaphorical and experiential to evade the consequences of the contradiction with his equally firm belief in the collective "will of the time," a contradiction which those who gave primacy to social justice did not have to face.

With the advent of the Nazi regime, inevitably, his ideas about freedom began to change. By March 1933, just after the Nazis had won the elections and Mies had started to make his designs for the Reichsbank, he wrote in a prospectus for the German plate-glass makers that the full potential of plate glass used with steel or concrete frames to permit "a measure of freedom in spatial formation" could be developed not in large utilitarian buildings but only in houses where the space could be united with the landscape—an obvious shift from his earlier self-referential concept of steel and glass in the skyscraper projects but also a retreat from the more universal ideal of freedom articulated in his lecture of 1928.[231] By the middle of 1935, after his comparatively closed and symmetrical projects for the Nazis, he could still exalt the "freedom of the open spatial form" in one of the last of his private commissions in Germany, the Hubbe House in Magdeburg.[232]

Because his ideal of freedom had become so private and purely metaphorical, he could put his work in the service of the Nazi regime as late as the summer of 1934, although his fellow modernists, more political than he, had come to believe that Mies had betrayed them. But when Mies arrived in this country, he changed his views about freedom and order one last time. In his inaugural address as director of architecture at the Armour Institute of Technology, delivered in November 1938, he said, "The long path from material through function to creative work has only a *single goal*: to create order out of the desperate confusion of our time [my italics]."[233] Neither then nor later did he speak again of freedom as a value in itself. When Peter Blake asked him in 1961, "Do you think that in a free-enterprise democracy, where everyone is free to do just about what he wants within very slight limitations, that it is possible to create architectural order?," Mies replied, "Yes, I think it would be an order in freedom."[234] Freedom was left to American politics; the task of architecture was order.

Notes

The following abbreviations are used throughout these notes:

BA: Bauhaus-Archiv, Berlin
BAK: Bundesarchiv, Koblenz
BDC: Berlin Document Center
LC: Mies Collection, Library of Congress, Washington, D.C. (Correspondence arranged under Private A, B, C, etc.)
MoMA: Mies van der Rohe Archive, The Museum of Modern Art, New York
UIC: Mies Collection, Special Collections, University of Illinois, Chicago

I presented the gist of this essay in a lecture at The Museum of Modern Art in March 1986, and in April for the Patronato del Pabellón Aleman de Barcelona in that city. For their comments on earlier versions of the text I wish to thank Barbara Miller Lane, Irving Lavin, Christian Otto, Francesco Passanti, and, especially, Joan Campbell for a detailed critique. In many conversations over the years, Franz Schulze has generously shared with me his great knowledge of Mies, and the essay has benefited from his suggestions as editor of this book. Rosa Maria Subirana invited me to talk on this subject in Barcelona; Fritz Neumeyer put me on to the importance of Romano Guardini for Mies; Larry E. Jones gave me advice about the *Hauszinssteuer*; Iain Boyd Whyte helped me locate an important illustration; Dirk Lohan, Mies's grandson, made his collection of Mies's books available to me; and Pierre Adler, Steven Bluttal, and Robert Coates of the Mies van der Rohe Archive of The Museum of Modern Art were unfailingly helpful. The late Arthur Drexler, as Director of the Museum's Department of Architecture and Design and the Mies Archive, gave my work indispensable support.

1. LC, Private F, unsigned copy, Mies to G. W. Farenholtz, November 14, 1925; *see below,* n. 50. Translations throughout this essay are mine unless otherwise credited.

2. John Willett, *Art and Politics in the Weimar Period: The New Sobriety, 1917–1933* (New York, 1978), p. 225.

3. Colin Rowe, "Introduction," in Arthur Drexler et al., *Five Architects* (New York, 1972), p. 3.

4. Donald Drew Egbert, "Socialism and American Art," in Donald Drew Egbert and Stow Persons, eds., *Socialism and American Life,* vol. 1 (Princeton, 1952),

p. 663; *see also* Donald Drew Egbert, *Social Radicalism and the Arts* (New York, 1970), p. 660.

5. Joan Campbell, *The German Werkbund: The Politics of Reform in the Applied Arts* (Princeton, 1978).

6. Joan Campbell, "The Politics of Cultural Reform: The Weimar Werkbund and its Architects" (lecture given at the Werkbund Symposium, Graduate School of Design, Harvard University, in 1980); I am indebted to Prof. Campbell for permission to quote from a copy of this talk.

7. Manfredo Tafuri, "U.S.S.R.–Berlin: From Populism to 'Constructivist Internationale,'" in *Architecture Criticism Ideology* (Princeton, 1985), p. 177.

8. Transcript of an interview with Mies for the *Bauwelt Archiv,* I (Berlin, 1966) (MoMA, English translation). Ludwig Hilberseimer, who like Mies clung to a prewar style at this time, wrote that his project was rejected along with Mies's (*Berliner Architektur der 20er Jahre* [Mainz, 1967], p. 30).

9. The drawing, dated 1919, present location unknown, resembles a description of the exhibition by Walter Riezler, "Revolution und Baukunst," *Mitteilungen des Deutschen Werkbundes,* no. 1 (1919), p. 19: "Es sind phantastische Gebilde, die manchmal an erstarrte Riesenpolypen erinnern, die ihre Arme nach allen Richtungen in den Himmel recken. Aus Wendeltreppen, die diese Arme entlang laufen, kann man schliessen, dass so etwas wie Aussichtstürme beabsichtigt sind." Iain Boyd Whyte, *Bruno Taut and the Architecture of Activism* (Cambridge, 1982), pp. 135–136, first published the drawing in connection with his discussion of the *Ausstellung für unbekannte Architekten,* and brought this quote to my attention. Walter Gropius, *Ausstellung für unbekannte Architekten* (Berlin, 1919): "Gebilde, die Zweck und Notdurft schafft, stillen nicht Sehnsucht nach einer von Grund aus neuer erbauten Welt der Schönheit, nach Wiedergeburt jener Geisteseinheit, die sich zur Wundertat der gotischen Kathedrale aufschwang."

10. Friedrich Naumann, *Werke,* 6 vols. (Cologne and Opladen, 1964); Theodor Heuss, *Friedrich Naumann, der Mann, das Werk, die Zeit* (Stuttgart, 1937).

11. Hermann Muthesius, "Leitsätze zum Vorträge," in *Die Werkbund–Arbeit der Zukunft* (Jena, 1914). Only in the hard times at the end of the war did Muthesius, in his *Kleinhaus und Kleinsiedlung*

(Munich, 1918), seriously discuss minimal dwellings.

12. Henry van de Velde, *Die Renaissance im modernen Kunstgewerbe,* 2nd ed. (Berlin, 1903), pp. 131–148, also pp. 50–67; *see also* idem, *Geschichte meines Lebens* (Munich, 1962), and idem, in *Die Werkbund–Arbeit der Zukunft,* pp. 49–51.

13. Fritz Hoeber, *Peter Behrens* (Munich, 1913), pp. 223–228; Tilmann Buddensieg et al., *Industriekultur, Peter Behrens und die AEG, 1907–1914* (Berlin, 1979), pp. D274–D291. His near silence on social topics is all the more remarkable because he built much housing for the AEG workers (Fritz Neumeyer, "Der Werkwohnungsbau der Industrie in Berlin und seine Entwicklung im 19. und frühen 20. Jahrhundert" (Diss., Technische Universität, Berlin, 1977–78), pp. 208–257.

14. Konrad Fiedler, "Bemerkungen über Wesen und Geschichte der Baukunst," in Gottfried Boehm, ed., *Schriften zur Kunst,* vol. 2 (Munich, 1971), pp. 429–479; Adolf von Hildebrand, *Das Problem der Form in der bildenden Kunst* (Strassburg, 1893); Joan Goldhammer Hart, "Heinrich Wölfflin, an Intellectual Biography" (Ph.D. thesis, University of California at Berkeley, 1981); Alois Riegl, *Stilfragen* (Berlin, 1893).

15. Bruno Taut, *Die Stadtkrone* (Jena, 1919), pp. 59–60; *see also* idem, *Alpine Architektur* (Hagen, 1919), pl. 16. On Taut's role in redirecting the political attitudes of the modernists, *see* Whyte, *Bruno Taut.*

16. "Haus des Himmels," *Frühlicht,* vol. 1, no. 1 (1920).

17. Rosemarie Bletter, "The Interpretation of the Glass Dream—Expressionist Architecture and the History of the Crystal Metaphor," *Journal of the Society of Architectural Historians,* vol. 40 (1981), pp. 20–43.

18. Helga Kliemann, *Die Novembergruppe* (Berlin, 1969), p. 119. In an interview with Peter Blake about 1961, Mies recalled: "I came to the Novembergruppe because a friend of mine knew that I had this modern glass skyscraper and said, 'You should show them [the drawings and models] in the Novembergruppe.' I didn't know what the Novembergruppe was." Mies also said that he was in charge of architectural exhibitions for the organization while he was chairman (Columbia University Oral History Project, tape one, published in part by Blake in "A Conversation with Mies," *Four Great Makers of Modern Architecture*

[New York, 1963], pp. 93–104); I am indebted to Peter Rutkoff for bringing this material to my attention.

19. "Hochhausproject für Bahnhof Friedrichstrasse in Berlin," *Frühlicht*, vol. 1, no. 4 (Summer 1922), pp. 122–124.

20. *G: Material zur elementaren Gestaltung*, no. 2 (September 1923), p. 1; *see* trans. by Philip Johnson, in his *Mies van der Rohe*, 3rd ed. (New York, 1977), p. 189.

21. *Bauwelt Archiv;* Peter Carter, *Mies van der Rohe at Work* (New York, 1974), p. 174. Behrens discussed his illusionary techniques in an article of 1910 on his AEG Turbine Factory, reprinted in Buddensieg, *Industriekultur*, pp. D277–D278.

22. Blake, "A Conversation with Mies," p. 95. It is characteristic of Mies that although he greatly admired Berlage, he paid no attention at all to the Dutch architect's concern with the social role and meaning of modern architecture.

23. Theo van Doesburg, "Zur elementaren Gestaltung," *G: Material zur elementaren Gestaltung*, no. 1 (July 1923); Ludwig Mies van der Rohe, "Bürohaus," *G: Material zur elementaren Gestaltung*, ibid.

24. Hans Richter, *Begegnungen von Dada bis Heute* (Cologne, 1973), pp. 53–54; Evert van Straaten, ed., *Theo van Doesburg, 1883–1931* (The Hague, 1983), pp. 98–100.

25. LC, Private V. The correspondence runs from July 28, 1923, to August 14, 1925. Mies takes up van Doesburg's ideas in his letters of the time, for example: "Das Problem unserer Zeit ist nicht formaler sondern konstruktiver Natur. Ich bin überzeugt, dass Arbeit, die ganz elementar aus ihren Bedingungen heraus gestaltet werden, ihrem Wesen nach zu einander passen, auch wenn die eine Arbeit Kurven aufweist und die andere nicht" (LC, Private J, Mies to Werner Jakstein, an architect in Altona, November 14, 1923, in a critique of the Bauhaus exhibition in Weimar).

26. Theo van Doesburg, "Anti-tendenzen Kunst," *De Stijl*, vol. 6, no. 2 (April 1923), pp. 17–19; for trans. *see* Joost Baljeu, *Theo van Doesburg* (New York, 1974), pp. 135–136; van Doesburg expressed some similar ideas as early as 1921 (ibid., pp. 113–114).

27. Ilya Ehrenburg and El Lissitzky, "The Blockade of Russia Moves towards Its End," *Veshch/Gegenstand/Objet*, nos. 1–2 (March–April, 1922), pp. 2–3; for trans. *see* Sophie Lissitzky-Küppers, ed., *El Lissitzky* (London, 1980), pp. 344–345. Lissitzky, van Doesburg, Richter, Karel Maes, and Max Burchartz issued a manifesto in 1922 declaring that the "creative Internationale . . . is not the result of some humanistic sentiment, idealistic or political, but of the same amoral and elementary principle on which science and technology are based" (*De Stijl*, vol. 5, no. 8 [1922], p. 116). Tafuri, "U.S.S.R.–Berlin," deduces from this that, "The avant-garde . . . was thus obliged . . . to declare once again not only its own non-political nature, but also its own *immoralism*." But Lissitzky clearly was far from renouncing his social and political concerns: *see also* Christina Lodder, *Russian Constructivism* (New Haven, 1983), pp. 228–229.

28. Justin Hoffmann, "Hans Richter und die Münchner Räterepublik," and Marion von Hofacker, "Biographische Notizen über Hans Richter 1888–1976," in *Hans Richter 1888–1976: Dadaist Filmpionier Maler Theoretiker* (Berlin, 1982), pp. 21–25, 55–57, 97–98; Willett, *Art and Politics*, pp. 148, 214; Gertraude Kühn et al., eds., *Film und revolutionäre Arbeiterbewegung in Deutschland 1918–1932* (Berlin, 1975) vol. 1, p. 126; vol. 2, pp. 230–233, 335–336, 412–414; *see also below*, n. 121.

29. On the Ring, *see* LC, BDA (*Bund Deutscher Architekten*), 1921–26: meetings of April 14 and 26, and May 3, 1924; February 17, March 19, April 3, May 26, July 7 and 10, August 10 and 22, and October 12, 1925; March 9, April 29, and May 26 and 29–30, 1926. *See also* Walter Curt Behrendt, in *Der Neubau*, VI (May 10, 1924), p. 104; (May 24, 1924), p. 114. Mies had been elected to the board of directors of the Brandenburg chapter of the BDA in August 1923 (LC, Private B, August 11 and 13). The Ring's efforts were directed particularly against Ludwig Hoffmann, an eclectic Wilhelmine architect who had just retired as chief municipal architect, but who continued to exert influence as the art conservator of Berlin.

30. The competition was open only to BDA members. Hoffmann had been one of the jurors. *See* Friedrich Paulsen, "Hochhäuser für Deutschland," in *Stadtbaukunst alter und neuer Zeit*, vol. 2 (Berlin, 1922), pp. 3–12.

31. So it was claimed by Heinrich Lauterbach, apparently on the basis of information from Häring (Heinrich Lauterbach and Jürgen Joedicke, eds., *Hugo Häring, Schriften, Entwürfe, Bauten* [Stuttgart, 1965], p. 10).

32. LC, BDA, meeting of August 22, 1924. Häring shared Mies's office in this period (Lauterbach and Joedicke, *Hugo Häring*, p. 10, n. 2). The expansion of the Ring is documented in Peter Pfankuch, ed., *Hans Scharoun, Bauten, Entwürfe, Texte*, Schriftenreihe der Akademie der Künste, vol. 10 (Berlin, 1974), pp. 58–61.

33. LC, BDA, meeting of April 26, 1924.

34. The other members at various times in 1924–25 were Walter Curt Behrendt, Otto Rudolph Salvisberg, Jürgen Bachmann, Walther Schilbach, Emil Schaudt, and *Geheimrat* Schüler.

35. "Sozialismus im unpolitischen, überpolitischen Sinne" (Taut, *Die Stadtkrone*, p. 59); according to his son, Taut never joined a party (Heinrich Taut, "Introduction," in Bruno Taut, *Die neue Baukunst in Europa und Amerika* [Stuttgart, 1979] p. vii [reprint]).

36. *Arbeitsrat für Kunst, Berlin, 1918–1921* (Berlin, 1980), pp. 14–16, 89 (exhibition catalogue).

37. Häring to Carl Lörcher, October 23, 1933, published by Matthias Schirren, "Was ist 'deutsch' Baukunst?," in Peter Hahn and Christian Wolsdorff, eds., *Bauhaus-Berlin* (Berlin, 1985), pp. 272–275. Lörcher had been appointed by the Nazis to reorganize the Werkbund and the *Bund Deutscher Architekten*. Despite Häring's special pleading, the points he made about the Ring do not conflict with other available evidence.

38. Ludwig Mies van der Rohe, "Industrielles Bauen," *G: Zeitschrift für Gestaltung*, no. 3 (June 10, 1924), pp. 8–10. Others besides Mies wrote of the need for inventing new materials for the new architecture: *see* Theo van Doesburg, "Von der neuen Aesthetik zur materiellen Verwirklichung," *De Stijl*, vol. 6, no. 1 (March, 1923), and Walter Gropius, "Wohnhaus-Industrie," in Adolf Meyer, ed., *Ein Versuchshaus des Bauhauses in Weimar*, Bauhausbücher, no. 3 (Munich, 1925), pp. 110–113.

39. The project is a critical reworking of the structural schema of an office building by Hans Poelzig in Breslau in 1911 (ill. in Julius Posener, ed., *Hans Poelzig: Gesammelte Schriften und Werke*, Schriftenreihe der Akademie der Künste, vol. 6 [Berlin, 1970] p. 80) in which the concrete floors also step out from bottom to top in the manner of medieval timber-framed buildings, but without the marked cantilevers of the end bays of Mies's project. The wider spacing of the bay next to the end in Mies's design

functions to distribute and absorb the stresses created by the cantilevers. Thus the forms are determined chiefly by structural and functional considerations, without reference to classical corner arrangements.

40. Theo van Doesburg, "Der Wille zum Stil: Neugestaltung von Leben, Kunst und Technik," *De Stijl*, vol. 2 (February 1922), pp. 23–32; vol. 3 (March 1922), pp. 33–41; Baljeu, *Theo van Doesburg*, p. 122.

41. Mies served as a juror for two housing competitions at this time. One was sponsored by the magazine *Bauwelt* for built-in furnishings of small dwellings (*Bauwelt*, vol. 15, no. 50 [December 13, 1923], p. 695; LC, Private B). The other, "Neue Wege des Wohnbaues," was sponsored by the Brandenburg chapter of the BDA. Among the other jurors were Käthe Kollwitz, Max Pechstein, and Hans Luckhardt (LC, Private B; *Die Baugilde*, vol. 6, no. 1 [January 17, 1924]). Mies, who was elected to the board of directors of the chapter in August 1923, gave a lecture on the topic, "Über neue Wege im Wohnungsbau," at the chapter's meeting on December 12, 1923 (LC, Private B). This was published as "Gelöste Aufgaben: Eine Forderung an unser Bauwesen" ("Fulfilled Tasks: A Challenge to Our Architecture") in *Bauwelt*, vol. 14 (1923), p. 719; and republished in Fritz Neumeyer, *Mies van der Rohe: Das kunstlose Wort, Gedanken zur Baukunst* (Berlin, 1986), pp. 301–303. The lecture was little more than a vague plea for greater functionalism in housing: in it Mies claimed that no modern housing met the needs of the time as well as primitive huts or modern ocean liners fulfilled their requirements, and called for the development of housing from the "organization of living . . . rational economic management . . . and the use of new technical means."

42. Mies van der Rohe, "Entwicklung und Aufbau der Miete," *Die Baugilde*, vol. 6, no. 5 (1924), p. 56. Mies thanked Tropp for the book in a letter of January 11, 1924 (LC, Private T), and wrote a slightly variant manuscript of the review on March 3, 1924 (LC, Private T). The published version reads: "Unter dem Titel 'Entwicklung und Aufbau der Miete' legt Paul Tropp die Resultate einer eingehenden Untersuchung unserer Wohnungswirtschaft in grosser Ausführlichkeit und Klarheit dar. Zum ersten Male wird hier unsere Wohnungswirtschaft von sachverständiger Seite scharf beleuchtet. Tropp zeigt, wie sie ist und wie sie sein könnte. Er setzt sich auseinander mit der bisherigen Wohnungs- und Steuerwirtschaft, mit Einkommen und Miete, mit Kapitaldienst, Bewirtschaftungs- und Instandsetzungskosten, Gestehungskosten und Grundmiete und zieht daraus als Fachmann seine objektiven Folgerungen. Zu begrüssen ist es, dass diese Schrift gerade in dem Augenblick erschienen ist, wo von allen Seiten die grössten Anstrengungen gemacht werden, die Bauwirtschaft wieder anzukurbeln und gleichseitig auf eine gesunde Basis zu stellen. Weil Tropps Arbeit hierzu einen wertwollen Beitrag darstellte, möchte ich diese Schrift allen interessierten Kreisen warm empfehlen."

43. I have been unable to locate a copy of Tropp's book. He summarized his ideas in an article, "Neue Wege der Wohnungswirtschaft," *Deutsche Wirtschaftszeitung*, vol. 21 (August 13, 1924), pp. 562–563, and in *Deutsche Bauhütte*, vol. 28, no. 20 (September 24, 1924), pp. 205–206. The latter was a polemically right-wing and often antimodernist architectural journal.

44. *Sozialdemokratische Partei Deutschlands*. In this essay I have referred to the party members more simply as Socialists.

45. For the discussions and vote on the basic law on rents (*Reichsmietengesetz*) of March 24, 1922 (*Reichsgesetzblatt*, vol. 1, pp. 273–279), see: *Stenographische Berichte des Reichstags*, I Wahlperiode, 1920–24, Bd. 352, Sitzungen 169, 170, 171, 172, 179, February 14–17 and March 3, 1922. Some background is given in Dan P. Silverman, "A Pledge Unredeemed: The Housing Crisis in Weimar Germany," *Central European History*, vol. 2 (1970), pp. 112–139, and Peter-Christian Witt, "Inflation, Wohnungszwangswirtschaft und Hauszinssteuer," in Lutz Niethammer, ed., *Wohnen im Wandel, Beiträge zur Geschichte des Alltags in der bürgerlichen Gesellschaft* (Wuppertal, 1979), pp. 385–407.

46. The tax was not debated in the Reichstag but put into effect directly by the Third Emergency Tax Decree of February 14, 1924 (*Reichsgesetzblatt*, vol. 1, pp. 74–91); it is discussed by Karl-Bernhard Netzband and Hans Peter Widmaier (*Währungs- und Finanzpolitik der Ära Luther 1923–1925*, Veröffentlichungen der List Gesellschaft, Bd. 33 [Basel, 1964], pp. 196–209). *See also* Larry E. Jones, "Inflation, Revaluation, and the Crisis of Middle-Class Politics: A Study of the Dissolution of the German Party System, 1923–28," in *Central European History*, vol. 12 (1979), pp. 143–168. The Socialists and Democrats opposed the tax and favored an increase in property taxes instead, the former because they believed the *Hauszinssteuer* would be a burden on poorer tenants, the latter probably because they thought it would be a greater imposition on house owners, although this point has not been clarified (Netzband and Widmaier, *Währung - und Finanzpolitik*, p. 207). I am most grateful to Larry E. Jones for his help on the DDP and the *Hauszinssteuer*.

47. Manfred Dörr, *Die deutschnationale Volkspartei 1925 bis 1928* (Marburg, 1964), pp. 334–335, discusses the party's attitudes toward landlords, mortgagees, and the housing market.

48. *Bauaufsichtsamt*, Wedding. The plans are dated November 16 and 18, 1925. The client was the Heimstättengesellschaft Primus; construction was carried out in 1926–27 (D. R. Frank and D. Rentschler, eds., *Berlin und seine Bauten*, vol. 4, Wohnungsbau, Bd. A [Berlin, Munich, and Düsseldorf: Architekten- und Ingenieur-Verein zu Berlin, 1970], pp. 268–269; *see also* Fritz Neumeyer, "Neues Bauen im Wedding," in *Der Wedding im Wandel der Zeit* [Berlin, 1985], pp. 26–34).

49. The evidence for this point will be presented by me and Christian Otto in our forthcoming book on the Weissenhof exhibition. Early in 1925, Mies was asked to let his name be put forward for the position of chief architect of Frankfurt-am-Main by Richard Lisker, an architect and teacher at the Kunstgewerbeschule there, and Lilly Reich, the interior designer who soon became Mies's collaborator. But the position was given instead to Ernst May (LC, Private L, Lisker to Mies, February 2 and 28, 1925; and Private F, Lisker to Mies, July 19, 1925).

50. LC, Private F, Farenholtz to Mies, October 10, 1925. Farenholtz wrote on the stationery of the firm of Gustav Hubbe–G. W. Farenholtz Gmbh. I do not know whether Gustav Hubbe was related to Frau Margarete Hubbe of Magdeburg, who is said to have met Mies in the fall of 1926 and who commissioned the 1935 project for the Hubbe House (Wolf Tegethoff, *Mies van der Rohe: The Villas and Country Houses* [New York, 1985],

51. Taut was elected *Stadtbaurat* of Magdeburg in 1921 with the Socialists voting for him and the other parties for a rival candidate; he held the position until he resigned in January 1924; *see: Deutsche Bauzeitung*, vol. 55, no. 24 (1921), p. 116; Christian Borngräber, "Bruno Taut a Magdeburgo e Otto Haesler a Celle," *Casabella*, nos. 463–464 (November–December 1980), pp. 42–45.

52. LC, Private F, Mies to Farenholtz, November 14, 1925. I have not been able to determine who succeeded Taut in the position.

53. LC, Private F, Mies to Farenholtz, December 7, 1925: "Ich selbst würde nie daran gedacht haben ein solches Amt zu übernehmen, wenn mir nicht daran liegen müsste einer neuen Baugesinnung an irgend einer Stelle Heimatsrecht zu erwerben, denn ich wüsste nicht, aus welch anderem Grunde ich meine freie künstlerische und um ein vielfaches bessere materielle Position aufgeben sollte. Da ich mich meiner Arbeit ganz bestimmte geistig-politische Ziele verfolge, so ist es für mich nicht schwer, eine Entscheidung darüber zu treffen, ob ich ein solches Amt annehmen kann oder nicht. Besteht nicht die Möglichkeit, an einer solchen Stelle meinem Arbeitsziel näherzukommen, so muss ich darauf verzichten dort tätig zu sein; deshalb muss Magdeburg sich entscheiden, ob man dieses Amt einem Routinier oder einem geistigen Menschen anvertrauen will."

54. Rolf-Peter Baacke and Michael Nungesser, "Ich bin, ich war, ich werde sein!," *Wem gehört die Welt—Kunst und Gesellschaft in der Weimarer Republik* (Berlin: Neue Gesellschaft für bildende Kunst, 1977), pp. 280–298 (exhibition catalogue). MoMA, Small Projects Folder 4C, Fuchs to Mies, March 24, 1926, reporting that the committee for the monument had asked that the project be ready for unveiling on June 13, Rosa Luxemburg's birthday, and asking for a final inspection of "all models" as soon as possible.

55. Egbert, "Socialism and American Art," pp. 661–662. The letter, undated in Egbert's publication, was written February 6, 1951; I am grateful to Egbert's widow, Mrs. W. S. Kilborne, for a copy of it. Mies claimed to have known Liebknecht as a neighbor in Paris (Oral History Research Office, Columbia University).

56. Gropius, letter of August 1, 1968, in Reginald Isaacs, *Walter Gropius, Der Mensch und sein Werk*, vol. 1 (Berlin, 1983), p. 465. In a letter to Egbert of October 14, 1948 (Egbert papers, as in n. 55 above), Gropius wrote: "The concrete memorial which I designed in Weimar was not designed for working men but for very various people of different circles of the population who fell in the upheaval of the *kapputsch* [*Kapp Putsch*]. It was ordered by a *staatsrat* in the Weimar Ministry who was a social democrat." But the monument was inscribed: *Den Märzgefallenen—1920— Die Arbeiterschaft Weimars*, and paid for by workers (Baacke and Nungesser, *Wem gehört die Welt; see also* Adalbert Behr, "Das Denkmal für die Märzgefallenen in Weimar," *Wissenschaftliche Zeitschrift der Hochschule für Architektur und Bauwesen Weimar*, vol. 14 [1967], pp. 459–464; and Emil Friedrich, "Aus bewegter Zeit," from the pamphlet published for the dedication of the monument [BA, GN 22/279–281].

57. Interview with Lisa Dechêne during Mies's visit to Aachen in 1968 (*Deutsche Volkszeitung* [September 5, 1969]; cited by Baacke and Nungesser, *Wem gehört die Welt*, p. 287).

58. Peter Blake (*The Master Builders* [New York, 1960], p. 184), gives a report with somewhat different implications: "Mies felt then (and feels today) that these two Communist leaders held honest convictions and lived according to them. He was not particularly interested in their party allegiances; he was interested only in their moral caliber. When they were assassinated by extremists of the Right, Mies felt honored to be chosen to build their monument. . . ." This was written shortly after the U.S. State Department had investigated Mies because of his work on the monument, and cleared him to receive a commission for a consulate building, according to Blake.

59. On the right and left wings of the DDP, *see* Bruce B. Frye, *Liberal Democrats in the Weimar Republic: The History of the German Democratic Party and the German State Party* (Carbondale-Edwardsville, Illinois, 1985), pp. 87–117.

60. Werner Schneider, *Die Deutsche Demokratische Partei in der Weimarer Republik, 1924–1930* (Munich, 1978), p. 45.

61. Ibid., 49ff.; Frye, *Liberal Democrats*, pp. 2–3, 87–117.

62. Schneider, *Die Deutsche Demokratische Partei*, p. 57.

63. The vote in the DDP for basic law on rents of March 3, 1922 (*see above*, n. 45), was six in favor, nineteen against, and eight absent.

64. I use the term "cultural reform" as developed by Joan Campbell in her study of the Werkbund (*see above*, n. 5) to mean a set of aesthetic and ethical policies, in order to distinguish it from the *Kulturpolitik* of the DDP, which was specifically concerned with educational policy.

65. Fritz Hesse, *Von der Residenz zur Bauhausstadt* (Bad Pyrmont [1963]), pp. 194, 196, 218. Dieter Rebentisch, *Ludwig Landmann, Frankfurter Oberbürgermeister der Weimarer Republik*, Frankfurter Historische Abhandlungen, vol. 10 (Wiesbaden, 1975).

66. Adolf Hofacker, representative of the DDP on the building committee of the city council (Stadtarchiv, Stuttgart, CIV A12 Bd46, 116.21, October 16, 1925; 116.28, November 12, 1925; 116.29, October 29, 1925). The political affiliations at this time of Gustav Stotz, the leader of the local chapter of the Werkbund and the main figure behind the exhibition, are not clear, but in a fragmentary and undated transcript of a letter, Stotz wrote to Mies: "Es liegt mir daran, dass den verständnislosen Kritikern der neueren Kultur gezeigt wird, dass die moderne Kunst und Architektur mit Politik direkt nichts zu tun haben, dass die sachlich einwandfreien Leistungen auf diesen Gebiet nicht in Feldwebelton abgetan werden könnten" (MoMA, Correspondence II, 262, transcript made by Ludwig Glaeser of documents in LC and MoMA; I could not locate the original).

67. These included Peter Bruckmann, president of the Werkbund during much of the late 1920s; Theodor Heuss, its most effective publicist; Robert Bosch, the Stuttgart industrialist; and Ernst Jäckh, an important Werkbund executive. *See* Campbell, *German Werkbund*, pp. 110–111.

68. Hesse, *Von der Residenz zur Bauhausstadt*; Rebentisch, *Ludwig Landmann*, p. 304, citing a letter of Landmann's to May of November 1, 1935; Hofacker (*see* n. 66).

69. Stadtarchiv, Stuttgart, CIV A12 Bd. 46, 116, meetings of the Building Committee of the City Council from October 1925 to October 1927; Karl Heinz Hüter, *Das Bauhaus in Weimar* (Berlin, 1976), p. 247; Hesse, *Von der Residenz zur Bauhausstadt*, p. 254.

70. Behne to Gropius, February 5, 1920, *Arbeitsrat für Kunst*, p. 124. His membership in the SPD was attested to by

his widow; *see* Marcel Franciscono, *Walter Gropius and the Creation of the Bauhaus in Weimar* (Urbana, 1971), n. 52.

71. *See* Gropius's letters in Hüter, *Das Bauhaus,* pp. 220–221, 229, and Claude Schnaidt, *Hannes Meyer* (Teufen, 1965), pp. 220–222.

72. *See above,* n. 35.

73. Wagner wrote to Paul Schmitthenner, a member of the Nazi Party, on June 10, 1934: "Obgleich ich selbst—wie Sie—Sozialist war und es auch heute noch bin, hätte ich an sich nicht die geringste Veranlassung, den 'offiziellen' Sozialismus zu verteidigen zumal ich mich von ihm in offenen Kämpfe und zu einer Zeit losgesagt habe." (BA, 13/100–108 [copy]).

74. Rebentisch, *Ludwig Landmann,* p. 133. May, who had been influenced by the Fabian socialists, joined the SDP after his selection as chief architect of Frankfurt in 1925; the SDP was the dominant party in the coalition that ran the city.

The politics of Otto Haesler, who built low-income housing projects in Celle and other towns, are not known; he makes no mention of them in his autobiography, written after the war in East Germany (*Mein Lebenswerk als Architekt* [Berlin, 1957]). His two early modernist housing projects in Celle, *Siedlung Italienischer Garten,* of 1924–25, and *Siedlung Georgsgarten,* of 1926–27, were built for a building society founded by a member of the right-wing DNVP, who sat with Haesler on the three-man board of directors. Haesler's later *Siedlung Rothenberg* in Kassel and *Siedlung Blumlagerfeld* in Celle were supported by coalitions of left-wing and middle-class representatives in the city governments (Angela Schumacher, *Otto Haesler und der Wohnungsbau in der Weimarer Republik* [Marburg, 1928]).

75. He wrote regularly for the revisionist *Sozialistische Monatshefte* during the 1920s, and was described in 1930 by Hannes Meyer, the Communist director of the Bauhaus, as "the Socialist architect, Ludwig Hilberseimer" (H. M. Wingler, ed., *The Bauhaus* [Cambridge, 1969], p. 164). *See* Richard Pommer, "More a Necropolis than a Metropolis: Ludwig Hilberseimer's Highrise City and Modern City Planning," in *Ludwig Hilberseimer, Architect, Educator and Urban Planner* (Chicago, 1988), pp. 16–53, esp. n. 13.

76. *See* p. 116.

77. Neumeyer, *Mies van der Rohe,* pp. 203–219, 311–316, dates the shift in Mies's approach to early 1926, as documented by an unpublished lecture, and ascribes it to the influence of Mies's friend, the architect Rudolf Schwarz.

78. *Bau und Wohnung* (Stuttgart: Deutsche Werkbund, 1927), p. 7.

79. "Vorläufiger Plan zur Durchführung der Werkbundausstellung 'Die Wohnung,'" June 27, 1925. Stuttgart Stadtarchiv, CIV A12 Bd46, 116, 3; "Wohnung der Neuzeit: Plan einer Werkbund-Veranstaltung in Stuttgart 1927," undated. MoMA 1/1/B; "Werkbundausstellung 'Die Wohnung,' Stuttgart 1927," MoMA 1/1/C.

80. On these expectations, *see: Die Bedeutung der Rationalisierung für das deutsche Wirtschaftsleben* (Berlin, 1928), especially the articles by F. Demuth and Julius Hirsch.

81. M. J. Bonn, "The Paradox of Rationalization," *Transactions of the Manchester Statistical Society* (1933–34), pp. 1–17. Otto Bauer, *Kapitalismus und Sozialismus nach dem Weltkrieg, I: Rationalisierung und Fehlrationalisierung* (Vienna, 1931).

82. Richard Ehrenberg, "Anfänge und Ziele industrieller deutscher Normalisierung," *Archiv für exakte Wirtschaftsforschung,* vol. 7 (1916), pp. 119–170.

83. Bruno Rauecker, "Die soziale Bedeutung der Rationalisierung," *Reichsarbeitsblatt* (Nichtamtlicherteil), N.F. VI (1926), pp. 267–273. Rauecker was an important figure in the left wing of the DDP: Frye, *Liberal Democrats,* p. 97.

84. D. Petzina, "Grundriss der deutschen Wirtschaftsgeschichte 1914 bis 1945," in *Deutsche Geschichte seit dem I Weltkrieg,* vol. 2 (Stuttgart, 1973), pp. 663ff.

85. W. Link, "Der amerikanische Einfluss auf die Weimarer Republik in der Dawes Plan Phase," in H. Mommsen et al., *Industrielles System und Politische Entwicklung in der Weimarer Republik* (Düsseldorf, 1974), pp. 485ff.

86. Barbara Miller Lane, *Architecture and Politics in Germany, 1918–1945* (Cambridge, Mass., 1968), pp. 135–138.

87. *Der deutsche Wohnungsbau,* Verhandlung und Berichte des Unterausschusses für Gewerbe, Industrie, Handel und Handwerk (III Unterausschuss) (Berlin, 1931), p. 25, report of an investigatory committee; p. 585, deposition by Gropius. Karel Teige, "Die Wohnungsfrage der Schichten des Existenz-Minimums," *Rationelle Bebauungsweisen* (III Internationale Kongresse für neues Bauen, Brussels, 1930) (Frankfurt-am-Main, 1931), pp. 64–70; Silverman, "Pledge Unredeemed," pp. 134–135. May's experiment with concrete plate construction was more expensive than brick construction: *Bericht über die Versuchssiedlung im Frankfurt a.M. Praunheim,* Reichsforschungsgesellschaft für Wirtschaftlichkeit im Bau- und Wohnungswesen, vol. 4 (April 1929), p. 101.

88. The lecture is in LC, Container 61. Except for Mies's comments on a few slides, it is the same as the lecture, "Die Voraussetzungen baukünstlerischen Schaffens," given by Mies in February and March 1928 in Berlin and elsewhere and published by Neumeyer from a manuscript in the collection of Dirk Lohan (Neumeyer, *Mies van der Rohe,* pp. 362–366). It contains numerous references to Mies's notes in MoMA, Manuscripts, Folder 7, which have now been published in Neumeyer, *Mies van der Rohe,* pp. 328–359.

89. The text of the lecture leaves space for these slides, but the names of the architects and some of their buildings appear only in the handwritten notes without specific indication that they were intended for the lecture; Neumeyer does not publish or discuss these lists.

90. He had stressed the importance of "life" as the ideal and measure of the new architecture in his dispute with Walter Riezler in *Die Form,* vol. 2, no. 1 (1927), p. 1; and no. 2 (1927), p. 59.

91. Romano Guardini, *Briefe vom Comer See* (Mainz, 1927), was published as "Briefe aus Italien" in 1923–25 in *Die Schildgenossen,* and republished as *Die Technik und der Mensch* (Mainz, 1981). Mies owned seven of Guardini's books and pamphlets published between 1921 and 1927 (UIC). Among them is *Briefe vom Comer See,* which Mies excerpted extensively in the notes in MoMA for his lecture. According to Neumeyer (*Mies van der Rohe,* p. 250), Mies almost certainly met Guardini by 1925. On Guardini see Hanna-Barbara Gerl, *Romano Guardini 1885–1968: Leben und Werk* (Mainz, 1985); Helmut Kuhn, *Romano Guardini: Der Mensch und das Werk* (Munich, n.d.). Although Guardini appears to have been overtly apolitical, the Quickborn youth movement at Burg Rothenfels of which he was a leader was notoriously antiliberal and antidemocratic: Heinrich Lutz, *Demokratie im Zwielicht: Der Weg der deutschen Katholiken aus dem Kaiserreich in die Republik 1914–1925* (Munich, 1963), pp. 114–116; Gerl, *Romano Guardini,* pp. 199–201. Rudolf Schwarz, the Catholic

140

church architect, who held ideas similar to Guardini's and who became a close friend of Mies, was also an important member of this movement from the early 1920s: Neumeyer, *Mies van der Rohe,* pp. 209ff.; Maria Becker, *Rudolf Schwarz 1897–1961: Kirchenarchitektur* (Diss., Technische Universität, Munich, 1979), pp. 70ff.

92. Friedrich Dessauer, *Streit um die Technik* 2nd ed. (Frankfurt-am-Main, 1958), with extensive bibliography, pp. 439–457. Idem, "Gedanken über Technik, Kultur und Kunst," *Hochland,* vol. 6, no. 2 (1907), pp. 47–61, 189–201. Ulrich Wendt, *Die Technik als Kulturmacht in sozialer und in geistiger Beziehung* (Berlin, 1906). Eberhard Zschimmer, *Philosophie der Technik: Vom Sinn der Technik und Kritik des Unsinn über die Technik* (Jena, 1914). Viktor Engelhardt, *Weltanschauung und Technik* (Leipzig, 1922). Jeffrey Herf, *Reactionary Modernism: Technology, Culture, and Politics in Weimar and the Third Reich* (Cambridge, 1984). Mies's notes for the lecture (*see above,* n. 88) also include references and excerpts from Friedrich Dessauer, *Philosophie der Technik* (Bonn, 1927), the most comprehensive book on the subject at the time, and Leopold Ziegler, *Zwischen Mensch und Wirtschaft* (Darmstadt, 1927). Mies's copies of these books, heavily underlined and annotated, are in the collection of Dirk Lohan.

93. The title of the *Jahrbuch des Deutschen Werkbundes,* vol. 1, of 1912, was "Die Durchgeistigung der deutschen Arbeit." Muthesius in his article "Wo stehen Wir?," *Jahrbuch des Deutschen Werkbundes,* vol. 1 (1912), pp. 11–20, argued for this spiritualization, but meant by this chiefly the introduction of artistic form.

94. Ernst Rudorff, "Über das Verhältnis des modernen Lebens zur Natur," *Preussische Jahrbücher,* vol. 45 (1880), pp. 261–276; Christian Otto, "Modern Environment and Historical Continuity: The Heimatschutz Discourse in Germany," *Art Journal,* vol. 43, no. 2 (1983), pp. 148–157.

95. Perhaps for this reason, Guardini is not mentioned in Dessauer's comprehensive study of the *Philosophie der Technik* in his *Streit um die Technik.*

96. *See below,* n. 231, for Mies's discussion of spatial freedom and opening to nature in his architecture in the early 1930s.

97. For example, the drawings for the Esters House in Krefeld of late 1927, and especially those for the Tugendhat House and the Krefeld Golf Club: *see* Tegethoff, *Villas and Country Houses,* pls. 7.2, 7.3, 11.6, 11.7 (which may be by Mies's shop), 13.2, 13.3. An early project for the golf club, with a circular glazed pavilion atop a small hill, offered the greatest freedom in, and concord with, nature through the agency of modern technology in Mies's work prior to the Farnsworth House: *see* Tegethoff, *Villas and Country Houses,* pp. 105–106. Mies's drawings in MoMA from his German years have now been catalogued and many of them reproduced in Arthur Drexler, ed., *The Mies van der Rohe Archive: Part I, 1910–1937,* 4 vols. (New York and London, 1986).

98. "Il est à sa juste place dans l'agreste paysage de Poissy." Of his project to transplant twenty Poissys to a rural field in Argentina, Le Corbusier wrote that the inhabitants would thus be "inserée dans un rêve virgilien" (Le Corbusier, *Precisions sur un État present de l'Architecture et de l'Urbanisme* [Paris, 1930], p. 133).

99. The philosophical background of Mies's balancing of polar oppositions is traced by Neumeyer (*Mies van der Rohe,* pp. 251ff.) to Guardini's book, *Der Gegensatz: Versuche zu einer Philosophie des Lebendig-Konkreten* (Mainz, 1925).

100. Georg von Schnitzler, quoted in L. S. M. [Lilly von Schnitzler], "Die Weltausstellung Barcelona 1929," *Der Querschnitt,* vol. 9, no. 8 (1929), p. 583.

101. The documents are discussed in Tegethoff, *Villas and Country Houses,* pp. 69–89. The Werkbund announced at a meeting of its directors on July 5, 1928, that Mies as artistic director was responsible for "the design of the various German sections and the creation of a German ceremonial space [*Repräsentationsraum*]" (ibid., p. 73, n. 17). Mies told an interviewer in 1966 (*Bauwelt Archiv*), that in meetings about the purpose of the Pavilion "it was concluded that it should only be a representation space without any special purpose. It should not contain any exhibit objects, nothing." Ludwig Glaeser has suggested that the combination of black, red, and gold colors in the ceremonial area of the Pavilion "may have had a symbolic reference to the colors of the German Republic" (*Mies van der Rohe: The Barcelona Pavilion, 50th Anniversary* [New York, 1979]).

102. MoMA, Later German Projects, Folders 6 and 7; Martin Kiessling in *Die Neue Wache als Gedächtnisstätte für die Gefall-*enen des Weltkrieges (Berlin, 1931); *Bauwelt,* vol. 21 (1930), pp. 986–987; Walter Curt Behrendt in *Zentralblatt der Bauverwaltung,* vol. 50 (1930), pp. 513–518. Mies was invited to take part in the competition on April 30, 1930; the jury made its decision on July 15; and the rebuilt monument was dedicated June 2, 1931 (MoMA, Later German Projects, Folder 6).

103. Otto Braun, *Von Weimar zu Hitler* (New York, 1940), pp. 333–335; Kiessling, *Die Neue Wache,* p. 10.

104. Braun wrote that the government reached its decision on March 27, 1931; but the competition for the Neue Wache was held in 1930.

105. MoMA, Later German Projects, Folder 7A, *Wettbewerbsprogramm.*

106. Kiessling, *Die Neue Wache,* p. 10.

107. "Tessenow baut das Berliner Ehrenmal," *Frankfurter Zeitung* (July 28, 1930). Another writer noted that the absence of inscriptions may have been in part a reaction to the long controversy between the Kaiser and left-wing politicians before the war over the inscription on the Reichstag—*Dem deutschen Volke*—which had been executed by Behrens: P. [Friedrich Paulsen], *Bauwelt,* vol. 21, no. 31 (1930), p. 987; Heinz Raack, *Das Reichstagsgebäude in Berlin* (Berlin, 1978), p. 43.

108. "Vom Votivraum der Gegenwart," *Deutsche Bauhütte,* vol. 34 (1930), p. 252: "Wenn dies zu spät errichtete Ehrenmal wirklich noch volkstümlich werden will, so muss es in Glyphen und Zeichen die Grösse des Ereignisses sichtbar machen, um die Schwere des gebrachten Opfers nachdenklich einzuprägen."

109. The other juror from the art world was Wilhelm Waetzold, director of the Prussian museums, whose position on the *Neue Bauen* is not known to me.

110. Only architects from the capital were invited because this was to be a Berlin memorial; the sixth architect was Hans Grube, a ministry official. Mies had gone out of his way to invite Tessenow to participate in the Weissenhof exhibition, but Tessenow withdrew: MoMA, Weissenhof, 4/2/D, Gustav Stotz to Mies, September 24, 1925; 6/1/F, Tessenow to Mies, September 6, 1926. On Tessenow's later opposition to the Ring, *see* Gerda Wangerin and Gerhard Weiss, *Heinrich Tessenow: Ein Baumeister 1876–1950* (Essen, 1976), p. 47. Blunck was a founder of the Block, which was formed in 1928 to counter the Ring.

111. The requirement of an atrium was waived by the jury: MoMA, Later German Projects, Folder 7A, *Wettbewerbsprogramm;* Folder 6, *Niederschrift der Sitzung des Begutachterausschusses;* Folder 7B, *Erläuterungsbericht.*

112. For a competition of 1910 for Bingen on the Rhine, illustrated in Franz Schulze, *Mies van der Rohe: A Critical Biography* (Chicago and London, 1985), p. 50.

113. MoMA, Later German Projects, Folder 6, *Niederschrift der Sitzung.* The third prize went to Poelzig.

114. The program was known as the *Reichsforschungsgesellschaft für Wirtschaftlichkeit im Bau- und Wohnungswesen* (RFG). It was initiated by Marie-Elisabeth Lüders; *see* her *Fürchte Dich Nicht: Persönliches und Politisches aus mehr als 80 Jahren* (Cologne, 1963), and BAK, Bd. 48, Lüders to E. Weber, April 4, 1928. *See also* E. Weber, "Die Aufgaben der RFG," *RFG Mitteilungen* (June 12, 1928).

115. Stadtarchiv, Stuttgart, CIV Bd. 2, 12, no. 11; BAK, Bd. 50, Lüders Nachlass, letters of February and March 1927.

116. Stadtarchiv, Stuttgart, CIV B5 Bd. 1, 2, no. 32. *Sitzung der Unterkommission des Hauptausschusses,* extract from the minutes. Report by Stotz on the renewal of negotiations with May for the construction of the concrete plate house at May's expense. The house is illustrated in Heinz and Bodo Rasch, *Wie Bauen?* (Stuttgart, 1927), pp. 50–51; and idem, in *Architecture et Urbanisme (L'Émulation),* vol. 68, no. 11 (November 1928), p. 74. According to the Rasch brothers, the house, which was intended for completion in two days, took ten.

117. Compare Gropius's project of 1926 for Törten with his plan of 1929 for the *Dammerstock Siedlung* in Karlsruhe, and May's project of 1926 for Praunheim and Römerstadt with his design of 1928 for the third section of Praunheim, in Liselotte Ungers, *Die Suche nach einer neuen Wohnform* (Stuttgart, 1983), pp. 81, 89, 121, 130.

118. Paris, Fondation Le Corbusier, Societé des Nations, EI-20: Mies to Le Corbusier, February 1, 1929: "Besonders in Deutschland, im Lande der Organisatoren, scheint es mir notwendig, mit aller Deutlichkeit zu betonen, dass Baukunst etwas anders ist, als nackte Zweckerfüllung. In Deutschland wird der Kampf gegen die Rationalisten schwerer sein, als gegen die Akademiker." Le Corbusier expressed similar but more general sentiments in a letter of June 10, 1931, to Alberto Sartoris, published in Sartoris's *Gli Elementi dell' Architettura funzionale* (Milan, 1932).

119. Schnaidt, *Hannes Meyer,* pp. 40–41. Meyer's political view of architecture emerges most clearly in his essay, "Über marxistische Architektur," written while he was in Russia in the 1930s and published in Lena Meyer-Berner, ed., *Hannes Meyer: Bauten und Gesellschaft* (Dresden, 1980), pp. 92–99.

120. Wingler, *Bauhaus,* pp. 169–171; Schnaidt, *Hannes Meyer,* pp. 121–123.

121. Hahn and Wolsdorff, *Bauhaus-Berlin,* pp. 47–53.

122. When the German League for Independent Film (*Deutsche Liga für unabhängigen Film*) was organized late in the spring of 1930, Mies joined as a member of its board of directors, along with his friends Hans Richter and Werner Graeff (LC, *Deutsche Liga für unabhängigen Film,* 1930–32). An offshoot of the International League for Independent Film, formed in 1929, the German group sought to defend avant-garde film production from capitalist exploitation and *Verkitschung.* Richter, who had close ties to Russian filmmakers, was the leader of the German group; the international organization was founded with the support of such well-known Communist writers and actors as Bertolt Brecht and Béla Balász (Hofacker, "Biographische Notizen," p. 97; Willett, *Art and Politics,* pp. 148, 214).

123. *The New York Times,* August 9, 1931, reprinted in Philip Johnson, *Writings* (New York, 1979), pp. 48–51; *see also* Wilhelm Lotz, "Die Halle II auf der Bauausstellung," *Die Form,* vol. 6 (1931), pp. 241–249.

124. Karel Teige, *Nejmensi Byt* [*The Minimal Dwelling*] (Prague, 1932), p. 182. Teige's discussion of Mies's house concludes: "The areas within the house are not enclosed but merge as in a labyrinth. The skeleton of the houses stands completely free, the steel frames [of the glass plates] and the supports are nickel-alloy. It is play, not architecture; luxury and snobbism, not a habitation." (Translations from the Czech by Irena Drobny.) Taut wrote: "Mies's house . . . is certainly very 'beautiful,' even paradisiacally beautiful; it is the house of the Superman, the 'blond beast,' to cite Nietzsche loosely, of the completely isolated individual being, the individual as such" (Bruno Taut, "Deutsche Bauausstellung Berlin 1931," *Bauwelt,* vol. 63, no. 33 [1977], p. 1110 [originally written for *Isvestia*]). The left countered with a *Proletarische Bauausstellung,* which dwelt on the causes of the failures in city planning and emphasized highrise buildings (ibid., p. 1109); an important role in it was taken by the Berlin architect, Arthur Korn, a leading member of the *Kollektiv für sozialistisches Bauen* (Martin Steinmann, *CIAM, Dokument 1928–1939,* Institut für Geschichte und Theorie der Architektur an der Eidgenössischen Technischen Hochschule Zürich, Schriftenreihe Bd. 11 [Basel and Stuttgart, 1979], p. 116).

125. Walter Riezler, "Das Haus Tugendhat in Brünn," *Die Form,* vol. 6 (1931), pp. 321–332.

126. Roger Ginsburger, "Zweckhaftigkeit und geistige Haltung," *Die Form,* vol. 6 (1931), pp. 431–434, with Riezler's rejoinder, pp. 435–437.

127. Sibyl Moholy-Nagy, in *Journal of the Society of Architectural Historians,* vol. 24 (1965), pp. 24–25, 80–84. Howard Dearstyne, who had been a pupil of Mies's at the Bauhaus, offered a rebuttal, ibid., pp. 254–255, and Moholy-Nagy a rejoinder, ibid., pp. 255–256. An article by Elaine Hochman, "Confrontation: 1933—Mies van der Rohe and the Third Reich," *Oppositions,* no. 18 (Fall 1979), pp. 49–59, is based almost entirely on long-known published sources and contributes little to an understanding of the complexities and ambiguities of these issues. Her more recent note, "The Politics of Mies van der Rohe," *Sites,* no. 15 (1986), pp. 44–49, adds little more other than material from Schulze, *Critical Biography.*

128. Philip Johnson, "Architecture in the Third Reich," *Hound and Horn,* vol. 7 (October–December 1933), pp. 137–139, reprinted in Johnson, *Writings,* pp. 52–54.

129. Hildegarde Brenner, "Art in the Political Power Struggle of 1933 and 1934," in Hajo Holborn, ed., *Republic to Reich, The Making of the Nazi Revolution* (New York, 1972), pp. 395–432.

130. Ibid., pp. 403–407.

131. At Ley's request, Goebbels appointed one of his own art experts, Hans Weidemann, as director of the section, and he in turn had Schreiber organize it: ibid., p. 410. The policies of Ley and his organizations in the patronage of architecture have yet to be clarified.

132. Ibid., n. 44.

133. Wolfgang Burde, "Neue Musik im Dritten Reich," in *Kunst Hochschule Faschismus* (Berlin, 1984), pp. 49–59.

134. Pius E. Pahl, "Experiences of an Architectural Student," *Bauhaus and Bauhaus People,* ed. Eckhard Neumann (New York, 1970), p. 231. This probably took place in the late fall of 1933: the *Reichskulturkammer* was created on September 22, 1933, and Pahl implies that this announcement was made before the end of fall. Hönig, who worked in Muthesius's office before the war alongside Martin Wagner, was looked upon by the modernists as closer to their cause than other Nazi functionaries: *see* Walter Scheiffele, "Das neue Bauen unter dem Faschismus: Aus dem Briefwechsel von Walter Gropius 1933–1936," *Kunst Hochschule Faschismus* (Berlin, 1984), p. 241.

135. "Brief aus München," *Das Werk,* vol. 20 (August 1933), p. xxxv.

136. Like all architects who wished to work in Nazi Germany, Mies joined the *Reichskammer der bildenden Künste* (BDC, letter of September 14, 1935, from the president of the RdbK to Mies, noting that Mies had to pay dues from December 15, 1933). Mies had earlier been a member of the Loan and Grants Committee of the *Reichsverband der bildenden Künstler,* which was absorbed into the *Reichskartell der bildenden Künste* (LC, Private R, letter of the president of the *Reichskartell* to Mies, August 1, 1933), but I was not able to learn anything about the function of these organizations.

137. LC, Private R.

138. LC, Private N.

139. Hildegarde Brenner, *Ende einer bürgerlichen Kunst-Institution,* Schriftenreihe der Vierteljahrshefte für Zeitgeschichte, vol. 24 (Stuttgart, 1972), p. 147.

140. Ibid., p. 125. Wagner, Mebes, Schmidt-Rottluff, and Otto Dix did leave at that time.

141. Ludwig Mies van der Rohe, "The End of the Bauhaus," *Student Publication, School of Design, North Carolina State College,* vol. 3 (April, 1953), pp. 16–18. Wingler, *Bauhaus,* pp. 194–196; Hahn and Wolsdorff, *Bauhaus-Berlin,* pp. 129–156.

142. Pahl, "Experiences of an Architectural Student," p. 2.

143. Mies van der Rohe, "The End of the Bauhaus," p. 18.

144. Johnson wrote in his article of 1933 (*see* n. 128): "Mies is respected by the conservatives. Even the *Kampfbund für deutsche Kultur* has nothing against him." Mies owned copies of Alfred Rosenberg, *Der Mythus des 20. Jahrhunderts* (Munich, 1932) and *Revolution in der bildenden Kunst?* (Munich, 1934) (UIC).

145. Hahn and Wohlsdorff, *Bauhaus-Berlin,* pp. 147–148. The petition appeared in the *Völkischer Beobachter,* the Nazi Party newspaper, on August 18, 1934. Among the other signers were Ernst Barlach, Erich Heckel, Georg Kolbe, Emil Nolde, Wilhelm Furtwängler, Richard Strauss, and Paul Schultze-Naumburg, a leader of the *Heimatschutz* movement who had played a major role in closing down the Bauhaus in Dessau.

146. On the competition, *see* Winfried Nerdinger, "Versuchung und Dilemma der Avantgarde im Spiegel der Architekturwettbewerbe 1933–1935," in Hartmut Frank, ed., *Faschistische Architekturen, Planen und Bauen in Europa 1930 bis 1945* (Hamburg, 1985), pp. 65–87, esp. pp. 66–73. The material on Mies's participation is in MoMA, Reichsbank.

147. Philipp Nitze, "Grundsätzliches zum Reichsbank-Wettbewerb," *Deutsche Bauzeitung,* vol. 67, no. 31 (1933), pp. 605–606. A list of the architects is in MoMA, Reichsbank, Folder 1, with a covering letter of February 10, 1933.

148. J. Tiedemann, "Wie wird die neue Reichshauptbank aussehen," *Völkischer Beobachter,* July 20, 1933: "Es ist unverständlich, heute wie damals, dass Namen wie Haesler-Celle, Gropius, Fahrenkamp, Poelzig, Mies van der Rohe und noch andere zu den Auserwählten für diesen aussergewöhnlichen Wettbewerb herangezogen werden konnten." More rabid is Lyonel Wehner, "Marxismus, Reichsbankneubau, Werkbund," *Der Reichsbote* (April 19, 1933) (BA, *Wettbewerb Reichsbank,* 1933).

149. *Bauwelt,* vol. 24 (1933), p. 1011.

150. For example, Kurt Frick and Pinno and Grund; *see below,* n. 156. Ludwig Ruff of Nuremberg, although not a party member, probably was also chosen as a sop to Hitler, who soon favored him with major commissions; *see below,* n. 186.

151. Erich Mendelsohn, *Briefe eines Architekten* (Munich, 1961), pp. 94–95, letter of February 11, 1933.

152. Nitze, "Grundsätzliches." Gropius, in a letter to Richard Döcker of June 17, 1933: "Die endgültige Sitzung mit den Reichsbanksdirektorium ist, da Schacht dauernd abwesend ist, zurückgestellt worden. Schacht hat sich vorbehalten, die Kuverts selbst zu öffnen" (Akademie der Künste, Berlin, Döcker Archive). I wish to thank Frau Cornelia Mirabelle Korfsmeier-Döcker and Dr. Achim Wendschuh, of the Akademie, for permission to quote from this material. Schacht was in fact due to sit at the final meeting but could not do so; instead, the vice president and board of directors of the Finance Ministry attended the meeting (MoMA, Reichsbank, Folder 2, "Pressnotiz . . . 8 Juli (1933)."

153. MoMA, Reichsbank, Folder 2, April 13, 1933. Nerdinger, "*Versuchung und Dilemma,*" p. 67, incorrectly states that Wagner was kept on as a juror; he was replaced by the Berlin *Stadtbaurat* Benno Kühn.

154. MoMA Reichsbank, Folder 1, Heinrich Wolff to Mies, March 3, 1933, inviting architects to visit the site; Folder 2, Mies to the *Reichsbank-Direktorium,* May 3, 1933, saying he had sent his project today.

155. The six projects and the jury's statements about them are reproduced in *Die Baugilde,* vol. 15 (1933), p. 716; other entries are illustrated in *Deutsche Bauzeitung,* vol. 67 (1933), pp. 607–614, 627–634. The six architects each received 4,000 marks in addition to the 5,000 marks given to each of the original competitors.

156. Tiedemann, *Die neue Reichshauptbank.*

157. *See* his competition project for the broadcasting center in Berlin and *Reichsgedankhaus* in Schneidemühl, both of 1928: *Paul Bonatz 1877–1956,* Stuttgarter Beiträge, vol. 13 (Stuttgart, 1977), pp. 67–68.

158. Edina Meyer, *Paul Mebes, Miethausbau in Berlin 1906–1938* (Berlin, 1972).

159. Nerdinger, "*Versuchung und Dilemma.*" The Reichsbank competition was particularly confused: Nitze ("Grundsätzliches") pointed out that the competitors were left in the dark about the best orientation of the building, the position of the entrance, and the development of an entrance plaza; yet the jury gave primacy to urbanistic considerations.

160. Heinrich Wolff, "Der Erweiterungsbau der Reichshauptbank," *Wasmuths Monatshefte für Baukunst,* vol. 21 (1937), p. 291, says Hitler ordered the construction of his project "aus städtebaulichen und architektonischen Gesichtspunkten." On the extant building, *see: Berlin und seine Bauten,* vol. 9 (Berlin: Architekten-und Ingenieur Verein zu Berlin, 1971), pp. 228–230.

161. Sergius Ruegenberg, "Ludwig Mies van der Rohe," *Deutsche Bauzeitung,* no. 103 (1969), p. 66. However, according to his own resume and a letter of recommendation from Mies in Ruegenberg's pos-

session, he did not work for Mies after 1931.

162. Johnson, "Architecture in the Third Reich," pp. 53–54.

163. Kenneth Frampton, *Modern Architecture: A Critical History* (New York and Toronto, 1980), p. 231.

164. Robert R. Taylor, *The Word in Stone: The Role of Architecture in the National Socialist Ideology* (Berkeley and Los Angeles, 1974), pp. 142ff., 264ff.

165. Adolf Hitler, *Mein Kampf* (1925), trans. Ralph Mannheim (Boston, 1943), p. 264.

166. The same is true for the competition projects for the Palace of the League of Nations (Ciro Luigi Anzivino and Ezio Godoli, *Ginevra 1927: Il concorso per il Palazzo della Società delle Nazioni e il caso Le Corbusier* [Florence, n.d.]). The competition for the Palace of the Soviets in 1930–32 produced a number of more radical projects in response to the Russian Constructivist tradition: Jean-Louis Cohen, "Le Corbusier and the Mystique of the U.S.S.R.," *Oppositions,* no. 23 (1981), pp. 85–121; Alberto Samona, ed., *Il Palazzo dei Soviet, 1931–1933* (Rome, 1976).

167. *Die Baugilde,* vol. 15 (1933), pp. 697, 713.

168. MoMA, Reichsbank, Folder 9, *Bericht der Gutachter. . . ,* May 27, 1933, no. 12.

169. *Deutsche Bauzeitung,* vol. 67 (1933), p. 631.

170. MoMA, *Deutsches Volk/Deutsche Arbeit,* advance flyer for the exhibition. Otto Riedrich, "Zum neuen Aufstieg! Ausstellung Deutsches Volk-Deutsche Arbeit," in *Deutsche Bauzeitung,* vol. 68, no. 1 (1934), pp. 325–329, 345–351; Hans Stephan, "Ausstellung 'Deutsches Volk-Deutsche Arbeit' Berlin," *Zentralblatt der Bauverwaltung,* vol. 59, no. 24 (1934), pp. 317–322.

171. The exhibition was arranged by the *Städtische Messeamt;* there is no evidence that it was overtly sponsored by the *Deutsche Arbeitsfront,* as claimed by Nerdinger (*Versuchung und Dilemma,* p. 75), although the *Deutsche Arbeitsfront* constructed a conspicuous pavilion at the exhibition.

172. Nerdinger, *Versuchung und Dilemma,* p. 75.

173. Siegfried Giedion, *Walter Gropius: Mensch und Werk* (Stuttgart, 1954), pp. 71–72.

174. On these exhibitions, *see* Brenner, "Art in Political Power Struggle."

175. Riedrich, "Zum neuen Aufstieg!"

176. Ruegenberg, together with another occasional assistant of Mies, Ernst Walther, designed the Hall of Honor of the exhibition (ibid., pp. 325, 327). Ruegenberg recalled in a recent interview ("Der Skelettbau ist keine Teigware," *Bauwelt,* vol. 77, no. 11 [1986], p. 350) that "the commission to plan the Hall of Honor came from people in the administration who had been responsible for Barcelona. I made a project with two large walls. Through these walls one proceeded—across a long room in the center—into the exhibition." (My translation.) The walls are shown in the photograph in Riedrich, "Zum neuen Aufstieg!" p. 347.

177. On the jurors for the competition, *see: Bauwelt,* vol. 25, no. 4 (January 25, 1934), p. 79; and Nerdinger, *Versuchung und Dilemma,* p. 75. On Speer's work for Goebbels and Hitler, and his appointment to the *Schönheit der Arbeit* unit, which was established on November 27, 1933, *see* Albert Speer, *Erinnerungen* (Berlin, 1969), pp. 39–40; 59, 67, 70; Rudolf Wolters, *Albert Speer* (Oldenburg, 1943), pp. 8–9; Anatol von Hübbenet, *Das Taschenbuch "Schönheit der Arbeit"* (Berlin, 1938), p. 17; Anson G. Rabinbach, "The Aesthetics of Production in the Third Reich," in George L. Mosse, ed., *International Fascism* (London and Beverly Hills, 1979), pp. 159–222.

178. Speer added that Mies, in contrast to other modernists, was taken seriously by the Nazis: *Die Zwanziger Jahre des Deutschen Werkbunds,* Werkbund Archiv, vol. 10 (Giessen/Lahn, 1982), pp. 292–309.

179. Mies's exhibit appears without his name in photographs in Riedrich, "Zum neuen Aufstieg!," p. 349. Ruegenberg recalled in a recent interview ("Der Skelettbau ist keine Teigware") that Mies "placed walls of coal and of stone in the hall. One wall was built of briquettes, another of rock salt, a third of something else. The only showpiece furniture was again the table for the visitors' book [i.e., as in the Barcelona Pavilion]. Once again he did not get away from using walls. In particular, my idea of entering through the walls preoccupied him again." (My translation.) But the freestanding and asymmetrically placed walls of Mies's exhibit were quite different from the centered and symmetrical walls of Ruegenberg and Walther's Hall of Honor (*see above,* n. 176).

180. MoMA, Brussels, Folder 1, *Richtlinien,* May 14, 1934, from Dr. Bährens, *Stellvertreter des Reichskommissars.*

181. MoMA, Brussels, Folder 1, *Entwurf,* undated and unsigned draft of a contract for participation in the competition.

182. Illustrations in *The Architect and Building News,* vol. 142 (May 17, 1935), pp. 179–180.

183. MoMA, Brussels, Folder 1, *Präsident der Reichskammer der bildenden Künste* to Mies, June 8, 1934, signed "Hönig."

184. Ruegenberg ("Der Skelettbau ist keine Teigware") claims that "Speer once again passed on a commission, namely for Brussels." On Speer's participation in Hitler's judging of the competition, *see below,* n. 196.

185. Fahrenkamp became a member of the Nazi Party in 1937 (BDC).

186. *Die Baugilde,* vol. 16 (1934), p. 577. The Kongresshalle, which goes back to Ruff's pre-Nazi design of 1927–28, was reworked by Ruff early in 1934 after he had been chosen by Hitler; construction was begun in 1935 after Ruff's death, but not completed (Eduard Brill, "Ludwig Ruff," *Zentralblatt der Bauverwaltung,* vol. 59 [1934], pp. 518–519; Armand Dehlinger, *Architektur der Superlative: Eine kritische Betrachtung der NS-Bauprogramme von München und Nürnberg,* vol. 1, pp. 64–68, MS 8/1a, Institut für Zeitgeschichte, Munich, which however offers a confused chronology; Taylor, *Word in Stone,* pp. 170–171 and figs. 46–47). On his career, *see* Brill, "Ludwig Ruff," and Ludwig's son Franz Ruff's resume in Thieme-Becker (1935). Ruff was an unpremiated competitor for the Reichsbank addition.

187. Schmitthenner's book was published in 1934 in Munich. He joined the Fighting League for German Culture (*Kampfbund für deutsche Kultur*) in 1932, was appointed its national professional leader for the visual arts (*Reichsfachleiter für bildende Kunst*) in 1933 (correspondence in BDC), and became a member of the Nazi Party: *see* Hartmut Frank, "Schiffbruch der Arche," introduction to a reprint of Schmitthenner's *Das deutsche Wohnhaus* (Stuttgart, 1984), pp. v–xvii.

188. He joined the party in May 1933 (BDC).

189. The final layout of the exhibition is illustrated in *Architecture et urbanisme (L'Émulation),* vol. 55 (1935), p. 119; the site of the German Pavilion was turned over to the "Hall International."

190. This description is based on Mies's drawings in MoMA and his descriptions in Brussels, Folder 6.

191. The drawings of the hall and court are MoMA 18.20, 18.3, 18.18, and the

more finished view in the collection of Dirk Lohan (Fig. 29). MoMA 18.20 (published in Schulze, *Critical Biography*, fig. 137) includes a small view from the court of honor toward the interior; the rest of the drawings look from the hall to the court. The height of the walls varies from drawing to drawing. The Lohan view shows the interior as described in the text of this essay. But in Mies's undated description of the project (*see above*, n. 190), he wrote that a bronze eagle of the Reich stood before one wall, and a swastika was carved in the other. It is not clear whether this or the Lohan view represent a later version of the project.

192. These volutes appear in the Lohan view (*see above*, n. 191) and, indistinctly, in MoMA 18.3, as Franz Schulze has pointed out to me. The MoMA drawing is reproduced in Schulze, *Critical Biography*, fig. 136.

193. Undated description, MoMA, Brussels, Folder 6 (*see above*, n. 190).

194. MoMA, Brussels, Folder 3, letter from Mies's office to Eduard Ludwig, July 24, 1934.

195. Ruegenberg, "Ludwig Mies van der Rohe." Idem, "Der Skelettbau ist keine Teigware" ("But this project [of Mies's] was not executed; instead, someone else's with great thick columns and great fanfare, and a pool in front of it. Even Speer gave in to it, although he had gone to great trouble, it must be said here quite clearly, to recruit Tessenow and Mies for such tasks"). (My translation.)

196. BAC, *Reichskanzlei*, R4311/330, pp. 61–94, recounts the history of the project in October and November 1934; I am indebted to Dr. Werner of the archive for aid in locating this material. Hitler's criticisms of the project, which was being supervised after Ruff's death by his son Franz, are recorded after a meeting of October 25. Hitler wanted the facade in solid stone or stone veneer rather than stucco or a compound, and the Hall of Honor to exhibit tall columns of porphyry decorated with bronze emblems of the Reich "als Höchstleistung der Baukultur des Dritten Reiches," as well as other changes. Albert Speer participated in these discussions. (Dr. Willuhn in the *Reichskanzlei* to Willecke, the *Reichskommisar* for the exhibition, November 10, 1934: "Präsident Willecke hat mit dem vom Führer und Reichskanzler beauftragen Architekten Speer eine Unterhaltung gehabt.")

197. Brussels, Folder 3, *Reichswirtschaftsminister* to Mies, August 6, 1934. Mies also transmitted correspondence and payments for photographs and blueprints to the other competitors.

198. Brussels, Folder 6, Mies to Mia Seeger, November 23, 1934. On Lilly Reich, *see* Schulze, *Critical Biography*, pp. 138–140 passim.

199. BAC, *Reichskanzlei*, R4311/330, ff. 72–94, record the discussions over discontinuing construction, which was well-advanced.

200. Brussels, Folder 6, *Zu dem Vorentwurf für ein Ausstellungsgebäude . . .*, July 3, 1934.

201. Adolf Hitler, *Die deutsche Kunst als stolzeste Verteidigung des deutschen Volkes* (Munich, 1934), speech delivered September 1, 1933.

202. Jeffrey Herf, *Reactionary Modernism: Technology, Culture and Politics in Weimar and the Third Reich* (Cambridge, 1984).

203. Ibid., pp. 195–197. The phrase comes from a speech by Goebbels of November 1933.

204. "Deutsch sein heisst klar sein," *Völkisher Beobachter* (Munich edition, September 6, 1934). Brenner, *Art in the Political Power Struggle*.

205. Lane, *Architecture and Politics*, pp. 147–184; Campbell, *German Werkbund*, pp. 242–287. Alan Windsor, *Peter Behrens, Architect and Designer, 1868–1940* (New York, 1981), pp. 169–173.

206. Scheiffele, "Das neue Bauen unter dem Faschismus," p. 241, Gropius to Hönig, December 31, 1936.

207. Häring to Carl Lörcher, October 23, 1933; Häring manuscript of January 1934, "Für Wiedererweckung einer deutschen Baukultur;" Gropius to Poelzig, January 24, 1934; Schirren, "Was ist 'deutsche' Baukunst?" pp. 253–282, Docs. 2, 3, 4. Gropius, however, did not himself take this position.

208. Brenner, *Ende einer bürgerlichen Kunst-Institution*, pp. 29–30; Wagner resigned in February 1933.

209. *Werk und Zeit*, no. 3 (1982), p. 36.

210. *See above*, n. 73.

211. BA, 13/44–54, copy of a letter of February 1, 1934, prepared by Wagner in collaboration with Gropius (*see also* Scheiffele, "Das neue Bauen unter dem Faschismus").

212. BA, 13/93–99, copy of a letter by Wagner to Carl Lörcher, chairman of the *Bund Deutscher Architekten*, June 8, 1934.

213. For example, Walter Schwagenscheidt, the city planner who worked for May in Frankfurt and in Russia, entered the competition for the House of German Labor in 1934, and worked for the *Deutsche Arbeitsfront* on city planning in 1934–35 (Burghard Preusler, *Walter Schwagenscheidt, 1886–1968* (Stuttgart, 1985)), pp. 110–111.

214. Gropius to Poelzig, June 15, 1933: *Die Zwanziger Jahre des Deutschen Werkbunds*, pp. 287–288; Gropius to Hönig, January 18, 1934, Hahn and Wolsdorff, *Bauhaus-Berlin*, p. 148.

215. Bruno E. Werner, "Wir brauchen jeden Mann! Kunst und Auslandspropaganda," *Deutsche Rundschau*, vol. 237 (1933), pp. 41–43. On Werner's position, *see* Lane, *Architecture and Politics*, p. 177.

216. LC, Deutscher Werkbund, 1933. Riezler had written that Paul Troost's House of German Art in Munich had shallow roots in tradition, whereas modern architecture—as in the work of Mies— was deeply rooted in its time (November 29, 1933). Wendland replied that he did not think Troost's museum pointed the way to the future, and that he too admired Mies (December 1, 1933).

217. Albert Speer, in an interview of 1978, recalled his own admiration for Mies's work, as a student, because he used "noble materials" and was a *Klassizist*, and added that Mies, in contrast to other modernists, was taken seriously by the Nazis: *Die Zwanziger Jahre des Deutschen Werkbunds*, pp. 292–309.

218. Letter from Rosenberg to Goebbels, in Ernst Piper, *Ernst Barlach und die nationalsozialistische Kunstpolitik* (Munich and Zurich, 1983), p. 11. Gropius to Donald Drew Egbert, October 14, 1948: Egbert papers, as in n. 55 above; Moholy-Nagy, in *Journal of the Society of Architectural Historians*.

219. Lane, *Architecture and Politics*, p. 204. Speer (*Die Zwanziger Jahre des Deutschen Werkbunds*, p. 306) referred to the Heinkel factories and steel works in Linz. Works by Rimpl's firm as well as other simple modernist buildings for the Nazis are illustrated in Gerdy Troost, ed., *Das Bauen im neuen Reich* (Bayreuth, 1938) vol. 1, pp. 103–112; vol. 2, pp. 66–70.

220. Philip Johnson, "Mies van der Rohe," in Henry-Russell Hitchcock, Johnson, and Lewis Mumford, *Modern Architecture: International Exhibition* (New York, 1932), pp. 111–128; Henry-Russell Hitchcock and Philip Johnson, *The International Style: Architecture since 1922* (New York, 1932). Mies's view of this

145

can be gathered from an exchange of letters with Johnson, then chairman of the Department of Architecture at The Museum of Modern Art, concerning a proposed exhibition of work by Mies's former students (MoMA, Philip Johnson File: Mies to Johnson, November 23, 1934): "Ich nehme meine Arbeit und die Bewegung des neuen Bauens viel zu ernst, als dass ich eine Verantwortung für Veranstaltungen und Arbeiten übernehmen kann, die ich nicht kenne; umsomehr als mir in letzter Zeit wi[e]derholt amerikanische Stimmen bekannt wurden, die das neue Bauen in Amerika immer mehr als eine Mode charakterisierten. Das ist sehr gefährlich." ("I take my work and the movement for the new architecture much too seriously to assume responsibility for events and works of which I have no knowledge, all the more because recently I've repeatedly heard from American sources who speak of the new architecture in America more and more as a fashion. That is very dangerous.") To this Johnson replied on December 5, 1934: "I have always had the highest respect for you and for the purity of the architecture for which you stand. I am not at all interested in modes or fashions in various kinds of modern." But he did, of course, see the new architecture as *the* modern style, the International Style.

221. "Baukunst und Zeitwille," *Der Querschnitt*, vol. 4 (January 1924), pp. 31–33; trans. in Johnson, *Mies van der Rohe*, pp. 191–192.

222. Albert Sigrist [Alexander Schwab], *Das Buch vom Bauen* (Berlin, 1930, and Bauwelt Fundamente, 1973).

223. Diethart Kerbs, introduction to the republication of ibid. Olaf Ihlau, *Die roten Kämpfer*, Marburger Abhandlungen zur politischen Wissenschaft, vol. 14 (Meisenheim am Glan, 1969), pp. 181–183.

224. Sigrist [Schwab], *Buch vom Bauen*, pp. 133, 156, 162. There is no evidence that Mies was a friend of Schwab, as claimed by Kerbs (*Werkbund Archiv*, vol. 1 [1972], pp. 159–163).

225. Sigrist [Schwab], *Buch vom Bauen*, p. 65.

226. Walter Rathenau, "Deutschlands Rohstoffversorgung," lecture delivered December 20, 1915 (published in *Gesammelte Schriften*, vol. 5 [Berlin, 1918], pp. 23ff.); *Die neue Wirtschaft*, Berlin, 1918 (*Gesammelte Schriften*, vol. 6, pp. 203ff.); *Von kommenden Dingen*, Berlin, 1917 (*Gesammelte Schriften*, vol. 3).

227. On the history of *völkisch* thought and the Nazis, *see* George L. Mosse, *The Crisis of German Ideology: Intellectual Origins of the Third Reich* (New York, 1964). For architecture, *see* Hubert Schrade, *Bauten des Dritten Reiches* (Leipzig, 1939) (1st ed., 1937). Taylor, *Word in Stone*, pp. 157–181. Karl Willy Straub (*Die Architektur im Dritten Reich* [Stuttgart, 1932], pp. 36–37) criticizes the earlier ideals of collectivism.

228. Mary McLeod, "'Architecture or Revolution:' Taylorism, Technocracy, and Social Change," *Art Journal*, vol. 43 [1983], p. 133, has argued that Le Corbusier, who during the 1920s was as overtly apolitical as Mies, nevertheless through his faith in rationalization held a "vision linking technology and social change." But this was clearly not the case with Mies in the late 1920s.

229. Hendrik Berlage, "Bouwkunst en Impressionism," *Architectura*, vol. 2 (1894), pp. 93ff.; idem, *Normalisatie in Woningsbouw* (Rotterdam, 1918).

230. *See* Ludwig Mies van der Rohe, "Die neue Zeit," *Die Form*, vol. 5 (1930), p. 406, and Mies's lecture of August 17, 1931, in Neumeyer, *Mies van der Rohe*, p. 375: "Zu der Sach- und Zweckstruktur der Bauten tritt das Künsterliche hinzu, oder besser gesagt, es vollzieht sich an ihr. Aber nicht in dem Sinne des Hinzufügens, sondern im Sinne des Gestaltens." Neumeyer (ibid., p. 204) asserts that Mies never again referred to the *Zeitwille*, the will of the times. But though he did not use the word, he clung to the idea, for example, in his notes dated by Neumeyer in the 1950s (ibid., p. 391): "Wer aber Baukunst will, muss sich entscheiden. Er hat sich den grossen objektiven Forderungen der Zeit unterzuordnen und diese baulich zu verwirklichen."

231. The manuscript of March 13, 1933, written for the *Verein Deutscher Spiegelglass-Fabriken*, is in MoMA and LC, and is published in Tegethoff, *Villas and Country Houses*, p. 66, and Neumeyer, *Mies van der Rohe*, p. 378. Tegethoff interprets this as a confirmation of his thesis that opening architecture to nature was a constant in Mies's work: *see* my counter arguments in *Journal of the Society of Architectural Historians*, vol. 43 (1984), pp. 88–89. In America after the war, Mies developed a type of "large utilitarian building," best exemplified by S. R. Crown Hall and the project for the Chicago Convention Center, with uninterrupted spaces and glazed outer walls—his so-called "universal space." Mies said of a similar project, for the Mannheim National Theater: "As you see the whole building is one large room. We believe that this is the most economical and practical way of construction. The purposes the building serves are always changing but we cannot afford to pull the building down. Therefore we put Sullivan's slogan 'form follows function' upside down, and construct a practical and economical space into which we fit the functions." (Christian Norberg-Schulz, "Ein Gespräch mit Mies van der Rohe," *Baukunst und Werkform*, vol. 2, no. 6 [1958], pp. 615–618; English version in *L'Architecture d'Aujourd'hui*, vol. 29, no. 79 [1958], p. 100). It is clear therefore that this concept of freedom referred to function only; it is certainly not experientially effective, since the clear spans and uniform glazing minimize the observer's awareness of change and movement. What mattered to Mies in these buildings was, as he said in the same interview, "clear construction," which, he added, "is the basis for the free plan." Such a structure represented order, needless to say, not freedom.

232. Neumeyer, *Mies van der Rohe*.

233. Ibid., pp. 380–381; Johnson, *Mies van der Rohe*, pp. 196–200. Mies also changed his position in asserting that neither the "mechanistic" nor the "idealistic" principles of order were sufficient, and in emphasizing instead the "organic" principle. Neumeyer, *Mies van der Rohe*, pp. 278ff., sees this talk as a continuation of Mies's European ideas.

234. Blake, "A Conversation with Mies," p. 100.

Addendum: Mies van der Rohe and Walter Gropius in the FBI Files

By Lee Gray

As recorded in files of the Federal Bureau of Investigation and related documents made available by the Freedom of Information Act, the contrast between the apolitical stance of Mies and the political activism or social concern of Walter Gropius in Germany during the Weimar and early Nazi years continued in evidence after they emigrated to the United States.

Mies was first investigated by the FBI in July 1939 because of a report that German spies were staying at Pike Lake Lodge in Park Falls, Wisconsin, where Mies and several companions were vacationing and working on architectural projects. The manager of Pike Lake Lodge told the FBI that Mies "did not hesitate to express his dislike for the Hitler regime and stated that it had practically ruined him financially in Germany," and that Mies had said further that "he had no desire or plans for ever returning to Germany."[1]

Another witness stated that "while Mies was opposed to the present dominant political party . . . [he] had not been sufficiently interested in his opposition to actively fight it."[2]

The FBI found only one "questionable" political association in its investigations of Mies. In 1946 it reported that Mies was listed as a member of the Midwest Board of Directors of the Independent Citizens Committee of the Arts, Sciences and Professions, which had been labeled a Communist front by the Congressional Committee on Un-American Activities in 1949 and 1951.[3] Nevertheless, Mies retained his membership, according to later checks by the FBI.

Gropius, by contrast, was repeatedly mentioned in FBI reports for his association with organizations labeled as Communist fronts, and for letters and petitions signed by him and printed in the *Daily Worker*. The FBI took note of his sponsorship of the National Wartime Conference of the Professions, the Sciences, the Arts, and the White Collar Fields, held in 1943 in New York, which was cited as a subversive group by a Congressional Special Committee on Un-American Activities in 1949.[4] The FBI recorded that as a member of the Committee of One Thousand, which was labeled a "Communist created and controlled front organization" by the California Committee on Un-American Activities in 1948, Gropius signed a petition in 1948 opposing the Mundt-Nixon Bill and calling for the elimination of the House Committee on Un-American Activities. In 1951, the FBI noted, he signed a petition circulated by the Civil Liberties Union in Massachusetts calling for the abolition of the Massachusetts Legislative Committee to Curb Communism. Various right-wing publications attacking Gropius in the 1950s and 1960s are also included in his FBI file.

Notes

1. FBI File No. 65–4656–2, pp. 4–5.
2. FBI File No. 65–4656–3, p. 4.
3. "Review of the Scientific and Cultural Conference for World Peace Arranged by the National Council of the Arts, Sciences and Professions," House Report No. 1954, April 28, 1958 (originally released April 19, 1949), p. 2. "Report on the Communist 'Peace' Offensive: A Campaign to Disarm and Defeat the United States," House Report no. 378, April 25, 1951 (originally released April 1, 1951), p. 12.
4. "Un-American Propaganda Activities," Hearings Before a Special Committee: 78th Congress (1949), Second Session, Appendix, Part II, pp. 1335–1338.

FRITZ NEUMEYER

Space for Reflection: Block versus Pavilion

In 1905, Ludwig Mies, the son of a stonemason, set off from his native Aachen to test his architectural talent in the metropolitan atmosphere of Berlin.[1] At the age of nineteen, he had only vaguely mapped out a course for himself. But the young Mies was well-schooled in the trades and had already gained a measure of professional experience as a craftsman.

Yet far more important than these practical accomplishments was an inborn sensibility, which, like an imaginary compass, would ultimately help him find his way with uncommon certainty through the vast aesthetic topography of architecture. If one grants credence to the sentiments of Adolf Loos, another stonemason's son, it was Mies's good fortune to make contact in his father's own shop with a narrow but important, even decisive, sphere of architecture. "Only a very small part of architecture is art: tombs and monuments," Loos wrote in his famous essay, "Architektur," of 1909. "All else, everything that serves a function, must be excluded from the realm of art. Only when the great misconception that art can be bent to a purpose has been disproved, will we have an architecture for our time."[2]

Both Mies and Loos had grown up with that "small part" of the building art. Contact with this specialized and essential architecture had made them sensitive to the symbolic nature of anything that is built: tomb and monument represented an absolute species of building, high in value both spiritually and formally. Metaphysical at the core, symbolic in its purpose, this architecture pointed beyond the visible, physical world to an incorporeal realm.

Mies's Catholic education as well as his exposure to Aachen's medieval architectural monuments may have contributed further to his awareness that a deeper stratum of meaning runs beneath appearances. The outer circumstances of his upbringing thus provided fertile ground in which an idealizing mind-set might mature. Nonetheless, it was only considerably later that Mies's inclination toward metaphysics came to the surface and found expression in words. In a lecture delivered in Berlin in February and March 1928 and significantly titled "The Prerequisites of Architectural Creation," Mies grappled with the material and spiritual existential problems of his time. Here, for the first time, he articulated his preoccupation with metaphysics. Inspired by the writings of the theologian and philosopher Romano Guardini, his near-contemporary whom he had met in the early 1920s, Mies argued that contemporary life must reconcile doubt and faith, *ratio* and *religio:* "It must be possible to enhance consciousness yet free it from the shackles of pure intellect. It must be possible to let go of illusions, to see our existence clearly and yet attain a new infinity, an infinity emerging from the spirit."[3]

Mies must have shown an interest in philosophy—an awareness of "infinity emerging from the spirit"—early in his life; while he was still in Aachen an architect invited him to dinner for the purpose of celebrating the philosopher Arthur Schopenhauer's birthday.[4] In his famous work of 1819, *Die Welt als*

Wille und Vorstellung (*The World as Will and Idea*), Schopenhauer had contended that the visible world emerges from the spirit: matter is constituted solely as the bearer of the spirit, as a vehicle of those forms and qualities through which ideas become manifest.

In Schopenhauer's work the existence of architecture was inferred similarly: the "fundamental bass notes of nature," i.e., "weight, cohesion, and rigidity," must be translated into the *"thorough bass* of all architecture"—into its "only constant theme: of support and load." Indeed, the final destiny of architecture was to reveal the order of idea and of will, as well as the "inherent laws of space."[5]

In his Aachen years Mies must have found such reflections somewhat beyond his reach. For all his intellectual yearning and despite the significant effect these ideas would have upon his later development, his initial encounter with philosophy seems to have come about by chance. One day while tidying up a drawing table in the office of the Aachen architect Albert Schneider, where he was briefly employed, Mies came across a copy of the magazine *Die Zukunft* (*The Future*) as well as an essay on the theories of the French astronomer Pierre Simon de Laplace, who in the eighteenth century had conducted major research into the movement of the planets. Mies studied his findings with great curiosity: "I read both of them [magazine and essay] and both of them went quite over my head. But I couldn't help being interested. So every week thereafter I got hold of *Die Zukunft* and I read it as carefully as I could. That's when I think I started paying attention to spiritual things. Philosophy. And culture."[6]

Reading *Die Zukunft* brought Mies in touch with a sphere of thought previously unknown to him. Published in Berlin by Maximilian Harden, this anti-Wilhelmine journal regularly aired the views of such reigning turn-of-the-century European intellectuals as art historians Julius Meier-Graefe and Alfred Lichtwark; architects and artists like Henry van de Velde and August Endell; writers like August Strindberg, Heinrich Mann, and Stefan Zweig; and philosophers like Georg Simmel and Alois Riehl.

The encounter with philosophy that began with the discovery in an Aachen drawing table, found its continuation in Berlin. Alois Riehl, a philosophy professor at the Friedrich-Wilhelm University in Berlin, whose work Mies had probably come across in the pages of *Die Zukunft,* proved to be his very first client, and his patron as well. One can only wonder what special conditions and sympathies enabled a twenty-one-year-old "architect," with neither a diploma nor an independent practice, to gain a commission to build a house for a prominent sixty-three-year-old university professor and his wife. Mies's own description of the circumstances, as offered in later interviews, only deepens the mystery.[7] It seems obvious that the decision was not based on what Mies had already achieved professionally. Indeed, Riehl, a most open-minded man, took it upon himself, at his own expense, to send his young friend on a six-week study trip to Italy.

Also, it is likely that Riehl supplied Mies with some works of classical literature to make the journey even more profitable. An 1885 edition of the Swiss art historian Jakob Burckhardt's *Die Kultur der Renaissance in Italien* (*The Civilization of the Renaissance in Italy*), bearing Riehl's autograph, is still in Mies's private collection, probably a loan that was never returned.[8]

Furthermore, Mies's client and mentor surely drew his young friend's attention to Heinrich Wölfflin, Riehl's colleague at the university in Berlin. Having succeeded Burckhardt in Basel in 1893, Wölfflin went on to teach in Berlin from 1901 to 1912. Mies and Wölfflin met at Riehl's house, and Mies certainly was not forgotten by Wölfflin; for Mies also met Wölfflin's young fiancée Ada Bruhn, won her for himself, and later, in 1913, married her.

It is hardly surprising, then, that several of Wölfflin's celebrated art historical studies may also be found in Mies's library, e.g., *Renaissance und Barock* (*Renaissance and Baroque*), in the third edition of 1908; *Kunstgeschichtliche Grundbegriffe* (*Principles of Art History*), in the second edition of 1917; and *Die Klassische Kunst* (published in English as *The Art of the Italian Renaissance*), in the 1908 edition, with a dedication, "November 1909 from H. W.," in the author's hand.[9]

Riehl's scholarly work, in turn, was not without significance in the development of art and art theory at the turn of the century. He was the first to publish, in 1897, a monograph on Friedrich Nietzsche, the poet-philosopher and visionary: *Friedrich Nietzsche: Der Künstler und der Denker* (*Friedrich Nietzsche: Artist and Philosopher*). This study was included in the renowned series *Klassiker der Philosophie*, and by 1909 had appeared in five editions as well as in Russian, Polish, and Italian translations. In Riehl's *Zur Einführung in die Philosophie der Gegenwart* (*Introduction to Contemporary Philosophy*), of 1903, a chapter titled "Schopenhauer und Nietzsche" dealt once again with the "philosopher of culture." The 1908 edition is also in Mies's library, the text underlined in many places.

Few, if any, thinkers matched the astuteness and eloquence with which Nietzsche had analyzed the ferment and unrest of his era. His theory of aesthetic salvation exerted a powerful impact on the intellectual life and the art of the turn of the century, and his influence continued to be felt in virtually all phases, movements, and institutions of the early modernist revolution, from the *Gesamtkunstwerk* of Art Nouveau, through Futurism and Dada, even to the Bauhaus. Henry van de Velde, August Endell, Peter Behrens, Bruno Taut, and Le Corbusier were only a few of the artists and architects to be deeply affected by their discovery of Nietzsche during the first decade of the new century. Both the development of the Nietzschean image and his reception as the philosopher of fashion at the turn of the century were largely due to Riehl's studies.[10] It stands to reason, then, that Wölfflin would have been interested in Riehl, for Wölfflin's concept of a *Sehgeschichte* (history of vision), which incorporated his view of style as the expression of an attitude toward life and form, and his postulation of a material and spiritual "culture of the senses," were significantly inspired by Nietzsche, who had seen art as the "reflection of the will" and the "symbol of feeling."[11]

This brief look at the complexities of a variety of relationships directly or indirectly affecting Mies may begin to explain what a giant intellectual step the commission of the Riehl House was for him. It was tantamount to immersion in a new universe, to induction into a realm of philosophy and aesthetics whose ethical system had to be as clearly understood and justifiable as any law in the real world. For Mies, Riehl was much more than just a conduit to that society from which his future clients were to be drawn: intellectuals and artists as well as bankers and industrialists.

1. Riehl House, Potsdam-Neubabelsberg. 1907. Facade

Until Riehl's death in 1924, Mies remained his faithful friend. In broadening Mies's spiritual horizons, Riehl both confirmed and reoriented the younger man's natural intellectual inclinations. The basic precept of Riehl's moral philosophy was autonomous will, a faculty qualified, however, by service to a metaphysical order. Thus, while stimulating Mies to self-discovery and self-definition, Riehl's system encouraged him to balance his drive toward freedom of action with the tempering tradition of religious thought in which he had been reared.

Riehl was also notable in both his teaching and his writing for the ability to express his ideas as simply and clearly as possible, the better to reach less-educated readers and interested laymen like Mies. His motto was "To stimulate, not to inculcate," and he directed his efforts, above all, to promoting an understanding of the philosophical movements of the day.[12] The wide circulation of Riehl's publications was a sign of the success of his struggle for clarity in communication, a habit which Mies may well have attempted to emulate. According to Riehl, contemporary thought was taken up largely with the conflict between the ancient faith in an existent, a priori order and the insistence of the modern self on making its own laws. This opposition between the bonds of mythology and religion and latter-day rational autonomy was at the root of the tensions of an era that had dawned with Nietzsche, a time in which people sought to free themselves from the grip of tradition in order to survey unfettered the opportunities that life might offer in the future.

Riehl's way of resolving the contradictions in the modern soul lay in the art of evolving new life views out of old ones. Not the *revaluation* of all values as propagated by the moral anarchist Nietzsche, but the *development* of certain values: this became the dictate of an ethical world view. Values, according to Riehl, could not be invented so much as discovered and recognized, like the

2. *Riehl House, Potsdam-Neubabelsberg. 1907. View from lower garden*

stars. Thus he said the maxim governing all action should be: "The ancient Good—hold fast to it! The new Good is but a transformation of the old." [13] Eduard Spranger, who said of Riehl that he forever needed a breath of greatness and an air of freedom in his inner world, characterized him further: "*Serving in freedom* was the substance of his life." [14]

One could almost have heard Riehl when Mies later called each of his own buildings "a demonstration" of thought, adding that "it must be possible to fuse into a harmonious whole the old and the new energies of our civilization." [15] Even the idea of "serving in freedom" was at the heart of his architectural efforts. Service was an imperative for Mies, [16] who regarded his creative work as striving toward a goal with philosophical implications: "to fulfill the law and thus to gain freedom." [17]

In light of the foregoing discussion, two significant aspects of the Riehl House of 1907 (Figs. 1, 2) may be perceived as constructed analogues of the client's thinking. The building reveals two faces, reflecting an ambivalence of concepts that can be related, in turn, to two different philosophical traditions. Moreover, the house can be read in terms of Riehlean development, with its design symbolizing the transformation of tradition.

In comparison with its neighboring villas and country houses, all of them executed in a variety of turn-of-the-century tastes, the Riehl House conveys an air of easy unobtrusiveness, traceable mostly to its harmony of proportions— qualities that are apparent in its smallest details as well as in the main body of the structure with its two-story elevation, stucco siding, high-pitched saddle roof, eyebrow dormer windows, and typical Potsdam gable fixed in the center of the upper floor. Clearly Mies had chosen to hark back to the local domestic architecture of the late eighteenth century, [18] a genre he must have known well, judging from his careful compliance with it. Such a proper bourgeois exterior was well suited to a country house in the residential suburb of Neubabelsberg on the outskirts of Potsdam, an affluent middle-class city in its own right that was once the dwelling place of kings.

In recalling the unostentatious neoclassicism of the eighteenth century, Mies was fully in tune with his times. Paul Mebes's *Um 1800* (*Around 1800*), a book of significant influence on German architectural thought, was published in 1908, at a time, that is, when construction on the Riehl House was just about completed.[19] Mies had already learned something about the influence of bourgeois neoclassicism on recent directions in German architecture while he was in the employ of Bruno Paul, an architect-designer who had made a name for himself with his elegant neo-Biedermeier furniture. In 1906, Mies had secured a place in Paul's studio, but gave it up in 1908 to join Peter Behrens.

According to Mebes, only a return to the lost bourgeois values of simplicity and *Sachlichkeit* could lead the world out of the hectic confusion of contemporary architecture. Such a revival was not really "a step backward following prolonged and fruitless floundering, but rather an advance—provided we resume the eighteenth century's attitude toward building."[20] This Mies had clearly sought to do in the Riehl House, a work regarded by several architecture critics of 1910 as close to model-perfect.[21] Behind its apparent ingenuousness, a new expressive concept was unfolding that was divinable neither in the outward style of the house nor in any specific treatment of its surfaces. Instead, it was in Mies's approach to space that his early work already bore his unmistakable signature.

In the disposition of the whole, as evident in the site plan (Fig. 3), two spatial realms confront each other. One calls to mind the world of man and his faculties—rationality and the capacity for abstract thought expressed through geometry—while the other evokes the world of nature already in place, whose richness of organic forms follows other, less clear-cut laws.

The dualism of these systems is reflected in the three-part division of the site. On the raised part of the site, order reigns and space for living is organized with mathematical logic by man. The upper garden in front of the house, artificially defined by the damlike wall, is part of this order. Here, accordingly, nature has been arranged into beds and borders set into a geometric grid. In the second part, the strip of garden below the wall, the different realms meet: on one side a pathway leads through the garden, while on the other, plants encroaching upon the space are superimposed on its underlying geometry. Here, two disparate forces maintain the balance between boundary kept and boundary abolished.

In the third and lowest garden zone nature comes into its own, with lush vegetation gaining an upper hand over man's formative plan. Only a narrow path winds through the green thicket, widening to make room for a small sitting area before providing access to the rest of the site and offering a view of the space beyond, which extends over Lake Griebnitz and the woods ascending the other bank, into infinity.

Indeed, the three-fold rhythm of Mies's plan can be read as a spatial sequence that establishes a relationship to infinity through transitions from one level of space to another. At one end of this bipolar field of tension is the open natural space, at the other, the intellectual, architectonic one, carved out of infinity, as it were, and given definable form. Similarly, in the interior of the

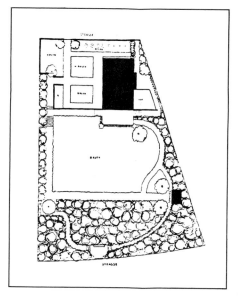

3. Riehl House, Potsdam-Neubabelsberg. 1907. Site plan

155

4. Riehl House, Potsdam-Neubabelsberg. 1907. Dining room

house (Fig. 4), an even rhythm of geometry in the central living hall pits the mathematical structure of the pure cube against the picturesque variety of the exterior world. The hall—the artificial spatial cell—is the center of gravity of the house. Here order is realized in its purest form, with the device that ideally symbolizes the delineation of space, the grid, decorating the walls in an orderly patterned relief.

Set into this metaphorical dichotomy between manmade environment and nature—cell and world—the house may be interpreted as both a refuge from the world and an entry into it. Riehl was, after all, a philosopher, and the name he affectionately bestowed on his abode, *Klösterli* (Little Cloister), figuratively suggests that it was inwardly conducive to concentration and contemplation, outwardly related to its natural surroundings. A philosopher's house ought to be a haven and a sanctuary as well as a meeting place, so that the self and the objective order may interact. Mies took this theme of bipolarity into account when he built the house. Nature and intellect were accepted as opposite realms of existence and at the same time as complementary parts of a whole. Their distinctive attributes and qualities demanded bonding in a form that basically affirmed their differences while establishing them as elements of a new unity.

In order to realize this complementary oneness, Mies needed a system of coordinates that would elevate a basically simple building to an implicitly higher field of reference. He employed a long, uninterrupted stretch of wall spanning the plot and serving as a baseline. It secures the necessary optical support for the house on its slope, while at the same time acting as an embankment, pulling the space of the terrace garden around to the front of the house. With openings inserted into it only under the body of the house itself, this rampart seems fixed in the ground, as if guaranteeing a firm sense of place within the softly modeled foundation of the natural surroundings.

5. Riehl House, Potsdam-Neubabelsberg. 1907. Altered photograph of view from lower garden with gables cut away

Above this base, with its imperturbable calm, there rises—off-center, and with discernible tension—a classical portico composed of a loggia and a high-pitched gable readable as a pediment. The house stands like a prostylos on its massive podium, and, thus exposed, communicates with the landscape. This contrasted orientation into the depth of space forms the second coordinate in Mies's axial system.

Although the long side of the house is visible from the street and centralized, in typical middle-class fashion, it is the side wall with its stately prostyle motif that offers a nobler aspect. This shift in weight establishes the two faces of the Riehl House: from the front it looks like a longitudinal, symmetrical bourgeois residence, a cubic mass, or block, situated like a flat crossbar in front of its terrace garden, while from the side view, it is transformed into an asymmetrical pavilion on a wide base, the pillared configuration serving to open up the building at a decisive place.

It is this opening that endows the pilasters on the long side of the house, which are arranged in precise relief on the tightly stretched wall, a deeper meaning. Mies does not simply present a variation on the elegantly decorative articulation that he might have lifted from Bruno Paul's villas. Instead, the Riehl House's double-facedness points far more to an advance in architectural typology, one that is overtly expressed as a cube, but ultimately meant as a skeletal construction. This intended ideal of the skeleton was more concealed than apparent in the pilaster order of the wall. Only when the pillars became structural did the tectonic and spatial intent become manifest, taking the form of a loggia and transforming the cube into a pavilion on the short side of the house. The pavilion is the secret subject of the Riehl House. It comes in at the side door, so to speak, but it imbues the building with a new order. This interpretation of the cube as a spatial weight-bearing structure is further justified by the two gutter cornices, which resemble slipped-on girders and, together with the supporting wall, define the spatial coordinate system. Extended

6. *New National Gallery, Berlin. 1962–68*

smoothly over the long side of the house, these sharp-edged architraves emphasize the direction of the longitudinal axis pushing powerfully away from the base, as if to reach out over the horizon. Without moldings or other details by which their ends might have been defined, they seem to thrust through the building. A clean cut across the profile firmly separates them at the base of the gable/pediment. The roof prism, proudly jutting over the loggia, sits securely on the strong pillars, which bear their burden with ease.

7. *Bruno Paul: Lawn Tennis Club, Berlin-Zehlendorf. 1907*

Into the primary bearing order of the pavilion, the cubic mass of the house was inserted, more or less as a secondary order, filling out the first. If one were to remove the cube of this modest house from its framework, one would be left (Fig. 5) with an illustration of the central theme that preoccupied Mies all his life, even to his last building, the New National Gallery in Berlin (Fig. 6), that is to say, the pavilion set asymmetrically on a classical base. In its compositional principles of order and freedom a dialectic of values oscillated, with classical and anticlassical tendencies, ancient and modern ideas locked in constant struggle.

The theme of the pavilion runs like a thread through Mies's oeuvre.[22] Not only the last but also the very first building of his professional career was taken up with it: the club house of the Lawn Tennis Club in Berlin-Zehlendorf (Fig. 7). Although Bruno Paul had received the commission, he assigned its execution to Mies, who worked on it quite independently.[23] Almost contemporary with the Riehl House, if with obviously different functional and spatial requirements, the Lawn Tennis Club features a classical prostylos clearly akin to the one that Mies employed in the Neubabelsberg house.

The decisive stimulus to the revival of this type of building may well have been Peter Behrens's Crematorium in Hagen (Figs. 8, 9). Built in 1906–7, this structure quickly gained "great prominence,"[24] conferring fame on its architect in the process. As early as 1906, drawings and photos of the model of this work had been published in a special folio edition by Ernst Wasmuth in Berlin,[25] in

8. *Peter Behrens: Crematorium, Hagen, Germany. 1906–7*

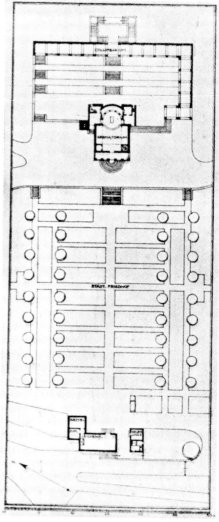

9. *Peter Behrens: Crematorium, Hagen, Germany. 1906–7. Site plan*

time, that is, for Mies to have been affected by it before beginning the Riehl House. It is safe to assume that Paul Thiersch, who had assisted Behrens in the design of the Hagen buildings and who was now chief of the Bruno Paul atelier, drew the attention of his office colleagues—Mies included—to this modern San Miniato.

The Crematorium in Hagen and the Riehl House have many essential characteristics in common. Both buildings are arranged on slopes in three levels and, in both cases, a long ground wall provides the base of the spatial arrangement while palpably increasing the physicality of the building.

But what in Mies's work is at most a hint of analogy, Behrens expressed with undisguised self-confidence: a prostyle temple that rises as the apex of an unrelieved axial-symmetrical complex, subjugating space to a formative will. Form is created for form's sake, in a solemn, relentless geometrization. Such thinking was alien to Mies, as was the rhetorical claim, manifest in Behrens's work, of the mastery of nature by intellect and will. The Crematorium, then, was a product of Behrens's "Zarathustra" style: in it space is symbolically offered up to the hallowed temple, at the feet, so to speak, of the *Übermensch*.

In Mies's case, the microcosm of the house with its clear arrangement of rooms was mathematically structured; the space itself was not. The grid of the paneling in the central hall of the main floor was equivalent to the precise geometry with which Behrens covered his whole plan. Behrens's argument was based on the Nietzschean concept of the "fervor of distance," expressing the desire for a world, which, having been given form by the artist's spirit, would rise above nature in pursuit of higher goals. In replacing myth with the abstract power of reason, science, and progress, modern man—in Behrens's view— would overcome the primal forces of old and confront nature with the rhythm of his own imposed geometry.

By contrast, Mies's pavilion was suffused with a more nearly late-Romantic atmosphere in which both orders, the manmade and the organic, retained their respective spheres of autonomy. His goal was the conciliatory interaction of intellect and nature, inner and outer, architecture and landscape; and the pavilion was the mediating space between these realms. Therefore, the house was to be understood as an independent three-dimensional object, which at the same time functioned as part of the greater unity it formed with nature.

This concept of complementary completion or reciprocal perfection, which would free the parts from the limitations of their isolation in order to fulfill a new reality, corresponded with the philosophical yearnings of German Idealism of about 1800. The dream of a new beauty that would reunite man with nature, regaining the lost identity of each, remained the desire of an era lately revolutionized by the Enlightenment and industrialization. In 1799, describing the relationship of landscape and architecture, Karl Friedrich Schinkel's friend and teacher Friedrich Gilly wrote that intellect and nature should "conserve each other's grandeur and freedom." Decades later, Schinkel affirmed an "informal combination" as his ideal of the "unity of absolute and relative order."[26]

The Riehl House was in fact closer to the tradition of *Um 1800* and to Schinkel's "informal combination" than to the modern "will to style" of Behrens, who went beyond the "lyrical constellation," in order to realize space as a function of modern "logical construction."[27] The neighboring parks of Potsdam and Glienicke were dotted with the perfect models built by Schinkel and his landscape architect and kindred spirit, Peter Josef Lenné, during the first third of the nineteenth century. Often taking the form of the Italian country house, Schinkel's vision of the union of landscape and architecture projected a kind of smiling classicism, made manifest in poetic spatial inventions of exceptional intensity. These buildings became a source of inspiration as well as an exacting criterion for generations of architects to come. Schinkel's proximity was more than geographical.

According to the classical ideal, a building was a freestanding sculpture. Perceiving its mass made the viewer conscious of space as a frame of reference. Such a relationship of building to surroundings was exactly opposite to the symmetry and spatial monotony of absolutist planning. Citing "Greek freedom" and its asymmetry, Schinkel was highly critical of the self-containment of Baroque building as univalent authority requiring subjugation of the individual. He stood, instead, for a continuum of open space, a generous expanse of nature and landscaped terrain interspersed with perfect buildings. The Romantic sensibility saw nature as the ideal mirror that confirmed man's newly won role as a subject and showed him the way to an understanding of himself. In these terms, the idealization of nature supported a confirmation of the new notion of the subject as well as the religious yearning to be enveloped in a wholeness. Heavily influenced by the philosophy of Johann Gottlieb Fichte, who had made the autonomy of the self and self-reflexiveness the crux of his theory, in harsh opposition to the concept of "universal monarchy," Schinkel tried to translate his idealistic concept of space into architectonic reality. The freestanding cube, diverging from the axial system of the Baroque and emancipating itself from traditional seigneurial claims, correspondingly stood for the modern self and for the middle-class appropriation of space. Its place in the city was confirmed by Schinkel's Bauakademie. Even his small pavilion at Charlottenburg Palace (Fig. 10), expressed a new point of view, with the energy of the grand Baroque axiality of the composition turned in upon itself so to speak (Fig. 11). Similarly, Mies emphasized the transverse axis when, in 1928, he selected the site of the

10. *Karl Friedrich Schinkel: Pavilion, Charlottenburg Palace, Berlin. 1824*

11. *Charlottenburg Palace, Berlin. Aerial view (Schinkel's Pavilion is circled at left)*

German Pavilion on the neo-Baroque fairgrounds of Montjuich Park in Barcelona (Fig. 12). In 1929 Walther Genzmer termed the choice of that site "perhaps the architect's most important creative act"[28] in the design of the Pavilion.

As a master of structure Schinkel understood the harmonies of noble proportions and the rhythmics of cubic precision; as a master of space he was no less assured in relating the building to its context. He designed so that he might initiate a dialogue between the architectural object and its "other," achieving this effect equally well in both natural and urban settings. The boundary between manmade and organic order was the conceptual locus to which Schinkel devoted his special architectural attentions. In this intermediate area he devised a multitude of interrelations, endowing even the smallest building with extraordinary inner spaciousness. Mies's three-fold, step-by-step transition from space to space in the Riehl House could be extensively studied in Schinkel's work. For example, in the Charlottenhof Palace in Potsdam. The simple prostyle manor house opens, like the nearby Riehl House, with a portico akin to a pavilion on three sides. Asymmetrically attached on one side is a long pergola (Fig. 13) that forms the border with the adjacent or "second" level of space, a raised terrace garden delimited by the semicircular exedra opposite the portico. On the other long side, opposite the pergola, the artificial plateau slopes down to the natural level of the park, so that the built space can become one with the landscape (Fig. 14); this became the ultimate goal of Mies's country houses as well (Fig. 15).

In elevating the viewer over nature, the "podium" at Charlottenhof creates an ideal space that emphasizes the autonomous self by distancing it, causing it to stand out, facilitating the relation with its "other." The poetic dialogue of man and nature articulated by architecture is carried further in the form

12. *International Exposition, Barcelona. 1929. Aerial view (Mies's German Pavilion is circled at left)*

of figurative sculpture and garlands of climbing plants that provide a green roof for the pergola (Fig. 16). This complex leads outward to a little hut made of branches. It is situated among the trees, which are the concluding elements, affording axial views toward the horizon and acting as coordinates that fix the site in space.

In urban settings as well, where, unlike the loose groupings of country houses, buildings are conceived as closed blocks, Schinkel demonstrated his integrative talents. The Altes Museum of 1824–30 (Fig. 17), which Mies called a "splendid building" from which all there was to know about architec-

13. *Karl Friedrich Schinkel: Charlottenhof Palace, Potsdam. 1826. View of pergola*

14. *Karl Friedrich Schinkel: Charlottenhof Palace, Potsdam. 1826. Stair between garden levels*

ture could be learned,[29] opens to space in a characteristic Schinkelesque manner. The row of columns on the portico joins the building to the cityscape and identifies it as a visibly public edifice, even from a distance.

Public space is in turn admitted into the building through this stoa, which amounts to an urban pergola, the counterpart to the pillar arrangements that firmly anchored those villas of Schinkel to the landscape. In the latter works pergolas are connected like elongated arms to the building on the outside, while the urban setting of the museum accounts for the incorporation of this motif *within* the cubic mass of the building.

The portico of the museum is complemented by another space that unfolds as the visitor enters the building. Behind the curtain of columns is a recessed niche accessible from a spacious staircase. This "urban loggia" was intended as a corridor leading to a "terrace" inside the building, whence the stroller might experience anew the view into the city (Fig. 18). As at Charlottenhof (Fig. 19), this podium lifts the viewer above the level of "nature," emphasizing the autonomy of each, and their interaction. The citizens for whom Schinkel meant this space are depicted in the engraving of his view from the upper level of this urban loggia. Curious about the vistas that beckon to him, one visitor leans on the balustrade. Others wander through this space completely absorbed with themselves in intimate dialogue. Elsewhere, other figures are involved in explaining or contemplating the art. In other words, the museum is not just a place for acquiring knowledge, but for promoting man's encounter with art, with himself, and with his surroundings. Schinkel meant it as a framework for "life;" thus by Mies's standards it stood for "genuine order," an order, that is, "which gives life the free space in which to unfold," and "the spirit room to realize itself."[30]

Mies's second residential commission, the Perls House of 1910–11, in Berlin-Zehlendorf (Fig. 20), in effect, bore witness to the influence of Schin-

15. *Tugendhat House, Brno, Czechoslovakia. 1928–30. Stair to garden*

16. *Karl Friedrich Schinkel: Charlottenhof Palace, Potsdam. 1826. View from end of pergola*

17. *Karl Friedrich Schinkel: Altes Museum, Berlin. 1824–30. Facade*

kel. Its resemblance to Schinkel's pavilion at Charlottenburg Palace is obvious. Less apparent are its references to the Altes Museum, which are hidden in its details. The parapets of the large second-floor windows of the Perls House (Fig. 21) are remarkably similar to the bannisters that decorate the gallery and stair of the museum's loggia. This suggests a reading of the ground-floor loggia of the Perls House as a pergola within the building (Fig. 22), moreover as a pillared hall pushed into the cube to form a tectonic skeleton whose structure has all but disappeared into the wall (Fig. 23). Its corners can be made out as a play of rabbet joints. In the inside corner of the loggia, set off by the plaster rabbet joints, the remains of the deepest interior pillar can be made out. Like the tip of an iceberg, only a fraction of its corner protrudes—no more than a centimeter (Fig. 24). This small detail indicates the autonomy of the tectonic

18. *Karl Friedrich Schinkel: Altes Museum, Berlin. 1824–30. Loggia*

19. Karl Friedrich Schinkel: Charlottenhof Palace, Potsdam. 1826. Portico

skeleton, whose pillars do not disappear but are submerged in the wall. Here Schinkel's philosophy is recapitulated in miniature: the autonomous parts form a unity of absolute and relative order.

This conflict between block and pavilion made manifest in the Riehl House by a first and a second architectonic order, can be observed in a different form at the Perls House. Here, too, the pillar system is the skeletal support, bearing the essential order, representing the *"thorough bass* of all architecture," in the Schopenhauerian sense: it is the carrier of historical memory and of new ideals—thus of Riehlian "development."

Since the Enlightenment, the pavilion as a building type has been the crucible of new concepts and spatial ideas. In his influential study *Von Ledoux bis Le Corbusier (From Ledoux to Le Corbusier)*,[31] Emil Kaufmann saw the breaking open of Baroque containment in the pavilion system as the decisive development in the architecture of the French Revolution. Comparably important in the rise of modernism, and traceable again to innovations in pavilion design, were the attraction to archetypes, the urge to pierce the block, and the attempt to bring the building into emotional harmony with the landscape.

Friedrich Gilly's 1798 project for a pillared hall (Fig. 25) inaugurated the idea of the pure skeleton building, a form destined to become one of the most important conceptual developments in modern architecture. Gilly's abstract construction skeleton was in a sense a distillate of architecture, both expression and symbol of ontological tectonics. Distinguished by its own special monumentality, the pillared hall emerged at the outset of a historic development as an architecturally experimental form. Yet it led well beyond that, to Schinkel's further pioneering efforts in the classical Romantic tradition (Fig. 26), thence to the early modern aesthetic of "bare building," and eventually to a profound reorientation of architectural priorities, as suggested by Karl Scheffler's notion of the "chaste beauty" of naked construction.

Scheffler, a conservative critic, prophesied that the "construction skeleton" of modern engineered buildings "could easily become the foundation of a new, higher building art." Thus Mies's own categorical imperative of "skin and bone" construction, formulated at the beginning of the 1920s, had been conceived earlier.[32] Scheffler's pre–First World War observation that "at present one gets

20. *Perls House, Berlin-Zehlendorf. 1910–11*

21. *Perls House, Berlin-Zehlendorf. 1910–11. Window detail*

the best architectonic impression from half-finished buildings,"[33] was echoed by Mies after the war, in 1922, in his first published declaration: "Only in the course of their construction do skyscrapers show their bold, structural character, and then the impression made by their soaring skeletal frames is overwhelming."[34]

When Mies went on to criticize the filling in of the skeleton with a "senseless and trivial jumble of forms," he was still harking back to Scheffler, who had considered it "madness" to cover iron structures with historical forms simply "in order to rescue some higher aesthetic."[35] Scheffler had attributed a "heroic monumentality"[36] to the structure of "pure iron construction" and by extension to the naked skeleton. Thus he proposed an aesthetic of the unfinished and the nascent, a point of view that was at the same time a reversal of

22. *Perls House, Berlin-Zehlendorf. 1910–11. Entry loggia*

23. *Perls House, Berlin-Zehlendorf. 1910–11. Loggia interior*

24. *Perls House, Berlin-Zehlendorf. 1910–11. Corner detail inside loggia*

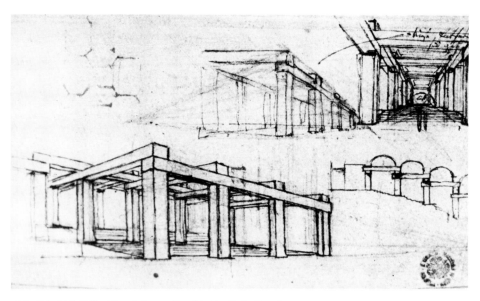

25. *Friedrich Gilly: Sketch for a pillared hall. 1798. Detail*

26. *Karl Friedrich Schinkel: Casino and pergola, Glienicke Palace, Potsdam. 1826*

the eighteenth-century Romantic passion for ruins. If the Romantic aesthetic of the unfinished saw the ruin as a symbol for what is past—for the futility of human endeavor—the modern construction aesthetic viewed the naked structural skeleton as an optimistic metaphor for the future—for progress.

Looking back now to the first two houses that Mies built, the Riehl and Perls houses, one can discern the initial tentative steps in the crystallization of a new understanding of space and mass. Thus both houses could be described as "way stations of becoming," to borrow a phrase of El Lissitzky's. They are the prelude to a creative process in Mies that began with the opposition of cube and pavilion and culminated in the establishment of the pavilion as an autonomous type in the Barcelona Pavilion (Fig. 27), the Farnsworth House, S. R. Crown Hall, and the New National Gallery.

Only with the conquest of modern construction and materials could there be a realization of the modern concept of spatial continuity that Schinkel had expressed for his own period in the poetic rapprochement of architecture and nature. In a manuscript of 1933 Mies described this relationship: "The glass skin, the glass walls alone allow for an unmistakable structural form in a skeletal building, and secure its feasibility." Only after the Barcelona Pavilion and the Tugendhat House, had steel, glass, and concrete become what he called "genuine building elements and supports for a new building art," because they had won a "measure of freedom in spatial design . . . that we will no longer forego. Only now can we structure space freely, open it and integrate it with the landscape. Thus modern man's need for space is fulfilled."[37]

What characterized that need for Mies was a "higher unity" between man, building, and surroundings, which had evolved from the philosophical tradition of German Idealism. Reciprocal perfectability and autonomy combined with responsibility toward the whole—those were the principles Mies honored most in his philosophy of serving in freedom: "Nature too should be allowed to lead her own life. We should beware of disturbing her with the bright colors of our houses. But we should endeavor to bring together nature, houses, and people in a higher unity. If you look at nature through the glass walls of the Farnsworth House, it assumes a deeper meaning than if you stand outside. More of nature is expressed—nature becomes part of a larger totality."[38]

To work for the realization of this "larger totality" and to make people more sensitive and responsible for themselves and the world around them: this constituted architecture's real duty in Mies's eyes. If the art of building fulfilled this spiritual human need, it could properly be called, in Nietzsche's phrase, *Architektur der Erkennenden* (architecture of those who realize). In 1886, the year of Mies's birth, Nietzsche envisioned an architectonic space under this rubric which brings to mind the spiritual qualities of the half-open foyer of Schinkel's Altes Museum and the glass pavilion of Mies's New National Gallery (Figs. 28, 29): "One day, probably soon, we shall need some recognition of what above all is lacking in our big cities: spaces quiet and wide, spacious places for

27. *German Pavilion, International Exposition, Barcelona. 1929. View toward pool with interior and entry reflected in glass*

28. *New National Gallery, Berlin. 1962–68. Corner*

29. New National Gallery, Berlin. 1962–68. Interior

reflection, places with long, high-ceilinged galleries that keep us from bad weather or from too much sun, that protect us from the noise of carriages and street vendors . . . buildings and cities that as a whole will altogether express the sublimity of contemplation and aloofness. We wish to see *ourselves* translated into stone and plants; we want to take walks *within ourselves* when we stroll around these buildings and gardens."[39]

Notes

1. Franz Schulze, *Mies van der Rohe: A Critical Biography* (Chicago and London, 1985), p. 104.
2. Adolf Loos, "Architektur," in *Adolf Loos, Trotzdem, 1900–1930* (Innsbruck, 1931), p. 101. Translations throughout this essay are mine unless otherwise credited.
3. *See* Fritz Neumeyer, *Mies van der Rohe: Das kunstlose Wort, Gedanken zur Baukunst* (Berlin, 1986), p. 365. (American edition in preparation.)
4. *See* Schulze, *Critical Biography,* p. 17.
5. Arthur Schopenhauer, *Die Welt als Wille und Vorstellung* (Leipzig, 1819), vol. 1, par. 43; vol. 2, ch. 35. Mies owned an edition of Schopenhauer's *Collected Works in 5 Volumes,* now in the collection of Dirk Lohan, Chicago.
6. Quoted in Schulze, *Critical Biography,* pp. 17ff.
7. Mies in a conversation with Dirk Lohan, in ibid., p. 23.
8. Books from Mies's collection are in the Special Collections Department, The University Library of The University of Illinois at Chicago. No. 254044: Jakob Burckhardt, *Die Kultur der Renaissance in Italien* (Leipzig, 1885), with autograph, "A. Riehl," on flyleaf.
9. Most probably the dedication was not for Mies, but for Ada Bruhn, who brought the book with her upon their marriage. In Mies's library, no. 240734/5, *see above,* n. 8.
10. *See* Neumeyer, *Mies van der Rohe,* pp. 88ff.
11. How important Nietzsche was for Wölfflin may be inferred from the fact that after the First World War he, Thomas Mann, and Hugo von Hoffmannsthal were board members of the Munich Nietzsche Society. *See* Jürgen Krause, *Märtyrer und Prophet: Studien zum Nietzsche-Kult in der bildenden Kunst der Jahrhundertwende* (Berlin and New York, 1984), p. 3.
12. Alois Riehl, *Zur Einführung in die Philosophie der Gegenwart* (Leipzig, 1903), Preface.
13. Ibid. (2nd ed.: Leipzig, 1908), p. 270.
14. Eduard Spranger, "Alois Riehl" [Obituary], *Der Tag,* no. 282, (November 23, 1924).
15. Ludwig Mies van der Rohe, "Baukunst unserer Zeit," in Werner Blaser, *Mies van der Rohe, Die Kunst der Struktur* (Zurich and Stuttgart, 1965).
16. *See* notebook entry by Mies of 1927 in Neumeyer, *Mies van der Rohe,* p. 355: "Philosophical comprehension reveals the proper order in our work and thus the worth and dignity of our existence."
17. Notes for lectures, c. 1950, Library of Congress, Washington, D.C., quoted in ibid., p. 392.
18. Renate Petras emphasizes this context in "Drei Arbeiten Mies van der Rohes in Babelsberg," *Architektur der DDR,* no. 23, vol. 2 (1974), p. 121.
19. An exact date cannot be given, as no documents survive (*see* ibid., p. 120).
20. Paul Mebes, *Um 1800,* vol. 1 (Munich, 1908), p. 17.
21. For discussions of the Riehl House *see* Anton Jaumann, "Vom künstlerischen Nachwuchs," *Innendekoration,* vol. 21 (1910), pp. 265–274; and "Architekt Ludwig Mies: Villa des Herrn Geheimer Regierungsrat Prof. Dr. Riehl in Neu-Babelsberg," *Moderne Bauformen,* vol. 9 (1910), pp. 20–24.
22. In this connection *see* Wolf Tegethoff, *Mies van der Rohe: The Villas and Country Houses* (New York, 1985), in which the villas from 1920 to the Farnsworth House of 1946 are analyzed.
23. *See* conversation between Mies and Dirk Lohan in Neumeyer, *Mies van der Rohe,* p. 76.
24. Fritz Hoeber, *Peter Behrens* (Munich, 1913), p. 62.
25. *Das Tonhaus und das Krematorium in Hagen in Westfalen von Peter Behrens* (Berlin, 1906).
26. In this context, *see* Fritz Neumeyer, "1789–1848: Zwischen zwei Revolutionen—Das Experiment Poesie," in *750 Jahre Architektur und Städtebau in Berlin* (Berlin, 1987), pp. 63–94. On the relationship between architecture and nature, *see* Eva Börsch Supan, "Architektur und Landschaft," in *Karl Friedrich Schinkel, Werke und Wirkungen* (Berlin, 1981), pp. 47–64 (exhibition catalogue).
27. Theo van Doesburg ("Der Wille zum Stil," *De Stijl 1922,* nos. 2, 3, pp. 23–42) uses this juxtaposition and talks about "heroic monumentality" as the characteristic of the coming new style.
28. Walther Genzmer, "Der Deutsche Reichspavillon auf der Internationalen Ausstellung Barcelona," *Die Baugilde,* vol. 11, no. 20 (1929), p. 1656. In this context, *see* the analysis of the integration of the Barcelona Pavilion in Tegethoff, *Villas and Country Houses,* pp. 85ff.
29. Peter Carter, in conversation with Mies, in *Bauen und Wohnen,* vol. 16 (1961), p. 213: "The Altes Museum was a splendid building. You could learn everything you needed for architecture from it—and I tried to do that."
30. Ludwig Mies van der Rohe, "Die Voraussetzungen baukünstlerischen Schaffens," 1928 (Unpublished manuscript, Library of Congress, Washington, D.C.); *see* Neumeyer, *Mies van der Rohe,* p. 246.
31. Emil Kaufmann, *Von Ledoux bis Le Corbusier: Ursprung und Entwicklung der autonomen Architektur* (Vienna, 1933).
32. Karl Scheffler, *Die Architektur der Grossstadt* (Berlin, 1913), p. 48.
33. Idem, *Moderne Baukunst* (Leipzig, 1908), p. 19.
34. Ludwig Mies van der Rohe, "Hochhaus Bahnhof Friedrichstrasse," *Frühlicht,* no. 4 (Summer 1922), pp. 122–124.
35. Scheffler, *Moderne Baukunst,* p. 15.
36. Ibid., p. 17.
37. Ludwig Mies van der Rohe, "Was wäre Beton, was Stahl ohne Spiegelglas?" Contribution to a brochure of the United German Mirror Glass Manufacturers of March 13, 1933, in Tegethoff, *Villas and Country Houses,* pp. 66ff.
38. Christian Norberg-Schulz, "A Conversation with Mies van der Rohe," *Baukunst und Werkform,* vol. 11 (1958), pp. 615ff.
39. Friedrich Nietzsche, *Die fröhliche Wissenschaft* (1886), *Werke in drei Bänden,* vol. 2 (Munich, 1981), p. 164.

Mies in America

Schulze: Your opinions of Mies take on special aptness in view of the rather uncommon combination of your closeness to him and distance from him. Having studied with him at Illinois Institute of Technology in Chicago, starting in 1948, you went on to practice architecture professionally in New York, briefly with Mies while he was working on the Seagram Building, later with I. M. Pei & Partners. In 1975 you returned to IIT to become dean of the School of Architecture, Planning, and Design. Thus, you occupied the same chair Mies had—nearly two decades after he retired and some six years after he died. In 1978 you resumed your affiliation with Pei's office in New York, where you have been a partner ever since. In short, you have known Mies not only as an architect but as the designer of an educational program that you studied under earlier and took over later.

Freed: It is important to keep Mies's several identities distinct because, in my view, Mies the teacher was not the same as Mies the builder or Mies the artist, however closely all these roles appear to be interrelated.

Schulze: Recalling that Mies came close in the mid-1930s to assuming the directorship of Harvard's Graduate School of Design before he accepted the offer from Armour Institute of Technology—later IIT—have you ever wondered what kind of architecture school he would have created in Cambridge? Might it have been substantially different from the one he put together in Chicago?

Freed: I think it might have been a different school, although Mies's own work would probably have had the same character. I suspect the school would have been different chiefly because of the nature of Harvard, which sees itself, after all, as The Great American University, and because of the sort of students who were drawn to it, not because Mies himself would necessarily have followed any other academic course. The students at Harvard, in large part because Harvard is a graduate school, would have brought a sophistication and worldliness with them that their counterparts in the undergraduate program at Armour/IIT did not possess. The latter were at that time mostly middle- and working-class students from Chicago and Chicago suburban public high schools—more intellectually innocent perhaps but no less eager to learn from a celebrated master. Perhaps they preferred learning what seemed concrete facts rather than seemingly speculative truths; it may have felt more practical to them.

On the other hand, Mies himself in his outlook and work would likely have been little affected by an American environment other than Chicago. To me, he was the only important modern architect whose efforts rested on the bedrock of principle (his, of course), which he put before anything else. It was a principle that dealt not at all overtly with aesthetic theory and only very little with social or political considerations—and it lost even that tenuous connection at the end. I will have to find a more specific definition of this as we go on, but

Mies's principle seemed to be about a moral way of behaving when you build, about an ethical, impersonal way of putting a building together so that the result remains valid and fresh over time. Mies felt, as we have heard and read many times, that architecture is the most important visible record of a unique spirit which civilizations leave in tangible form. Architecture existed physically for him, not simply as an idea in the history of ideas, which might lend itself to interpretation in a variety of ways, but as the idea of culture frozen and fixed. It was for him not a performance art like music. The performance of Mies's art was completed when his building was up.

It is not surprising that he consequently developed a profound reverence for permanence, not only as an expression of the building as a valued artifact but as a means of safeguarding evidence of the phenomenon that obsessed him, the putative spirit of the age, the *Zeitgeist*.

To be sure, his understanding of the *Zeitgeist* was unique and unlike our view of culture today. We don't use the word much anymore, and we don't quite trust it. Mies trusted it, believing as he did in universal fact, in a world of facts imbued with idea. We are far less sure of facts or their general validity, at any rate less sure that we can define them or rank them in a hierarchy of importance. He did not suffer from such doubt or uncertainty. He felt sure of his concept of *Zeitgeist* and firm in his conviction that architecture must be an expression of it—that it could, in fact, be nothing else.

Indeed, in his best work he makes a powerful case for that conviction. He did, after all, consider seriously the process, techniques, and materials by which we build today; he taught us that you cannot ignore or deny industrialization of technique but showed that you could work with it as process. And then, as he would say, you raise the building to a higher plane when you refine what is essentially a coarse way of building, and, by that refinement, make poetry out of technique.

Still, in neglecting to deal with opinion—which in its own right in the contemporary world can be said to qualify as fact—Mies was an absolutist, who permitted an unchecked temper of absolutism to grow in the school he directed. The teaching at IIT, over time, took on rigidity and suffered from the inability to provide a flexible, moving development of the principles he laid down—principles that, I believe, if sound, can be developed and found in other basic architectural forms than those in which Mies found them.

I'll have more to say about Mies the teacher later, but here I want to address the greater complexity of Mies the architect. While he was certainly not what I would call a socially conscious designer or a lover of the urban framework, he was neither irresponsible nor frivolous. He felt quite seriously that he had the trust and therefore the obligation to dispose wisely of the surplus economic wealth that accrued to a people already well fed and clothed who, living well above the subsistence level, can entrust an architect with the commission to do buildings for them that may define their cultural and communal being. With this view implicit, not stated, he gave his students a kind of moral basis for building—not for making buildings *look* a certain way but for taking seriously the assignment of disposing of the economic surplus in a creative, impersonal way, not willfully or as a means of self-aggrandizement. Thus a priesthood of the *Zeitgeist* was created. I think that is the reason why he finally reduced his palette to primary forms: to remove anything from the creative act except what was essential to the most direct and impersonal and to him unwillful construction of buildings.

Schulze: If to him his buildings were physical manifestations of the *Zeitgeist,* did he also see them as metaphors of fact, of the fact to which he was so devoted?

Freed: I think so.

Schulze: But if you acknowledge that his teaching system in America led to a kind of rigidity, why can you not also argue that the work he did in America was comparably inflexible and rigid? Especially if it stood for a fact he considered incontrovertible?

Freed: Some of it was, surely. But Mies could be and was at times flexible, resourceful, and, in a limited way, responsive to the city frame and fabric. He was not as totally indifferent to context as the current view makes him out to have been. The Seagram Building (Fig. 1) does everything the postmodernists say a building should do, but uncapriciously. It does so with dignity, not to

1. Seagram Building, New York. 1954–58

mention a freshness that makes many latter-day so-called contextual buildings look withered by comparison and, interestingly enough, off the pace. It is, however, instructive to add that his buildings fit in best by opposition, that is, by becoming the unique monument rather than by merging with the fabric.

Apropos of Seagram, I don't think Mies would have built or disposed the parts of a building in that fashion on another site. Consider the Racquet Club opposite, a low building, a *palazzo.* If he had built Seagram, tall and modern as it is and given over to offices, on the very front of his site, there would have been none of the lively exchange that now takes place between the two works. Mies's building would have simply been part of the wall of Park Avenue. Now, on the other hand, sitting back behind its plaza, it engages the Racquet Club in a dialogue (Fig. 2). Mies authentically wedded an old building to a new one.

Remember, too, that he has often been accused of providing his buildings with no front, back, or sides. Seagram does have these features, in a modest way. It has an emphatically frontal approach, yet it adjusts itself adroitly to the slope of Fifty-second and Fifty-third streets. It is positioned as an iconic object would be. An icon of modernism, one might call it, since more than many of his other towers, it goes back to his European buildings. For it is a distinctly more asymmetrical building than his still later, sometimes deadly symmetrical structures.

Schulze: But it is axial, the way his American work as a whole often is.

Freed: Axiality doesn't mean it's symmetrical, only that it's frontal. But its sides are very different, while the "bustle" to the east ties it quite naturally to the building—I think it was the YWCA—that originally stood behind it. There was, as I recall it, a scheme developed in the course of planning that showed what might happen if the rest of the block were cleared and the build-

2. *Seagram Building, New York. 1954–58. View toward New York Racquet Club*

3. *Seagram Building, New York. 1954–58. South facade*

ing would extend to and look out on Lexington Avenue from its back as it faced
Park Avenue from its front. There were lots of stairs coming down to Lexington. He gave the building four distinct aspects without ever losing the quality
of a tall, unmistakably modern structure conceived according to his habits and
principles. As to the shear walls he was forced to build in order to provide wind
bracing (Fig. 3), if he had left them to appear solid, without the frame/screen
that covers them, I think the scale of the building would have suffered. Besides, Seagram is a building that is all grid and all frame; the structure is articulated only at the corners.

Schulze: Was Mies so conscious of context in his other American buildings?

Freed: I think the 860–880 Lake Shore Drive Apartments in Chicago is a
good example (Fig. 4). You would never build "860" deep in a city; it would not
make sense to create so plastic a composition on anything except an edge condition. Mies encountered two edge conditions at "860:" the Outer Drive and
the lake. His solution also reminds me somewhat of his European work. I see
"860" as one building, not two. It closes and opens and shapes itself as you

4. 860–880 *Lake Shore Drive Apartments, Chicago. 1948–51*

move around it, yet it always addresses the lake and it always holds the street. And it generates all of this from a trapezoidal site. It is a very complex building, a powerful piece of work.

I must add that it seems to me it grew from Mies's deeply poetic view of, for want of a better term, disposing the elements of a building. He taught that the space between parts of the building-object was as important as the object, perhaps even more important. Altogether too many buildings today are aspatial, I believe. They deal not with space but with form, or with surface. When this is the case, more often than not space is negated because the surfaces, the walls, are so active and aggressive. Mies's lambent space stirs me still. When you walk up to one of his good buildings—those he spent a lot of time on, not the indifferent ones—you become aware of the exterior space that has been activated by his building (Fig. 5), and when you walk inside, you sense space as a palpable presence.

The ability to see space and to animate it this way is, so to speak, an acquired taste. Some societies do not possess it. The Renaissance did; it used space lavishly. Even though Mies talked very little about the Renaissance, he

5. 860–880 *Lake Shore Drive Apartments, Chicago. 1948–51. Entrance*

approached design in a not dissimilar way. Renaissance public spaces—the spaces in front of Renaissance buildings—were remarkable. No building was placed in those spaces except that it enlarged them or closed them but always made them active. "860" behaves similarly. It is not so much a building *in* space as a building that *makes* space. That **L** shape yields a strong contained space. It brings to mind Mies's notion of free space, but in effect it is not really free so much as it is closed—as closed as a Renaissance piazza.

All this—to return now to his instructional method—he taught by example. I remember the excitement in school whenever one of his new projects was shown; the example of what he did and how he did it was more important than theory. He never taught theory as theory. He taught in an extraordinary way, by silence—a silence that forced you to look at things, to see them again and anew, to stare at them for a very long time until you became aware of what was working or what wasn't, aware, that is, of the principles at issue.

Schulze: Was a good deal of his effectiveness dependent on your own awareness as a student that you were simply in the presence of a great architect, so that you became exceptionally alert on that very account? Could anyone other or less than he convey such lessons to you?

Freed: Yes and no. Mies created a unique program. It owed a lot to the Bauhaus while it distanced itself from that program; it was less experimental. He felt it was strong, airtight, and consistent, and he believed therefore that the people close to him could teach it as well as he could. To some extent he was right, because his program was most certainly clear. But he was the only one who appreciated it for substantially more than its clarity. I remember him now and then studying a student's solution that one would seldom if ever associate with Miesian architecture—a circular opening in a brick wall, for example—and praising it for its intelligence, for its exquisite execution. On the other hand, two or three generations of teachers seeking to apply that program of Mies's with nothing but the letter of it in mind turned it from a program into a liturgy. I suppose that may be the fatal flaw in any curriculum that depends on an undisputed master for its formulation and guidance.

Schulze: You said earlier that you regard Mies as unique among major modern architects in the degree of his devotion to principle. By implication, then, others were less devoted to principle. How do you see Le Corbusier or Frank Lloyd Wright relative to that argument?

Freed: I'll answer that circuitously, first making a distinction between principle and aesthetics. I would propose that there is a gulf between them, between a theory of aesthetics and a belief-system of principle. Aesthetics, as I think of it, is the composition of parts to create a whole based on a fundamentally philosophical point of view. Cubism is an aesthetic but not a principle. One can imagine many other ways of interpreting a visual reality based on Cubist thought. But Mies's commitment to principle was not the same thing. He was fearful of interpretation, of subjectivity, of what he called aesthetic speculation, and he evoked the specter of that subjectivity so as to alert and forewarn his students, and to stress by contrast the desirability of and the need for permanence of form as well as of value. Yet it is also rather revealing how his supposedly unsubjective outlook colored the content of his own coursework at IIT in terms of history: we studied Greek architecture, Egyptian, Romanesque (*not* Roman, ever), and Gothic. Then we stopped and went straight to the modern movement. It was as if the wholeness of the building, or the building as object, or as exemplar of universal principle—I want to say logic, but I'll stick to principle—was what Mies was after. There was, in other words, a prejudice in his own summation of history. He always felt, I think, that the Renaissance and, even more, the Baroque were too subjective, in the sense of being insufficiently guided by principle. I remember one slide we saw at IIT, of the Foundling Hospital in Florence, which showed its stone construction with an iron tension rod drawn across a vault. This was offered to us as an example of bad architecture, because if you build in stone, build in stone; don't use iron rods. In fact, I can see such a juxtaposition as quite wonderful—*today,* not then. I have come to think that of course one may legitimately use iron rods with stone or without stone, depending on the situation. The IIT insistence on principled consistency resulted in a kind of closure of invention that I have to lay, finally, at Mies's feet.

Now to Wright and Le Corbusier. I think both were guided by aesthetic theories that dealt with compositional effect. So Le Corbusier, who was as rigorous as Mies in deploying structure and in not faking anything he did, nevertheless did not design buildings to stand as unique paradigms. Rather, he left a less absolutist corpus, which meant that you had to look at many of his buildings in order to distinguish what he was after. This difference between the two men led to a difference in the effect they had on architects working after them. Le Corbusier left a lot of room for other people to explore, since he dealt with the comparative positions of things: structure positioned to enclosure in one way, structure composing with space in another. On the other hand, Mies toward the end of his American career seems to have decided to remove everything from his architectural work that was compositional. Thus, with the exception of some of the buildings we have discussed here, which were more or less compositional, he ended with buildings that too often did not make space but stood neutrally in it (Fig. 6).

Schulze: Examples?

Freed: The IBM Regional Office Building in Chicago (Fig. 7); the New

6. Colonnade Apartments, Newark, New Jersey. 1958–60

7. IBM Regional Office Building, Chicago. 1967–69

181

8. *New National Gallery, Berlin. 1962–68*

National Gallery in Berlin (Fig. 8); and, more marginally, the post office and its accompanying federal towers in Chicago. These last, which comprise the Federal Center (Fig. 9), do make space, but for my part it is a space that breaks down. It is so vast in contrast with the rest of the city. Instead of opening to nature, as "860" does at the lake, a literal edge condition, the Federal Center opens to the city, as the city was before and as the city is afterward. It just marches through, making that opening, but it is built as if to attract attention to the way the three component buildings work as objects alone by themselves rather than to the way they function interactively in an urban setting.

If Mies had remained in Europe, I doubt he would have built the same way he did in America. Conditions here were tailor-made for the tall solitary buildings he became associated with. Traditionally, in Europe, you build less on a *tabula rasa* than you do in America. And one can't blame Mies for the *tabula rasa*. Americans have always wiped out urban spaces. Whole cities in the Midwest have been wiped out, especially by the automobile. Parking lots are installed in, rather than around, their inner cores. In a European city the center tends to hold. I think Mies would have been less encouraged in Europe to carry out his tower-in-the-park idea, which flourished in America in the 1950s and 1960s and which is, in a way, reflected in the Federal Center.

I am reminded of other differences between Europe and America. In the early years following Mies's arrival here, Americans by and large perceived only the slenderest connection between ideology and art. They cared little for the political meaning, language, or consequences of buildings. Idea in architecture interested them hardly at all. Europeans, needless to say, took a quite different view of things; hence, as a European, Mies had long since positioned himself ideologically, curiously enough, in *opposition* to ideology, political or otherwise. He wrestled endlessly with ideas, principles, and philosophical rationales, as we know from those terse, chiseled statements he wrote in the 1920s.

His early relation to the *Neue Sachlichkeit* was touched with political overtones. That movement, which was a response to the destruction of so much of Europe in the First World War, had implications for all the arts, including architecture. A new treatment of the individual building was proposed that discarded all historicist decoration associated with a discredited past. The *Neue Sachlichkeit* took an equally radical view of the context of buildings, offering as an alternative system another way of seeing the social construct: the city, the urban plan.

Ludwig Hilberseimer figures importantly in all this. He was Mies's friend

9. *Federal Center, Chicago. 1959–64*

from the 1920s and a political radical clearly affected by the *Neue Sachlichkeit*. Hilberseimer was a city planner in Berlin long before he emigrated to Chicago to join Mies at IIT, and I think it was from him (in Europe) that Mies learned most about the possibility of the freestanding building.

The protagonists of *Sachlichkeit* maintained that fact was all, logic was all; and if a building were built logically, factually, it would be structurally uniform on all sides, *ergo,* it would require openness on all sides. This meant that it could not fit into traditional urban patterns, into the sort of city that had changed only gradually over the centuries. It tended to demolish that city and to introduce a new kind of space to live in. In Hilberseimer's planning classes at IIT we were taught to let the park enter into the city and float through it, with unclustered towers only punctuating the park. We destroyed the network of streets, with the result that we throttled city life. The process was meant finally to suburbanize the city, but it was also a throwback to the *sachlich* yearning to effect an equalization of the political body, a homogenization of society. (Needless to say, Mies never took to the "political" core of the idea.)

When Mies arrived in America, he found that Americans at that time were not much interested in theory or argumentation. In Chicago, *doing* was the thing most valued and held in highest regard. What pleasure it must have been for Mies to come here and be free to apply his principles in a more artistic way than he had been encouraged to do in Europe, where he had constantly to defend the building and argue for it, not only for the building but for the place of it in the city and the place of the park in the city. It is enough to remember his 1928 project for the Remodeling of Alexanderplatz (Fig. 10), where tall buildings rise quite independent of the old street system.

Schulze: And Hilberseimer's resounding defense of that project at the time.

Freed: Mies came to Chicago and found a city that had been run down over the years, especially its South Side. In his plan for the Armour/IIT campus on the South Side he introduced the image of the building in a park (Fig. 11). Unfortunately, that scheme did not build a brave new city; it eventually eroded the old one, without offering a viable alternative.

I retain a vivid recollection of a visit I made to Isfahan in the 1970s. Shortly before, the Shah had built a national highway through the old bazaar that originally spanned the space between the great Shah Mosque and the Friday Mosque. The bazaar had been a locus of city life, a compound of heterogeneous people and tribal types. After the highway was built, the bazaar was disconnected from its two anchors, and it slowly dwindled. It ceased to function as a vital social connection between the two mosques. Heterogeneity and individuality were compromised in the process.

I don't think Mies had any such disruptive notion in mind when he brought the idea of the freestanding building to America. But the pleasure he must have found in being able to build that building type here—as an artist building an artwork—freed from the burden of dialogue and argumentation, must have been great, must have offered a clue to him of how he could proceed.

One more thing: since he emigrated just before the Second World War, by the war's end he had educated his first groups of students. And also by that time America was looking around, realizing that since the Depression it had had virtually no new construction. Big institutions were then bursting, eager to put up new buildings, to raise a new architecture.

10. *Remodeling of Alexanderplatz, Berlin. Competition project, 1928. Photomontage with drawing. Whereabouts unknown*

11. *Preliminary Campus Plan, Armour Institute of Technology, Chicago. 1939. Photomontage with model. The Museum of Modern Art, New York, Mies van der Rohe Archive*

The demand was huge and almost instantaneous, requiring a major change in the nature of architectural practice at the national level. Offices grew larger, more corporate and institutionalized, as they responded to a postwar economy whose urgent need to catch up was inversely proportional to the need to build with culturally meaningful decoration or form.

In a sense, it can be said that Mies cleared the way. He had already produced a group of graduates who saw positive value in building simply, if schematically. When these graduates began to enter the architectural work force, moreover, when it became possible to transfer much of the building process to factories and to carry it out less exclusively in the field, Mies found he had a significant constituency among architects who proceeded to establish the preeminence of the Miesian building. They were, however, as a group unable to turn their work into the high art of Mies's buildings. They started from a set of premises that from the beginning promised less poetry than functional logic. They proposed that there was a rational way to make buildings, that large teams could be effectively put to work, particularly when you separate interior from exterior, when you start with primary forms, and when you isolate structure and are no longer required to carve, shape, or compose a building. When that happened, a compellingly easier if less lively method of building seemed to have evolved, without losing the culturally based notion that one was indeed making architecture.

Mies himself never saw it that way. He always thought his way of work made the task of building harder. Yet he was pleased that so many of his ideas had become effective on so wide a front. He talked about the "war" of modern architecture, which he wanted to win and which he saw as a battle for the minds and sensibilities of the public. He appeared to be winning that war at last, and as the normative system changed in accommodation to him, he changed in accommodation to the system. Things gradually reached a point where it was in everyone's interest to maintain the new, clearly successful form of corporate architecture. Meanwhile, now and then Mies would do a building that he really cared about, like "860" or Seagram, that pointed up the difference between his work and the work of his constituency. Yet I am inclined to believe that he might have been less tolerant of what they—and he himself to a degree—finally accomplished if he had been younger. After all, he grew old in America, during the years his building tended toward radical simplification.

Schulze: Prior to Mies's arrival in Chicago, architectural instruction at Armour Institute of Technology had been based on the Beaux-Arts system, as was true of most American schools at the time. The changes Mies wrought were radical. He drew up a curriculum, painstakingly conceived and written down, which qualitatively altered the character of the school. Would you comment on the effect of that?

Freed: In the Beaux-Arts system, design and composition were everything. Originally one worked in a master's studio, where one learned planning principles derived from past examples: the cruciform plan, square plan, U-shaped plan, etc. It was a typology of form that had been tested historically and empirically, and it is what came to be the skeleton of building. I can think of nothing that would have been more alien to Mies than to start with a planometric spatial skeleton of a building. He began with the structural skeleton of the building. Karl Friedrich Schinkel's Altes Museum (Fig. 12) would be incomprehensible, or surely unacceptable, in the world of Miesian architecture, since it was an articulated, particularized space, defined by structure. For Mies, space was neutral and floating, and the structure was just a grid. But Mies, of course, loved Schinkel.

The Beaux-Arts system assumed that the student was an integrated mem-

12. *Karl Friedrich Schinkel: Altes Museum, Berlin. 1824–30*

13. *Architecture, City Planning, and Design Building (S. R. Crown Hall), Illinois Institute of Technology, Chicago. 1950–56*

ber of society, that he had imbibed with mother's milk certain social norms and typologies and their meanings. These he was free to modify and develop but not to destroy or radically change. The language of architecture was presented to him as his inheritance.

In that respect, too, Mies was a revolutionary. He could not accept the inheritance of the tradition immediately preceding his era. He started teaching from the premise that people's perceptions had to be changed. To this end he employed a combination of *Sachlichkeit* and visual training. The visual training was perfectly abstract; problems given the student for individual study were always abstract. *Sachlichkeit,* in turn, took the form of such assignments as putting bricks together, in a variety of structural patterns, some of them extremely subtle. The process informed the student that there was no *given* form, that it was *structure* from which an architecture would derive; thus the spatial development typology dear to the Beaux-Arts was no longer valid or called for. All functions could take place in just two or three types of buildings, such as the tall building or the pavilion, simply by letting the function shift internal walls around.

Yet what spoke of the deeper Mies—not the teacher or the builder or the articulator and preserver of principles, but the artist—was the way, the nearly perfect way, he adjusted the walls in the first place. So, in fact, one couldn't just shift them around willy-nilly. Imagine shifting the core around in Crown Hall (Fig. 13)! But the theory was established, which held that the hierarchical disposition of typological formal plans was not the modern way of building. Such a view generated favorable responses outside the school, since it appeared no longer necessary to do anything much to the inside of buildings. Up until then, buildings had been laid out, with interior spaces reflecting the basically planometric approach. But here comes *free* space! And with it, free planning. And here, in the loft building with its infinitely flexible plan, the architect has only to build a shell. What pleasure! What profit!

At Armour/IIT, the laying of bricks had its two-dimensional counterpart that took the form of the most meticulous exercises with the pencil. You first learned how to make a drawing—with that famous precisely hand-sharpened pencil—and to make it as nearly flawless as possible. For in an architecture

186

that sought to become *beinahe nichts* (almost nothing) what is done has to be done with the most impeccable craftsmanship. Mies's early students emulated the master even in their manner of dress—how their buttons were sewed on. They wore the most conservative suits, and their clothes always seemed beautifully tailored.

Here we see the limits of materiality in Miesian work. After all, if you build a complex building with lots of shaping and lots of sculpture, it is additive. And additive buildings can hide various imperfections. But Mies's buildings were reductive. And when you are reductive, you *have* to be perfect.

So perfection was taught early. There followed a series of exercises running through the fourth year. You were not allowed to design anything by yourself until the fifth year. The exercises took you through more and more complex buildings, but unfortunately those exercises had a way of eliminating all other options, so that by the time you got to the fifth year you didn't know what to do except what you had already done.

This raises the question of whether and to what extent the study of architecture should consist of education or of training. I am constrained to believe that much of Mies's program at IIT when applied by others was only training. Education implies free will; and there was little of that there. What I personally wanted to do when I took over the directorship of IIT was to distinguish and perhaps separate form from principle, to free one while underscoring the other. That initiative failed, probably because it was not translated in detail into a program. I believe in development, not in revolution, and that is an attitude that doesn't lend itself easily to programmatic restructuring. Yet, without a clearly defined program, I was unable to deflect attention from an already very clearly defined curriculum.

It seems to me, in any case, that modernism as we have lately thought of it is not exhausted. It seems true enough that we need to develop a serious critical literature. The past generation has come to value the city more than the park and we now find in history not only a treasure worth mining and preserving but a vital source of creative ideas in contemporary work. I think, in fact, that messy New York City has just the right number of buildings by Mies and Wright, one from each. The best recipe for a city—Siena is a prime example—is to be composed of many similar, sound, but undistinguished buildings topped off by several real masterpieces. This seems to me to be preferable to a community where architects are uniformly trying too hard to turn each building into a monumental foreground building.

Schulze: Are you suggesting that New York is a more urbanistically gratifying town than Chicago?

Freed: Yes. But let me return to the matter of modernism and my belief that it is not yet used up. If Mies's followers failed to develop a viable architecture based on his own example, this did not happen in the case of Le Corbusier, whose open-endedness prompted a group of designers who were sufficiently inventive to establish a creative momentum of their own.

Is such a thing really impossible with Mies's heritage? I like to think it is not, and I am brought back to principle, the noble legacy he left to architecture. To build solidly, to put things together positively, with unfailing rigor and scrupulous self-criticism, to foreswear all attempts at "effect" (not to mention jokes!); all these ideas I have earlier called Miesian principles can be as valid now as they ever were. Unfortunately, too many have been distracted from them by yard-goods Miesian reductivist form. The problem, the objective, ought to be to see the principle behind the form. There is a pretty irony here, for we should have learned to distill the essence of Mies's method—to abstract it, that is. And yet his detractors as well as his admirers have paradoxically materialized him, this maker of the most abstract, the most immaterial of architectures! It is a kind of reification at work.

Schulze: Or idolatry.

Freed: Obviously, as we have said, Mies contributed to all this. Still I find myself forever wanting to balance each minus with a plus and vice versa. Make a few allowances here: it must have been hard for him late in his life, covered as he was with honors, to warn his followers of the dangers of idolatry, if indeed he could see them as such. And since there is inevitably a psychological dimension to all this, let us keep in mind the sheer force of his personality. He was overwhelming, a genuinely charismatic presence. He was the one who brought the light to these young people. Many of his Chicago students, as I noted, came from unsophisticated backgrounds. They had little experience with artistic matters, so that Mies's asceticism became the standard by which they learned to judge art. And after five years' experience with the master's lean deterministic approach to the art of building, it became difficult for them to reshape their tastes. Small wonder they could not separate form from principle, for to do so would necessitate striking out into the darkness again. Much better to live comfortably with the form that embodies the principle. That's actually a very Beaux-Arts notion, isn't it! IIT became an academy rather than an outpost of the avant-garde.

Schulze: There is darkness and there is darkness. What you say suggests another image: Mies as a great black hole. He sucked everything and everyone into his gravitational field.

Freed: Yes, his absolutist field. At IIT there never was a jury system for critiques. Each professor was independent of all his colleagues in judging the work of a student in his class. There was no discussion among teachers, no exchange of views that the student might hear and profit from. Consequently, the student was left with the notion that he was invariably getting absolute truth, whatever the origin, since there were only single, autonomous sources of judgment. The assumption was that jury critiques were not necessary because there is a right way and a wrong way, and the instructor will let you know if you're doing something wrong, whereas if you're doing it right, well, as they used to say, "The work speaks for itself." So there was no dialectic involved. It was not an intellectual procedure, but rather a craftsman's method.

Schulze: More irony. Despite his role in the modern revolution, Mies retained more than a trace of his origins in the crafts. He grew up in the family of a stonemason and the crafts provided him with his first work experience, in Aachen. The child begat the man.

There are other ironies as well, which prompt me to return to the matter of Mies's move from Europe to America, and its ramifications. You argued earlier that the architecture of *Sachlichkeit,* manifest in Hilberseimer's city plans and Mies's variations of them, had political meaning. You suggested that the isolated tower could be understood as a metaphor of revolution; and you added that such a notion, when transported to the United States, was picked up by

American corporations, which found it attractive not because it was revolutionary but because it was convenient and practical. The result—and here is the irony—was the curious consonance of Mies's former radical theoretical position in Germany and the cheerful pragmatism of postwar corporate America.

Freed: I also argued that Mies himself eventually aestheticized that revolutionary view. Indeed, by the time he left Germany he seemed to have lost all interest in the politics at issue, and he evidently had little enough to begin with. Instead, he had begun to emphasize the importance of his building as the carrier of the cultural norm, much the way he read the architecture of the Gothic period. In order to do this he had to chuck whatever little ideological baggage he still had. And the Americans themselves, committed far less to ideology than to an easy and rational way of building, only hastened this normalization process, which in turn enabled Mies to pursue his own goals with even less encumbrance.

Now as to his goals: clearly, then, he wanted an art of architecture, not a politics of architecture. He was, after all, no longer content with *Bau* but increasingly insistent on *Baukunst.* In the course of all this, however, I think a certain confusion about the relationship between art and politics arose in his mind. I have already discussed the late stages of his career, when he allowed the uncomposed, freestanding building to take up more of his creative energy and, as a type, to become more readily associated with his name than was good for architecture as a whole or, indeed, his own reputation. At the very time—the late 1920s—when he was producing some of his most beautiful, most personal, most architecturally powerful work—the Barcelona Pavilion (Fig. 14), the Tugendhat House (Fig. 15)—he was also developing his vision of the remodeled Alexanderplatz (Fig. 16), consisting of large isolated slabs in an almost endless, triumphantly anti-urbanist row. This design was a precursor of his later American efforts. It also—speaking of metaphors—prefigured the bureaucratization of society that went into high gear in Germany during the Nazi period; the Nazis, in fact, took over the national government just a few years

14. *German Pavilion, International Exposition, Barcelona. 1929*   15. *Tugendhat House, Brno, Czechoslovakia. 1928–30. Garden facade*

16. *Remodeling of Alexanderplatz, Berlin. Competition project, 1928. Photomontage with drawing. Whereabouts unknown*

after the Alexanderplatz project. Mies must have sensed bureaucratization as a fact of the international future that was to some extent already then apparent.

In addition to a good eye, then, he had a good nose, for better or worse: a nose for fact. And with those big, deadly Alexanderplatz slabs you can see already a diminishing interest in space and a growing interest in the wall as a defining element in space. He seems not to have cared what went on behind the wall. I see a considerable difference between the lively facade of the Concrete Office Building of 1922–23 (Fig. 17) and those grim boxes he did five years later for Alexanderplatz. The latter stand more for the corporate nature of modernity, and at the turn of the 1930s in Germany they could be seen also

17. *Concrete Office Building. Project, 1922–23. Perspective. Charcoal and crayon on tan paper. The Museum of Modern Art, New York, Mies van der Rohe Archive. Gift of the architect*

as representative of that most bureaucratic of all political entities: government. Mies might have been willing to stay in Germany, regardless of the kind of government there, if the state had adopted the iconography of steel and glass he longed for. I recall a story I heard—which may be apocryphal—about his reaction to the design carried out for the Chicago Civic Center (Fig. 18) by one of his ablest students, Jacques Brownson. Mies, who liked that building, is said to have asked what its purpose was: "Is it for government?" Reportedly, when he was assured it was, he said, "Good. Then we will yet win the war of modern architecture." The ratification by government was the ultimate sanction.

But this brings us back to the question of the relation between the morality of art and the morality of politics, and the uneasiness of Mies's position between them. As if to seek relief from this condition, he developed another meaning, or mythos, another kind of moral which didn't pertain to the city or bureaucratization or government or people. It was a primarily self-referential moral, that dealt almost exclusively with the *way of building*. The only message we really heard at IIT was that it was moral to build in the image of the *Zeitgeist*, immoral not to. But the "spirit of the time" was never seen in terms of something like a struggle for workers' rights, or for better housing in more vital cities. Instead, we were told that, in a self-referential way, a building wants to do such and such because such and such is how you build with steel, or how you build with brick, or with concrete.

Schulze: Was this architectural morphology?

Freed: Right, although I prefer to call it self-referential. So what Mies arrived at finally was a morality of building dissociated from a morality of use, or from a politics of use. Thus, he gave meaning to architecture for people who had lost all other sense of belief or meaning. He showed them how to approach their work: you build in a way that verifies the materials and techniques of the *Zeitgeist*. To build is a moral act.

However, at this point he stepped well ahead of the parade he had organized and was leading, and proceeded to design those exquisitely proportioned buildings where a beam didn't really have to be the size he made it, where it could have been smaller but if it had been smaller it would have been bad for the proportions. He didn't have to use eight-inch-wide flanges, as in the Seagram Building; he could have employed six-inch pieces more economically—which he did in fact in One Charles Center in Baltimore (Fig. 19), to the detriment of the proportions there. But the people trained in the Miesian mode could no longer clearly see the difference between Seagram and One Charles Center. And Mies moved ever further ahead, free to make changes at will and ultimately no longer required to justify them. He still could turn his buildings into sculptural evocations of space, structure, form, and proportions. Then he was at liberty to do a Bacardi Building (Fig. 20), as no one else was; he could break his own rules, because they were not subject to any other form of validation— not to a social ethos or a political philosophy that others could join or critique, only to the making of form in the most beautiful way. He could get away with the 50 by 50 House (Fig. 21), because no one else would have thought of it. It was a house that had no source in the vocabulary of forms he normally dealt with. Some called it an unstable building: "You can't build that way." But Mies made it so beautiful, and he saw to it that it worked, because of that rigid plane

18. *Jacques Brownson of C. F. Murphy Associates: Civic Center, Chicago (now Richard J. Daley Center). 1965*

19. *One Charles Center, Baltimore, Maryland. 1960–63*

20. *Bacardi Office Building, Mexico City, Mexico. 1957–61*

21. *50 by 50 House. Project, 1950–51. Model*

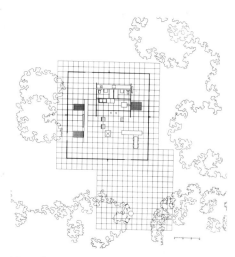

22. *50 by 50 House. Project, 1950–51. Plan.*
The Museum of Modern Art, New York, Mies
van der Rohe Archive

of welded steel above it. And the asymmetrical way he interlocked the gridding of the paving—it has the touch of mastery about it (Fig. 22). None of his followers would have done that. They would have put a symmetrical pad under it and let it go at that.

Schulze: Mies was an artist, first and foremost, was he not, whose view of himself and society was shaped by the lingering romantic values of the late nineteenth and early twentieth centuries that saw the Artist, with a capital **A**, as a special figure, inspired, sovereign, unique, and bound only by those bourgeois conventions, and no others, that suited his purpose.

Freed: I suspect Mies's sympathies were always with the people who ran the world. It's hard to believe that he could ever have identified himself with a workers' class. If he was, as I believe, basically more interested in "the art of this" than in "the meaning of this," then the Karl Liebknecht–Rosa Luxemburg Monument of 1926 begins to make sense, as does his design for a German Pavilion for the Brussels World's Fair of 1935. The former was a Communist commission, the latter sponsored by the Nazi government. He was not just apolitical; he was an artist who would take any formally promising assignment that came along. In this respect, strikingly, he was not unlike Philip Johnson, whose architecture seems directed 180 degrees the other way, caring little about the relationship of the morphology of the building or the form of it to its internal conception or the provenance of it, wanting instead to make an art object out of it that has nothing to do with the city or the other buildings around it (Fig. 23).

Mies's instincts in much of his work were those of an artist. Walter Peterhans, another German emigré at IIT, and Hilberseimer, both of them socially involved and politically committed, always touted Mies as a great artist, not a notable revolutionary.

Schulze: Have you any more thoughts on the difference between Mies's European and American work? Any further speculations on why the increased symmetrization in America, the move closer and closer to the use of the compact box, the freestanding tower?

Freed: I have a few. I've thought about this chiefly taking the Brick Country House of 1924 as a point of departure (Fig. 24). To begin with, I see that project as the most radical of all his works, and, at the same time, the most modernist. The Brick Country House explodes the building and throws the pieces all over the countryside. In its unfixed, dynamic fragmentation it has definite affinities with modernist thought in other disciplines. How could it not have been so, with Mies so close in those days to that restless soul Theo van Doesburg?

Well, from that point onward, after doing the Brick Country House, Mies conceived no designs that were so totally freeflowing. The Barcelona Pavilion (Fig. 25) is admittedly asymmetrical, but it turns on itself; it's caught in a courtyard. The court houses, by definition, are houses with courtyards. The model house for the Berlin Building Exposition, although originally open, has only a tentative stub of a wall poking out (Fig. 26).

I infer a significant intention here. It seems to me that the problem of the Brick Country House was that it led to many other possible organizations of the building. It isn't a reductive object. It allows people to design buildings every which way; it offers choice. The moves made in it are willful moves that are then transformed by Mies's proportioning of them. But they do not convey or lead to a belief system. There is no suggestion of a *way* of building, no minimalization, no intimation that such a design, if followed in other projects, could have provided him with something he could hold up and say, "*This* is iconographic." Or, alternatively—as he might later have said—"Here we have, by contrast, the Farnsworth House (Fig. 27). We have taken away from it everything we could take away, and what is left, sings." It sings because it is now truly *beinahe nichts.* But in the Brick Country House, as in most modernist designs, there are options left us. We end up with something variable, something additive.

And here is where I think Mies broke with the modern movement. The asymmetry and openness of modernism encouraged options. I think he reflected on this and said, "That's all well and good, but how will I be able to let people know what the hallmarks of the age are?" With modernism anybody can move the design around and conceivably make it very beautiful, with many sequences of spaces—but it will offer nothing that is a touchstone of where we are, nothing that guarantees where excellence should go.

Perhaps this doesn't explain why he closed the box in America, but it does propose a possible clue as to why he left the aesthetic of the Brick Country House behind him. The process was not, I think, conscious; it was gradual. But it *is* perceptible. In the European designs that follow it, walls slowly shrink and shrink as the definer of internal space until at last they are gone, and Mies is left with his crystal, his reductive crystal. In a way, he had hinted at it already, in his Friedrichstrasse Office Building (Fig. 28). He could make that design because the fledgling European modern movement had never positively identified how you do a skyscraper and how you loosen it up.

Schulze: It happened that his search for the reductive crystal coincided with the bureaucratization of the modern age and the development of his huge rectilinear slabs in the late 1920s, didn't it?

Freed: If you reflect on the idea of the tall building, how do you make it

23. Philip Johnson: 885 Third Avenue, New York. 1987

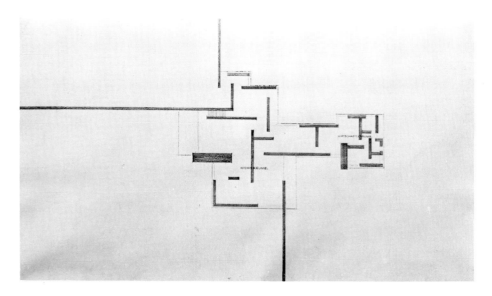

24. Brick Country House. Project, 1924. Plan. Whereabouts unknown

absolute? How might Mies explain it to the people who would wish to have it built? I remember a conversation with a former Mies student who took me around Chicago one day, showing me buildings. Of the old shaped skyscrapers he said, "Of course they're not very good." "Why not?" I asked. "Because they're willful," he said. "And if they are willful, where will it all end? With a simple rectangular prism, you remove the personal agenda, and you gain universality."

Schulze: How could something so hermetic as an "absolute building"—one that does not stand for political or religious values or anything outside itself—how could that be said to manifest the spirit of the time?

Freed: In fact, who is to say who the interpreter of the *Zeitgeist* is? Or that we live in a world with one *Zeitgeist?* Our world seems to have a lot of them: different people, different perceptions, other ways of living in this world than what we associate with the industrial West.

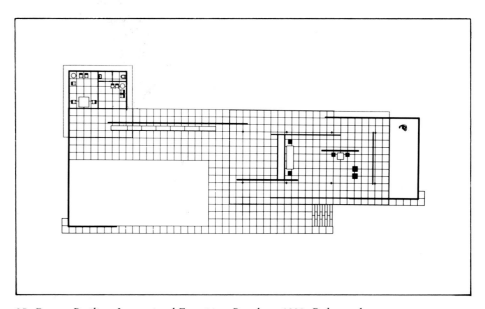

25. German Pavilion, International Exposition, Barcelona. 1929. Redrawn plan

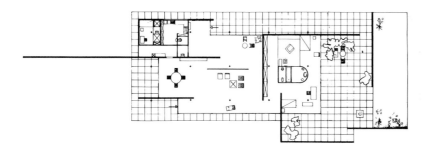

26. *Model House, Berlin Building Exposition (destroyed). 1931. Altered preliminary plan*

On the other hand, if Mies hadn't proposed his moral terms, he would have left his people and himself in a difficult position, because he would have had to admit that his building is actually as willful as any other. So what he did with the *Zeitgeist* was . . . fuzz it. He fuzzed it by identifying it as a phenomenon of building, not of cities, or social classes, or economics, or whatever. He narrowed his vision. He said, the *Zeitgeist* has an icon: it is the building, which shows that we build as no societies before us could build.

Schulze: The famous technology argument. Such a view would also provide a way of taming modern chaos and securing a new order.

Freed: Absolutely. When you identify the *Zeitgeist* as he did, you assume that there is *one* overarching spirit of the age, and that we are ready to throw everything out except what is built in that spirit. Having given us the concept of the spirit of the age, however, Mies was never forced to divulge much more.

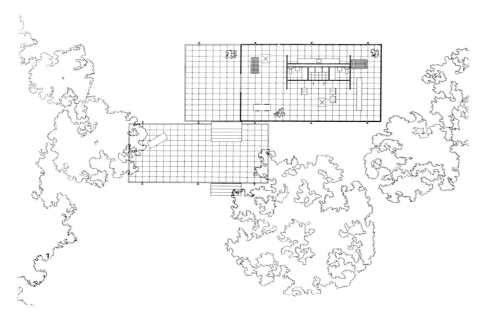

27. *Farnsworth House, Plano, Illinois. 1946–51. Plan*

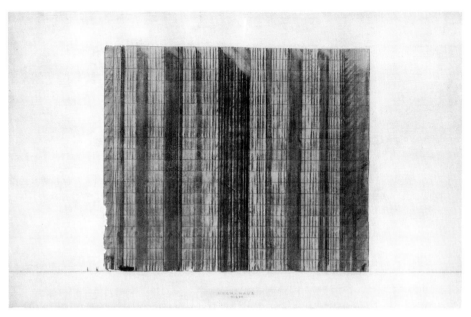

28. Friedrichstrasse Office Building, Berlin. Competition project, 1921. Elevation (east side). Charcoal and pencil on brown paper. The Museum of Modern Art, New York, Mies van der Rohe Archive. Gift of Mary Callery

And when you recall the poverty-stricken state of architectural theory at that time, his pronouncements were like a breath of fresh air. You could believe, as you surely had not recently believed. All right, we won't solve the problems of the age—but Mies never said we would. He said we *build* in the *spirit* of the age.

Schulze: The eye of the needle through which Mies passed the world: was it not to some degree a concept traceable to his own mental makeup? Psychologically speaking, was he not himself a freestanding construct, isolated, absolute? He never took kindly to marriage or parenthood, and rarely lived intimately for any length of time with anyone. And his natural inclination to remain alone must have been strongly reinforced by the professional ostracism through which he lived during his last years in Nazi Germany. America may have liberated him and left him free to do with his architecture all that you have suggested, but remember that he came here at the age of fifty-two, almost totally incapable in English and content to live for well over a year in hotel rooms. If his emigration cost him none of his excellence and sensitivity as an artist, might not his search for an immutable and ineffable truth have been intensified by his psychic isolation over here? The Farnsworth House was drawn up a little more than a generation after the Brick Country House, but conceptually the two works are an age apart. In Farnsworth the dynamism of the Brick Country House has given way to a contained stasis, at least within. All movement occurs without. One sits in a vitreous prism of pure form and contemplates, in stillness, an ever-changing nature (Fig. 29). Farnsworth is a shrine.

Freed: Or a temple. Or a metaphor for a house, not a house in the psychological or physical sense. As he goes on, Mies sheds programmatic restrictions right and left, and ends up with inhabitable sculpture. A wonderful thing, that house. It really is an icon of our age and it has, by Mies's definition, *Zeitgeist* written all over it. But it hardly works well for people who look to architects to give form to their environment. It is the last station on the Weimar road that starts with an optimistic attempt to change, if not society, at least its (public) norms of perception and ends in a private pavilion in a private landscape to be privately enjoyed.

As to the psychological, or spiritual, aspect of all this, it applies to others than Mies. His disciples performed their own priestly acts developed from their worship of him—acts of self-abnegation in which they sought to design the building by paring it away, thus calling to heel any internal self that wanted to individuate. This could be deeply satisfying to people who had no other belief system that seemed valid at that time, roughly mid-century. Yet, as one studies the period with a greater measure of historical perspective, one grows more and more suspicious that a faith founded on the way one builds a building may be a symptom of anomie, a reflection of a lack of workable normative standards in modern social life. Those who lived by this faith sometimes displayed a fortress mentality, as if they were ready to draw their wagons in a circle and fend off the Indians. Such a defensive posture only strengthened their belief, and because it did they found it was easy to ignore such distressing extra-architectural problems as the cities and the poor people in them.

Schulze: Even if the order Mies sought eluded him, it has also eluded the rest of us. Perhaps we now recognize that his dedication to fact was illusory because this world, as you said, is a world of opinions in collision rather than of facts and transcendent truths. How much better off are we for knowing that? Have we offered anything better in consequence of our knowledge? Have we done much more than recognize that we must learn to live with chaos?

Freed: I wouldn't call it chaos. Cacophony, perhaps. Look, there are obviously gains and losses in this. We lost utopia. Some loss. But I submit that we have come to appreciate the city as a pretty good place for human interaction. I draw a distinction between the twentieth-century city that I know, the one I think we will have to inhabit and cope with, and, on the other hand, the city as envisioned by Leon Krier—a city that rejects industry and technology and, in a curious way, life. That city is what Mies was fighting, just as I would fight it. In the end much of Mies's artistry will be seen, even in respect to its lack of urbanism, as a part of what we have gained. Lest we create an exaggerated notion of a "sealed off" Mies, let me recall what we said earlier about his ability, when he wanted to turn it on, to build well in the city with all its problems. The message he sent is that we can make art out of technology. The message we want to send is that it is possible to sustain and re-create the city as the place that has inspired the most intense speculations of man and given rise to the most interesting episodes in the history of human culture.

Here Mies's example is useful. Seagram is a building of the highest intrinsic order, yet it exists in the city by the rules of the city as we best can make them out. Indeed, it is a building, curiously, that is now unique in the city without being alienated from the city. In the midst of all the various shapes and bits and pieces that have attracted the compulsive attention of architects over the last decade or so, it stands out like a Gothic cathedral. With all our new jagged towers, a building that is Platonic in its intentions becomes the centerpiece. It is only that Mies neglected to consider that you cannot have thirty Gothic cathedrals in a single city.

29. Farnsworth House, Plano, Illinois. 1946–51

To sum up, by extending my earlier statement: Mies the architect has more to teach us today than Mies the teacher. We can learn most from his own work. What he projected was his belief in the singularity and truthfulness of his art. What he stood for was the principled, ethical worker—architect, designer, or craftsman—who possesses the will to build to last. Too often now we build *not* to last. In order to build to last you must know how to put buildings together, moreover, in ways that are architectonic and poetically evocative. I quite agree that there is poetry latent in the act of putting together bricks or putting together steel. But all poetry doesn't have to be in the same sonnet form in which Mies composed.

He also stood for the sensitive handling of space, especially spaces between things, which is an ability we have so little cultivated lately in our fascination with decorating the wall, that space has become for us only dimension. Mies may have been the last great spatial innovator. Large-scale sculpture can sometimes treat the "in-betweenness" of space, but only architecture can teach us space as the sequential experiencing of a thing. That Mies knew this is evident from the way he put free walls in space, making space active, not just making walls or enclosures active.

So what have we? What did he leave us? A commitment to work toward excellence, a commitment to building that rises to the level of the architectonic and, in turn, may be elevated to poetry. And a commitment to space, which has a value of its own. I think that is more than enough.

Trustees of The Museum of Modern Art

Photograph Credits

Pierre Adler: 128
© Akademie der Künste, Berlin: 38 left, 41 top
Apeda: 41 bottom
Courtesy Art Institute of Chicago: 164 top and bottom, 165
Bauhaus-Archiv, Berlin: 109, 123 bottom
Courtesy Bildarchiv, Berlin: 46, 115
Robert Damora, FAIA: 11
From *Frühlicht,* vol. 1, no. 71 (1920): 102
Alexandre Georges: 177
From Fritz Hoeber, *Peter Behrens* (Munich, 1913): 101, 158 top and bottom
Hedrich-Blessing: 98 top and bottom, 107, 124 top, 169 left, 178 top, 180 right, 181 top and bottom, 191 top left and right, 198
David Hirsch: 157 top
Hochschule für Architektur und Bauwesen, Weimar: 49 bottom
Courtesy Philip Johnson: 193
Kate Keller: 15 top, 49 top, 59 bottom
Balthazar Korab: 22
Koster: 121 top
From Le Corbusier, *Oeuvre Complète,* vol. 2 (Zurich, 1935): 123 top
From *L'Émulation,* vol. 68, no. 11 (November 1928): 116
Courtesy Dirk Lohan: 99 top, 129, 131
Kunsthalle Mannheim: 54
Rollie McKenna: 76
The Museum of Modern Art, New York: 17 bottom, 18, 19, 34, 35, 38 right, 39, 40, 42 left and right, 44, 51, 53 top and center, 55, 57, 60 left and right, 61, 62 top and bottom, 69 top and bottom, 71 top and bottom, 77, 79, 81, 82, 83 top and bottom, 84, 85, 86, 99 bottom, 112, 113 top, 120 top and bottom, 127, 161, 163 left, 166 top, 167 top, 169 right, 178 bottom, 180 left, 183 top and bottom, 185 right, 188 right, 189 top and bottom, 191 bottom, 192 left and right, 194 top and bottom, 195 top and bottom
Courtesy National Archives: 126
Fritz Neumeyer: 156, 160 top, 162 top and bottom, 163 right, 166 bottom, 167 bottom left and right, 168 bottom, 170
From Josef Popp, *Bruno Paul* (Munich, 1916): 157 bottom
Rolf Petersen: 105, 196
Rasulo: 56
F. A. Russo Inc.: 100 top
From Alfred Rietdorf, *Friedrich Gilly* (Berlin, 1914): 168 top
Courtesy Franz Schulze: 12, 14, 66, 80
Seidman: 188 left
Ezra Stoller: 25, 175
Soichi Sunami: 15 bottom
Courtesy Plansammlung, Universitätsbibliothek, Technische Universität, Berlin: 121 bottom
Wolf Tegethoff: 64 right
From Paul Westheim, *Das Kunstblatt* (February 1927): 52, 59 top
Courtesy Iain Boyd White: 100 bottom
Williams and Meyer Co.: 155
T. Paul Young: 36
From *Zentralblatt der Bauverwaltung,* vol. 54 (1934): 124 bottom
Zentralinstitut für Kunstgeschichte, Munich: 53 bottom, 72, 75 left and right, 76, 124 bottom

Index